TALKIN' UP TO THE WHITE WOMAN ABORIGINAL WOMEN AND FEMINISM

Dr Aileen Moreton-Robinson is a Geonpul woman from Quandamooka (Moreton Bay). Previous to her appointment as Lecturer in Indigenous Studies at Griffith University in Brisbane, she taught Women's Studies at Flinders University in Adelaide. She has been involved in the struggle for Indigenous rights at local, state and national levels, and has worked for a number of Indigenous organisations. Her writing in the area of native title, whiteness, race, and feminism has been published in anthologies and journals here and abroad.

TALKIN' UP TO THE WHITE WOMAN

ABORIGINAL WOMEN AND FEMINISM

Aileen Moreton-Robinson

University of Queensland Press

First published 2000 by University of Queensland Press
PO Box 6042, St Lucia, Queensland 4067 Australia
Reprinted 2002, 2005, 2009, 2012, 2015, 2016, 2017, 2019 (three times)

www.uqp.com.au

Typeset by University of Queensland Press
Printed in Australia by McPherson's Printing Group

This project has been assisted by
the Commonwealth Covernment through
the Australia Council, its arts funding
and advisory body.

Sponsored by the Queensland Office
of Arts and Cultural Development.

Cataloguing in Publication Data
National Library of Australia

Moreton-Robinson, Aileen.
   Talkin' up the white woman: indigenous women and white
   feminism.

   1. Feminism — Australia. 2. Aborigines, Australian — Women.
   I. Title.

   Bibliography.
   Includes index.

305.420994

ISBN 978 0 7022 3134 6

*For the warrior women of Quandamooka
especially my nan Lavinia Moreton (1905–1989),
my mum Joan Moreton and my daughter
Rhiannon Moreton-Robinson.*

Contents

Chapter Seven
Conclusion: Talkin' Up to the White Woman *179*

Acknowledgments

Writing this book was one of the hardest things I have ever had to do, for reasons too numerous to mention. I acknowledge and thank the ancestral spirits of Quandamooka and the Minjerribah and Mulgumpin Elders. I am indebted to the many Indigenous women warriors who have gone before me, who walk beside me, whose spirits carry me and who continue to protect, nurture and sustain me. Many of their faces are on the cover of this book. They have created a path on which to walk. My love and appreciation go to my grandmother, Lavinia Moreton, my mother, Joan Moreton, Aunty Milly Moreton, Aunty Shirley Moreton, Aunty Irene Egert, Aunty Estelle Bertossi, Aunty Margaret Islien, Aunties Eileen and Irene Borey, Aunty Thelma Campbell, my sisters Denise and Leonie Coghill, Kerry and Lynn Charlton, Donna Ruska and Shelly Moreton. To my grandfathers, uncles, fathers and brothers, thank you for your support, your teachings and for believing in me. Outside my country I am indebted to women warriors who lead by example. I thank Aunty Jean Phillips, Aunty Janey Arnold, Aunty Lois Gulash, Aunty Nellie Bunda, Aunty Mary King, Aunty Eileen Broderick, Grace and Leena Coolwell, Maureen Kirk, Leslie Ahwang, Ravina, Denise and Bernice Waldren, Lila and Maureen Watson, Cheryl Buchanan, Sue Morgan, Helena Gulash, Hope Neill, Henrietta Fourmile, Kay Mundine, Jackie Huggins, Leesa Watego, Coralie Ober, Isobel Tarrago, Pat Turner and Kerry Tim. There are also five remarkable Indigenous women warriors who deserve a special mention for their wisdom, courage, tenacity and unconditional support: Glenis Charlton, Auriel Bloomfield, Angela Barney-Leitch, Raelene

Baker, and Tracey Bunda; words fail to express my gratitude and appreciation.

I have also depended on a network of colleagues. My appreciation extends to Belinda Mckay, Jane Haggis and Gillian Cowlishaw; I have benefited immensely from your friendship and intellectual support. I am especially grateful to my friend and colleague Fiona Nicoll for her constructive criticism, positive energy, intellectual commitment and encouragement as well as for teaching me to appreciate the finer points of drinking beer. Thanks also to my colleagues Yvonne Corcoran-Nantes and Sue Sheridan in the Women's Studies Department at Flinders University in Adelaide. I benefited from working with them and having the opportunity to teach Women's Studies. A special thanks also to Sue Abbey at Queensland University Press for encouraging me to publish this book.

Finally, there are the three most important people in my life to thank: my children, Adam and Rhiannon, and my soulmate, Ian. Thank you for believing in me, the numerous cups of tea you made, the massages you gave and your unconditional love. I could not have climbed the mountains, swum the rivers, crossed the deserts and run the miles on this intellectual and emotional marathon without each one of you.

Preface

In this important and beautifully written book, Aileen Moreton-Robinson gives us a compelling analysis of white Australian feminism seen through Indigenous Australian women's eyes. She unpacks the unspoken normative subject of feminism as white middle-class woman, where whiteness marks their position of power and privilege vis-à-vis Indigenous women, and where silence about whiteness sustains the exercise of that power. And she examines the consequences of such practices for Indigenous women and white women.

The argument is theoretically sophisticated and well situated in the context of feminist scholarship and critical race theory, drawing on works from the United States, Canada and Britain as well as Australia. Moreton-Robinson takes seriously the key understanding that perception and knowledge depend upon one's social standpoint, and that standpoints offer partial knowledge. It has often been asserted, but seldom shown so clearly, that the standpoint or subject position of whiteness in general and white feminism in particular is also partial despite its dominance and self-representation as universal truth. The second chapter offers a masterful analysis of a large and complex body of scholarship. She includes those works developed by scholars and activists who work from subject positions that are non-white. These works develop perspectives on whiteness as difference, as "Other", and show the difference that non-white standpoints make for feminist understandings and practice in different nations and areas of the world.

The structure of the book is a dialogue between white feminist thought and Indigenous women's thought where Indigenous women's standpoints are the centre and illuminate those of white Australian feminists. Moreton-Robinson alternates between interrogating how white Australian women have constructed Indigenous women in ethnography and in feminist writings, and how Indigenous women's life writings and interventions in white feminist discourse reveal different self-presentations, subjugated knowledge and resistance to white representations. In a final chapter, Moreton-Robinson argues that white feminists in the academy are still unable or unwilling to interrogate the power and privileges of whiteness or its status as the measure of the normal and the desired. Too, race remains for them a category that applies only to non-whites. What is needed, Moreton-Robinson argues, for inter-subjectivity — the ability to examine an issue from a number of perspectives — to develop is academic and social relationships of white feminists with Indigenous people where the power of whiteness is not institutionally defended, where white freedom to imagine "others" is challenged and resisted by Indigenous people. The conclusion develops the concept of inter-subjectivity — the importance of whites seeing themselves and Indigenous people through Indigenous eyes — as a way station to developing less partial knowledges. Such knowledges would make visible to whites their everyday participation in practices of racial domination, alternative ways of acting and knowing, as well as making possible feminisms that recognise the importance of Indigenous women's priorities.

I think it's important to say that this is an optimistic work, and one with political intent. The intent is to begin the hard conversation with white feminists about whiteness and what it does to women and to a feminist agenda. One consequence of whiteness unspoken is that white feminist perspectives, practices and political priorities have marginalised, denied and disrespected the perspectives and priorities of Indigenous women — that is, whiteness is bad for Indigenous women. Another consequence is that the whiteness of feminism also compromises and narrows its agenda as well as implicating white feminists in white male privilege — in other words, it's also bad for white feminists. The optimism, manifest in the care and clarity of the analysis, is that such a conversation is possible and can be productive of a more inclusive politics.

Professor Karen Brodkin
Anthropology Department
University of California, Los Angeles

Introduction:
Talkin' the Talk[1]

> Recent work on whiteness has engaged a range of questions ... This
> scholarship helps make it evident that the formation of specifically
> white subject positions has in fact been key, at times as cause and at
> times as effect, to the sociopolitical processes inherent in taking land
> and making nations (Frankenberg 1997:2).

The protocol for introducing one's self to other Indigenous
people is to provide information about one's cultural location,
so that connections can be made on political, cultural and social
grounds and relations established.[2] Following this protocol, I
introduce myself to the reader. Unlike the majority of white
people in Australia, I belong to the Koenpul people of the
country known as Quandamooka. White people, who thought
they discovered our country, named it Moreton Bay. It is a bay
formed by a group of islands, approximately 16 kilometres from
the mainland, which surround the coastline from north of the
Brisbane River to Southport on the Gold Coast in Queensland,
Australia. As such, I am of the salt water and sand; I am Yulubir-
ribah. I am also of the owl people; I am Mookmook, and my yurri
is Kabool, the carpet snake. I was born in the 1950s, a time when
governments separated "half caste" children from their families
and country. My grandparents, Lavinia and Alfred Moreton, on
Minjerribah (Stradbroke Island) raised me. They taught me not
to be afraid to speak my truth to white people. Many times I have
been given the responsibility by women elders in my community
and in the Brisbane Indigenous community to talk up to white
people.

This book is an extension of my communal responsibilities; I am representing an Indigenous standpoint within Australian feminism. The explicit acknowledgment of this standpoint does not make my work a special case because the standpoint of each and every academic is embedded in their texts. In recognition of this I have — where possible — refused to use the third person plural "they" to refer to other Indigenous women. My role as an academic analyst is inextricable from my embodiment as an Indigenous woman.

An Indigenous woman's standpoint is informed by social worlds imbued with meaning grounded in knowledges of different realities from those of white women. And we have become extremely knowledgeable about white women in ways that are unknown to most of them. I use the term "white" in this book because skin colour is the marker for objectifying difference in the social construction of "race". All Indigenous women share the common experience of living in a society that deprecates us. An Indigenous woman's standpoint is shaped by the following themes. They include sharing an inalienable connection to land; a legacy of dispossession, racism and sexism; resisting and replacing disparaging images of ourselves with self-defined images; continuing our activism as mothers, sisters, aunts, daughters, grandmothers and community leaders, as well as negotiating sexual politics across and within cultures (Collins 1991). Such a standpoint does not deny the diversity of Indigenous women's experiences. Indigenous women will have different concrete experiences that shape our relations to core themes.

In Australia, in the 1990s, I was situated in three particular contexts in feminism as an embodied Indigenous subject. It was in these contexts that I experienced white feminists engaging with my racialised difference. The first experience involved Indigenous women, including myself, challenging a white feminist anthropologist's right to speak on behalf of all Indigenous women about rape in our communities. Certain white feminists vigorously opposed the challenge (some in public and others in private) on the grounds that all women have the right to speak out about violence. The second experience was teaching in the same faculty with a young white feminist. She lectured on inequality and was intolerant of racism in the classroom, but her idea of working with me as an Indigenous woman meant in practice my working for her. The third experience came as a result of being asked by a university (with one day's notice) to be part of a welcoming committee to meet a white feminist professor at the International Airport at 5:30 a.m. The professor had been invited to receive an honorary doctorate from the university, but she threatened not to come to Australia unless she was met and welcomed by Indigenous women. This seemingly noble but colonial gesture by the professor was soon eroded by her questioning us on what we were going to do at the Sydney Olympics about the denial of Indigenous rights in this country. She offered her unsolicited advice about what we should do and wanted us to advise her about what we might want her to do. Finally I responded by asking her to tell us what the limits were to what she would do. She did not answer my question — instead she changed the subject.

On each of these occasions the white feminists positioned themselves as anti-racist women who were doing the right thing, unaware that their actions were not interpreted by Indigenous women in the same way. The Indigenous women involved, including myself, perceived their actions as those of white middle-class women who were acting from a subject position of dominance. I use the concept "subject position" to denote a socially constructed position whereby one's behaviour is significantly shaped by what is expected of that position rather than by conscious intention. I use the term "middle class" in this book in the Weberian sense to refer to one's social status and prestige based on capital, occupation, skill and education. Indigenous women are familiar with this "white middle-class woman" subject position because we have become accustomed to its presence in our daily interaction.

These experiences led me to an exploration of feminist texts where I found women of colour, African American and lesbian feminists contesting the homogeneity of the category "woman". Their collective work identified "woman" as diversity, multiplicity and heterogeneity through highlighting the specific concrete particularity of different women in different contexts and herstories (Moraga & Anzaldua 1983; Smith 1983; Minh-ha 1989; Collins 1991; Mohanty, Russo & Torres 1991; Chaudhuri & Strobel 1992; Busia 1993; Moghadam 1994; Momsen & Kinnaird 1993; Prakash 1995). Critiques by these writers facilitated a politics of difference within feminism and disrupted representations of the white middle-class woman as the universal woman. Some western feminists responded to these critiques by redefining the way in which "difference" had been theorised. There was a shift from theorising the subject in relation to categories of "difference" (such as sexuality, gender, class and race) to theorising these categories as "differences" within the subject. In spite of this shift, white feminist discourse on "difference" continues to be underpinned by a deracialised but gendered universal subject.

In Australia, a small number of feminists have written within the framework of a feminist politics of difference, including Bottomley et al. (1991), Jeffreys (1991), Gunew & Yeatman (1993) and Pettman (1992). The Australian works vary in their focus, from asking what is "difference" in feminist theory and practice, to addressing how feminists theorise and operationalise "difference" in practice. "Difference" becomes a marker of that which is not the same. Even though this literature acknowledges in theory that some "differences" are irreducible and incommensurable, in feminist political practice "differences" are managed by allowing "Others" voice and space within already established forums. This practical form of managing difference incorporates all "Others" into a homogenous sameness.

In the Australian literature whiteness is not interrogated or named as a "difference", even though it is the standard by which certain "differences" are measured, centred and normalised. Whiteness as race, as privilege and as social construction is not interrogated as a "difference" within feminist political practice and theory. This is not to say that some feminists have not made whiteness visible. In recent years, in Britain and the United States, thinking and writing about whiteness has begun to generate new intellectual and practical approaches to living in a multi-racial society. This emerging literature on whiteness is slowly impacting on the study of race in Australia. However, despite — or perhaps because of — feminism's commitment to a politics of difference, thinking and writing about whiteness has not yet had widespread impact on theorising difference. Whiteness remains the invisible omnipresent norm. As long as whiteness remains invisible in analyses "race" is the prison reserved for the "Other".

However, some feminists have addressed whiteness by examining the relationship between theory and standpoint. Perhaps the first piece to be written specifically on whiteness was by Adrienne Rich (1979) who argued that white feminists practise white solipsism; they view the world through a form of tunnel vision of which their experiences of the world are the centre. Marilyn Frye (1983, 1992) later explained that white women practice whiteliness as "an ingrained way of being in the world". Frye and Rich both suggest that feminists should be disloyal to whiteness by refusing the material and ego rewards conferred on them through their association with white men; they should actively work against their white race privilege. Elizabeth Spelman (1990) demonstrated how the white middle-class woman is centred in feminist theory. She urged white feminists to be conscious of the ways in which the legacies of white privilege appear "in our confusing imagining women with knowing them; in priding ourselves on tolerance; and in appropriating others' identities through our desperate rush to find similarity" (1990:185). Ruth Frankenberg's (1993) seminal work on the social construction of whiteness elucidated how race is salient in shaping the lives of white women. She argues that racial hierarchies need to be changed in material and discursive forms in order to redistribute power in society. Connected to this transformation is the altering of the meanings of white and other racial and cultural identities. Kate Davy theorises white womanhood as an institution in the service of white supremacy based on a form of civility "that encompasses a plethora of values, morals, and mores that determine sexual propriety, as well as the tenets of respectability in general" (1997:213). It is an institution containing different ideologies which are invoked differentially depending on the historical conditions and needs of white control. Davy's political strategy is to "out" whiteness by examining how white women participate in and use a politics of respectability. Peggy McIntosh's (1992) much quoted paper on white privilege and male privilege identifies forty-six conditions of unearned white race privilege. For McIntosh, silences and denials about unearned privilege protect systems of inequality and she asks herself what she should do with such knowledge. Minne Bruce Pratt (1992), reflecting on her white identity, discusses aspects of her race privilege as she walks through her white neighbourhood. Pratt concluded that rather than appropriate the other's experience of racism she needs to do work on her own racism and privilege.

The work of these feminists recognises that white race privilege makes a difference to women's life chances. Yet these authors fail to appreciate that their position as situated knowers within white race privilege is inextricably connected to the systemic racism they criticise but do not experience. "The situated knower is always also a participant in the social she is discovering. Her inquiry is developed as a form of that participation. Her experience is always active as a way of knowing whether or not she makes it an explicit resource" (Smith 1999:6). In other words, feminists' knowledge of systemic racism is easily abstracted from their embodied experience as white middle-class women.

In this book I show that white middle-class women's privilege is tied to colonisation and the dispossession of Indigenous people. Notions of race are closely linked to ideas about legitimate ownership and formation of the nation, with whiteness and nationality woven tightly together. In America and Australia, white men who governed the nation state limited naturalised citizenship to white immigrants (Lipsitz 1998). In Australia, blackness was, and is, congruent with Indigenous subjugation and subordination. In the emerging feminist literature on whiteness and race in America, the black/white binary distinction works to reserve "race" for the African American Other. First nation people remain largely invisible due to this distinction. However, the social construction of whiteness in America is tied to the appropriation of Indigenous lands and the incarceration and enslavement of Indigenous people by colonial and subsequent governments. This is evident in the literature on whiteness outside feminism, which illustrates that the creation of white subject positions is inherent to, and an outcome of, colonisation and the development of nationhood (Brodkin 1999; Delgado and Stefancic 1997; Nakayama and Martin 1999; Allen 1994).

The British invasion and subsequent colonisation of Australia began the process whereby whiteness became institutionalised. The Australian mode of production is derived from, and is part of, the western system of capitalism; Australian systems of government are based on both British and American models; the system of law is British as is the system of education. Decisions that affect the nation in politics, bureaucracies, policy and business are made predominantly by white males. Australia's immigration policy up until 1962 was "whites only", and although government promotes a multicultural and tolerant society our institutions remain white in ethos and practice.

The work of feminists such as Rich (1979), Frye (1983, 1992), McIntosh (1992), Ware (1992) and Frankenberg (1993) provides valuable insights about white race privilege. However, it derives from and is limited by the standpoint of these authors. This book is not about how white women perceive their whiteness. Instead, the experiences and writings of Indigenous women and our herstories inform the book. And it is informed by my embodiment as an Indigenous subject situated in particular feminist contexts. This book reveals how whiteness as ideology and practice confers privilege and dominance in power relations between white feminists and Indigenous women.

This book makes whiteness visible in power relations between white feminists and Indigenous women through examining their respective self-presentation and representation in various discourses. I use the term discourse to mean "those distinctive forms of social organisation that are like conversations mediated by texts and are carried on by and co-ordinate subjects situated in multiple local sites" (Smith 1991:159). Postmodern feminists influence my approach. They argue that multiple subject positions and the relations between those positions constitute subjectivities. However, the limit of theorising subjectivity in this way is that it has the effect of equalising subject positions. It fails to connect subjectivity to relations of ruling whereby white racial difference shapes those on whom it confers privilege as well as those it oppresses. My research demonstrates that there are dominant subject positions in society that are implicated in relations of ruling. These subject positions are historically constituted and are represented in discourse through and beyond the activity and experience of individual subjects. I argue that the subject position middle-class white woman is structurally located as an ideological position within whiteness. Examining a variety of discourses, I show how the representations of this dominant subject position collide with the self-presentations of Indigenous women.

This book draws on the postcolonial critique of epistemological foundationalism to argue that all knowledge is situated and therefore partial. Spivak identifies two dimensions to the act of representation (Spivak 1988a, 1988b). One dimension is to perceive representation as "speaking for"; the other is to comprehend representation as involving interpretation. The latter Spivak identifies as re-presentation; thus all representations are based on interpretation. I utilise Spivak's definition of representation in my work, and the concept "self-presentation" is operationalised to distinguish between how one represents oneself through interpretation as opposed to how one is represented by another. Representations are more than mere symbols. They are a means by which we come to know, embody and perform reality. Our different representations of reality arise "out of differences in the position of knowing subjects in relation to the historicity of interconnected relationships of domination and contestation" (Yeatman 1991:17). Although my work is centrally concerned with representation, it does not seek to answer questions about the causes of white representation. Nor does it posit that the subject position middle-class white woman is constituted the same way in all social and historical locations. As a consequence this book is not so much a study of white womanhood as an exposure of an invisible racialised subject position that is represented and deployed in power relations with Indigenous women through discourse.

My methodology provides a new framework for analysing whiteness as a dominant subject position. In comparing the self-presentation and representation of the subject positions "middle-class white woman" and "Indigenous woman", my research provides a context for different bodies of knowledge to meet and disrupt each other. Consistent with this meeting, I use both Indigenous English and standard English in the title of my chapters. In the first chapter I argue that Indigenous women's self-presentation in our life writings — as state-indentured domestic servants — reveals that our experiences are grounded in a different history from those who deploy the subject position middle-class white woman. Indigenous women are the bearers of subjugated knowledges and our ethics, behaviour and values repudiate the moral and intellectual hegemony of white domination and oppression.[3]

Indigenous women's life writings unmask the complicity of white women in gendered racial oppression. They reveal the imperative to negotiate Indigenous subjectivity in relations with white women. We are conscious of a dominant subject position that we actively resist through the deployment of a variety of subject positions. Our resistances are therefore not reducible to overtly defiant behaviours. They are multifaceted. Our resistances can be visible and invisible, conscious and unconscious, explicit and covert, partial and incomplete and intentional and unintentional. They are profoundly political acts that are neither one dimensional or fixed and they do not always lead to conflict or self-destruction.

In Chapter 2 an overview is provided of feminist literature from different countries, whose debates on "difference" such as "race" inform the Australian feminist conceptual landscape. By mapping the white feminist literature on "difference" I show how the identification, interrogation and elucidation of whiteness as "difference" is absent, as is an engagement with an Indigenous critical gaze. What my review of the literature most clearly demonstrates is that whiteness is not perceived as a category of difference by most white feminists, yet it is a standpoint and subject position from which they view the world, theorise and practise their politics. In the third chapter I examine representations of the "Indigenous woman" by white feminist anthropologists. I argue that they position Indigenous women in contradiction and juxtaposition to the subject position middle-class white woman and deny the subjectivity of Indigenous women through methodological erasure. I further argue that their representations of the "Indigenous woman", in the knowledges they have constructed about us, conceal the colonising process by relegating Indigenous women to the imagination. White feminists draw on these representations without interrogating them or recognising their importance in shaping the subject position middle-class white woman.

The subject position middle-class white woman has been historically shaped, redefined and represented in Australian culture as the embodiment of true womanhood. In Chapter 4 I argue that white feminists have been and continue to be implicated in the colonising process. My analysis of the history of feminist relations with Indigenous women reveals that first- and second-wave feminists defined, normalised and represented themselves within feminist discourse through their centring as the all-knowing subject who constructs the Indigenous "Other". First-wave feminists, by deploying respectability and sexual propriety embodied in the subject position middle-class white woman, sought to remake Indigenous women by civilising us (in particular our sexuality) to minimise racial impurity. Second-wave feminists in Australia seek Indigenous women's ideological reconstruction as middle-class white woman feminist, despite their theorising of difference and incommensurability.

The degree to which white feminists today in Australia understand that they belong to the white centre and are implicated in power relations that have been historically constituted is assessed in Chapter 5. Through their self-presentation in interviews, white feminist academics illuminate the contradictory and inconsistent nature of their positioning on race, gender and cultural differences. "Race" and "racism" are important intellectually to feminist politics. However, white feminist academics' anti-racist practice is reduced to teaching within a limited paradigm, which has little impact on their subject positions within and outside the university. I argue that feminists need to analyse and interrogate this subject position and its relationship to the dominant white male centre of Australian society in order to understand how such a subject position is represented, complies with and maintains the racial order. The knowledge produced from such analyses can inform feminist theory and be used in anti-racist practice.

In Chapter 6 I show how Indigenous women have challenged the authority of white feminist knowledge through their self-presentation in a counter hegemonic discourse. Indigenous women do not want to be white; our politics are concerned with sustaining and maintaining our cultural integrity and achieving self-determination as a people. The subject position middle-class white woman is embedded in particular material conditions which shape the nature of power relations between white feminists and Indigenous women. These inter-subjective relations reflect the structural relationship between white society and Indigenous society.

For Indigenous women all white feminists benefit from colonisation; they are overwhelmingly represented and disproportionately predominant, have the key roles, and constitute the norm, the ordinary and the standard of womanhood in Australia. White women are not represented to themselves as being white; instead they position themselves as variously classed, sexualised, aged and abled. The disjuncture between representation and self-presentation of both Indigenous women and white feminists means that the involvement of Indigenous women in Australian feminism is, and will remain, partial. This partiality in practice requires white feminists to relinquish some power, dominance and privilege in Australian feminism to give Indigenous women's interests some priority. To do any less means that the subject position middle-class white woman will remain centred as a site of dominance participating in maintaining the racial order in Australian society.

White people may find this book difficult to read because my representations will challenge and discomfort them. My hope is that this book stimulates new ways of thinking about racialised inter-subjective relations and contributes to the development of an understanding of, and respect and appreciation for, each other in the struggle for racial justice and Indigenous rights.

CHAPTER ONE

Tellin' It Straight:
Self-Presentation within Indigenous
Women's Life Writings[1]

> Aboriginal women's autobiographies announce their cultural differ-
> ence from the dominant white culture. This difference is quite
> complex and exists on a number of levels, some of which are difficult
> for white readers to perceive, so strong is their inclination to incor-
> porate everything they read into their own experience (Brewster
> 1996:39).

White Australia has come to "know" the "Indigenous woman"
from the gaze of many, including the diaries of explorers, the
photographs of philanthropists, the testimony of white state
officials, the sexual bravado of white men and the ethnographies
of anthropologists. In this textual landscape Indigenous women
are objects who lack agency. The landscape is disrupted by the
emergence of the life writings of Indigenous women whose
subjectivities and experiences of colonial processes are evident
in their texts. The term "life writings" has been used because the
Indigenous women's texts that have been analysed do not fit the
usual strict chronological narrative of autobiography, and they
are the product of collaborative lives. In these life writings experience is fundamentally social and relational, not something
ascribed separately within the individual. Indigenous women's
life writings are based on the collective memories of inter-genera-
tional relationships between predominantly Indigenous women,
extended families and communities, hence the inclusion of the
works of Morgan (1987), Huggins (1994a) and Pilkington
(1996), who have written their mothers' life herstories. These

relationships are underpinned by connections with one's country and the spirit world.[2] In all of the life writings, Indigenous people are related either by descent, country or place or shared experiences. In this sense the life writings of Indigenous women are an extension of Indigenous relationality in that they express the self as part of others and others as part of the self within and across generations.

Indigenous women's life writings have been edited by white people to different degrees and some have been written in collaboration with white people.[3] Literary relations such as these are representative of power relations between coloniser and colonised. Indigenous women's knowledge in itself can not be accommodated, but must be redefined to conform to the requirements of white literary practice. However, although white editing or scribing may influence the writing of the text, it does not erase the subtext, which is informed by the knowledge and experience of Indigenous women. These women are not the site of a mastering gaze, but are voices reclaiming Indigenous experience as the locus of relationships in their life writings. The gaze of Indigenous women on themselves is inscribed into the text through their self-presentation. There is little room made available for the reader to be distracted from the inter-subjective meeting or to objectify them. "The eye is not given its solitary freedom. The women depicted function as subjects of their own looking or their activity, within highly specified locations of which the viewer becomes a part" (Pollock 1988:87).

As subjects of their own gaze, the personal is political in Indigenous women's texts. Mudrooroo refutes this in both his books on Indigenous literature. He argues that Indigenous women's life writings are not "political" because white editing of these texts makes their message one of understanding and tolerance (Narogin 1990:162–63). Narogin's critique is spurious because he separates Indigenous women's lives from the Indigenous struggle. He relies on a white patriarchal definition of what it is to be political, thus denying subjectivity as a site of resistance, and he is overly concerned with how the text is written — its form, rather than what is written. Indigenous women's life writings make visible dimensions of the hidden history and colonial legacy of this country through their gaze as subjects. Indigenous women's life writings are testimony to colonial processes that shaped subjectivity and they illuminate the pain and loss of dispossession in its many forms. The life writings also reveal various creative strategies developed and deployed for survival and resistance. As Larbarlestier notes, "in contemporary Australian society, 'living black' and writing about it can be seen as a process of political confrontation" (Larbarlestier 1991:90). Indigenous women's life writings challenge and disrupt both Narogin's claims and anthropological representations of the "Indigenous woman" because self-presentation by Indigenous women is a political act.

This chapter examines the content of Indigenous women's life writings to describe certain aspects of the social construction of Indigenous women's subjectivity. Indigenous women's experiences are grounded in a different history from that which is celebrated and known in white domains, and our experiences and subjugated knowledges offer insights about differences and incommensurabilities between white women and Indigenous women.[4] In the life writings Indigenous women speak of the practical, political and personal effects of being "other". Through self-presentation they are the subject of their own gaze rather than the object of white anthropological scrutiny and knowledge (Brewster 1996:38). Indigenous women use experience as a criterion for accumulating and producing subjugated knowledges which reflect their world view and inform their social practice in Indigenous and white domains (Collins 1991:206). Indigenous women's self-presentation in their life writings challenges anthropological representations of the "Indigenous woman". The chapter begins by making connections between colonising processes and Indigenous women's lives by linking government policies to their lived experiences. It then demonstrates how Indigenous women's subjectivity has been shaped by experiences of these processes and resistance to such processes through subjugated knowledge. Indigenous women's encounters with the subject position middle-class white woman in white domains is then discussed, and the chapter concludes by looking at how subjectivity is a site of activity, meaning and resistance in the cultural borderlands.[5]

The social construction of Indigenous women's subjectivity

Herstory: dispossession, domination and domestication

The British government did not colonise Australia overnight, nor was it a consistent project; nevertheless the dispossession, domination and denial of Indigenous people's sovereignty provided the foundations for the modern Australian state. In *Follow the Rabbit-Proof Fence*, Doris Pilkington gives us an insight into what the arrival of white people meant for the Nyungars around Swan Bay in Western Australia in the 1800s (1996:1–17). At first the Nyungars thought the British were gengars, spirits of the ancestors, returning to their country and the gengars' behaviour seemed non-intrusive, but it soon became apparent that they did not act according to Nyungar lore.[6] These new gengars were taking land that was not theirs and would not share it to hunt and gather. Instead they murdered Nyungars who resisted them or got in their way. Stories of their atrocities soon spread through Indigenous camps in the Kimberley and fear crept into the hearts and minds of Nyungars. Similar stories were spread in different Indigenous camps in the south, north and east of Australia. On Mornington Island in Queensland, Elsie Roughsey's grandfather told his son: "Never kill a white man, because that fellow got plenty more people like him, to come here and kill us all" (Roughsey 1984:3).

Why did white people come and take our land? is a question asked many times over by Indigenous people. Different versions of white history give different answers (e.g. Blainey 1966; Morris 1989; Clark 1969; Reynolds 1987, 1989). Whatever the reasons for British colonisation of Australia, during the first five years of the colony the relationship between Indigenous people and white colonists involved violent confrontation as more and more land was appropriated to establish a new economy and society. The white colonists' pursuit of stock and land meant that hunting and pastoral economies could not coexist within the same boundaries (Stanner 1979; Reynolds 1981; Burgmann & Lee

1988; Morris 1989; Cowlishaw 1988). Coupled with overt acts of violence was the development of a new hegemonic ideology born out of a patriarchal society whose imperative was the establishment of a capitalist mode of production. Indigenous people who suffered rapid dispossession of their land underwent cultural changes in response to their new position: most notably, they became fringe dwellers living on the edges of towns. Guns, poison or disease exterminated indigenous people who did not survive. Indigenous women were raped and children were murdered or mutilated. The oral tradition of Tasmanian Aborigines records that white men used babies' heads as balls in polo practice and cut off Indigenous men's scrotums for use as tobacco pouches (pers. com. Michael Mansell 1990). As an indication of the number of Indigenous deaths, it is estimated that there were 11,500 Indigenous people in Victoria at the time land was taken up at Port Phillip, but 100 years later the population was only 800; 93 per cent had been killed or displaced (Rowley 1972b:5). Similar stories and statistics can be produced for other states. It is estimated that approximately 100,000 Indigenous people lived in Queensland in the late 1700s, but by 1901 the population had been reduced to 26,670.

Frontier violence was related to the fact that Indigenous people and white colonialists came from diametrically opposed cultural backgrounds. Land was essential to the survival of both peoples, but cultural differences meant that there were widely divergent attitudes towards its use. The white colonists' desire for land provided the rationale for the unofficial policy of extermination that was implemented and supported by the colonial government of New South Wales (Stanner 1979:90–191). Indigenous hunter-gathering practices and philosophies entail a complete aversion to any thought of owning nature, and are inexorably tied to the land. Conversely, the religion of the early colonists was tied up with the virtues of work, production and progress. For Indigenous people the land was the basis of spirituality and the sole means of subsistence, and it was defended in frontier battles from 1788 up until the 1930s, during which time virtually all land that the colonists considered to be economically viable was expropriated (Reynolds 1981). Reynolds notes that "the intensity and duration of conflict varied widely depending on terrain, indigenous population densities, the speed of settlement, the type of introduced economic activity, even the period of first contact" (Reynolds 1981:50). Dispossessed of their land, many of the remaining Indigenous population were forced to live on the fringes of towns where they suffered from malnutrition and introduced diseases. In northern Australia, where white occupation occurred later, some Indigenous people were able to maintain a predominantly hunter-gather existence until the late 1880s (Lippmann 1981). However, the new means of subsistence established by many Indigenous people in response to their dispossession led to a more sedentary lifestyle (Morris 1983:504–5). At times, due to a shortage of white labour, Indigenous men, women and children worked in the pastoral industry under dismal conditions (Berndt & Berndt 1987; Wade-Marshall & Loveday 1985).

By 1911, with the exception of Tasmania, most state governments and the Northern Territory had legislated for state control of Indigenous people through establishing either white "Protectors" or an "Aborigines Protection Board" to manage Indigenous affairs (Wilson 1997:28; Morris 1985:85–89). Ida West, a Tasmanian Indigenous woman, talks of her childhood from 1919 to 1925 as being a period of freedom on Flinders Island, where she says "we lived at Killiecrankie for a time before I started school, and never saw anyone except our relations" (West 1987:3). Land was made available for reserves and missions throughout Australia. The reserves were managed and controlled by either the local police or a government-appointed manager. Missionaries of various denominations controlled the missions. The shift in government policy was from one of extermination to protection, which some have argued was brought about by the political activity of the anti-slavery and humanitarian movement in Britain. This movement was influenced by the theory among the British scientific community that Australian Indigenous peoples were a dying race in need of saving (Western 1983:200). The Indigenous people referred to were those classified as being of "full descent" or biologically pure. In 1997, the National Inquiry into the

Separation of Aboriginal and Torres Strait Islander Children from Their Families found that:

> By the late nineteenth century it had become apparent that although the full descent Indigenous population was declining, the mixed descent population was increasing. In Social Darwinist terms they were not regarded as near extinction. The fact that they had some European 'blood' meant that there was a place for them in non-Indigenous society, albeit a very lowly one. Furthermore, the prospect that this mixed descent population was growing made it imperative to governments that mixed descent people be forced to join the workforce instead of relying on government rations. In that way the mixed descent population would be both self-supporting and satisfy the needs of the developing economy for cheap labour (Wilson 1997:29).

De Lepervanch argues that the change in Indigenous policy could be linked to the way in which "economic expansion had provided the setting in which some political and social reforms could be made without sacrifice by or danger to the existing order" (1975:90–91). White social structures had been put into place and the dominance of white Australian society firmly established. Indigenous people who were placed on, or had moved onto, reserves and missions were subject to restrictive laws and repressive control. In 1902, in New South Wales, Ella Simon's family moved onto 12 acres that had been set aside and named the Purfleet mission, which was controlled by missionaries until 1932. Ella's people worked for nearby farmers in the early years, but by the Depression, when numbers had increased on the mission, the state extended its control by appointing a manager who had wide-ranging powers. In Western Australia, Doris Pilkington's grandparents and extended family moved from the desert region in the 1900s to the perceived safety of Jigalong mission station because of the appropriation of their lands and fear of the white man's treachery. Stories of murder and mutilation spread among Nyungars along the coast and throughout the north.

In 1937, when it became obvious that the Indigenous population was not dying out but continuing to increase due to white men either raping or having consensual sexual relations with Indigenous women, the first joint State-Commonwealth conference on Native Welfare was held (Wilson 1997:32). After this conference most state governments moved to a policy of assimilation (Cowlishaw 1986c; Lippmann 1981:35). Miscegenation was again the catalyst for the new policy because it disrupted racial purity but offered white society a pool of cheap labour. Mothers and the children from such unions were usually removed from the Indigenous community. Indigenous women's sexuality was policed and contained and their children removed from the influence of kin and community. Connie Nungulla McDonald and her mother were taken to the Forrest River Mission in 1933. McDonald stated:

> Documents show that the protector for Aborigines at Wyndham, Sergeant J. F. Flinders, had consulted with his fellow protector, Dr Webster, and they decided that it was in my mother's "best interests" for us to be taken to the mission. They feared that left in Wyndham, "she would become a victim to the lust of degenerates — whites and Afghans" (McDonald et al. 1996:3).

In 1931 Monica Clare and her brother were taken by Child Welfare some years after the death of her white mother because of the impoverished conditions she and her brother were living under with her Indigenous father (Clare 1978:34). Marnie Kennedy of Palm Island in Queensland, whose mother was a Kalkadoon woman named Rose by the station owners she worked for without payment, says:

> As she grew older and began to blossom like the flower she was named for, the white man soon had his way. She had three children to the white man. That was her crime and she was sent to Palm Island as punishment — no blame to the white man. My elder brother was kept to work on the station while my mother, myself and baby brother went to Palm (Kennedy 1990:2–3).

In theory the policy of assimilation was aimed at resocialising and educating Aborigines to be able to function in the white-man's world. However, in practice, it involved cruelty, discipline and punishment for Indigenous girls and boys who received minimal training to become indentured Indigenous servants for Australia's emerging white middle-class. Children were removed from their parents by force or coerced through deceit. Pilkington in Western Australia says of the removal of her "half caste" mother and aunty:

> Molly and Gracie sat silently on the horse, tears streaming down their

cheeks as Constable Riggs turned the big bay stallion and led the way back to the depot. A high pitched wail broke out. The cries of agonised mothers and the women, and the deep sobs of grandfathers, uncles and cousins filled the air. Molly and Gracie looked back just once before they disappeared through the river gums. Behind them, those remaining in the camp found strong sharp objects and gashed themselves and inflicted wounds to their heads and bodies as an expression of their sorrow (Pilkington 1996:44–45).

Alice Nannup, also identified by white officials as a "half caste", recalls:

> There were three of us kids that went with the Campbells down south; two girls and a boy. The boy was from another station and he was brought over two or three days before we all left. Now that I'm older, I often think back to this time and I think everything was arranged before we ever left the North. It was a cunning way to get me, to trick my mother by telling her I was going off to be educated, then brought back to be with them when I turned eighteen (Nannup et al. 1992:45).

In Victoria, Margaret Tucker was taken from her mixed descent parents at Moonachulla Reserve to work as a domestic at the age of 13 in 1917 (Tucker 1983:91–93). In Western Australia, Glenyse Ward was removed as a baby from her mother and has no recollection of the event (Ward 1988:1). Arthur Corunna tells Sally Morgan of the removal of himself, his brother Albert and sister Daisy (Sally's grandmother) from their mother at Corunna Downs to "the Swan Native and Half Caste Mission" (Morgan 1987:180). In Queensland, Elsie Roughsey was removed from her father's care at the age of eight and placed in the dormitory of the mission that had been established on her country, Mornington Island. She says they went to the mission at first only for the day and obtained meals: "Each day it happened, until there was that time when the missionaries desired to have us put in the dormitory to stay with the other children and go to school" (Roughsey 1984:7). Rita Huggins recalls her family's removal to Barambah reserve in the 1920s:

> One winter's night, troopers came riding on horseback through our camp. My father went to see what was happening and my mother stayed with her children to try to stop us from being so frightened. One trooper I remember clearly. Perhaps he was sorry for what he was doing, because he gave me some fruit — a banana, something as

unknown to me as the whiteman who offered it. My mother saw, and cried out to me, "Barjun! Barjun!". Dadda and some of the older men were shouting angrily at the officials. We were being taken away from our lands. We didn't know why, nor imagined what place we would be taken to (Huggins & Huggins 1994: 9).

Rita and her brothers and sisters were removed from their parents and placed in the dormitory on Barambah Reserve. In contrast, Ella Simon (1987), Ruby Langford (1988), Della Walker (1989), Evelyn Crawford (1993) and Eileen Morgan (1994) in New South Wales were not separated from their kin by the dormitory system; instead they lived with family confined to the reserves and missions. Mabel Edmund, who is of Aboriginal and South Sea Islander descent, was never placed on a mission or reserve but she and her parents worked on cattle stations. She was raised in north Rockhampton: "the white community called this area Kanaka Town, but to the South Sea Islanders who lived there, it was known as Northside, or Moores Creek, or Ford Street, or Creek Street" (Edmund 1992:6). The assimilation policy impacted differently on these women's lives, but they all became domestic servants working for middle-class white women and white men.

By the 1950s some of these Indigenous women were still living on reserves or missions, while others were in domestic service. Embedded within the rhetoric of the assimilation policy was the notion that Aborigines were to achieve equality with the rest of the Australian public. The fact that they were clearly not in an equal position as a result of colonisation and domination often served as evidence of their supposed intrinsic inferiority as human beings (Lippmann 1981). The life writings of Indigenous women show that the attitudes of white mistresses towards their Indigenous female servants were that they were born to serve them, as Margaret Tucker's recollection of having to continue with chores, even though she was ill, reveals:

My mistress asked me why I was limping. I had to show her the leg. She gave a gasp and ran out of the room to the telephone. She called the doctor. I was sitting on the garden seat near the kitchen door when he came. I don't know what she told him, but she said later that if the wound had gone a fraction deeper it would have reached the bone, and I would have had to have my leg off. She also said the doctor said Aborigines had no feeling, we were like animals, our wounds just healed without any trouble. It didn't worry me. Things could not have been any worse anyhow. I had to sit every day for nearly a week under the trees out the back on that garden seat with my leg up. She brought the dishes out to me to wash up. I cleaned the silver and peeled the vegetables, all because the doctor said I had to sit down and I was not to use the leg. She grudgingly gave me food such as broth, because the doctor said I was to have it. I never told her how the sore started. I suppose it would not have made much difference. One morning I was washing up outside with my legs up. I did not do something properly. She was in a bad mood and I copped it as the saying is. She boxed my ears as she held me by the hair. She slapped my face as I cried, "Don't, you are hurting me." (Tucker 1983:119–20).

In attempting to assimilate Indigenous women as domestic servants, the government was constructing and defining who they were and how they should behave. Government and popular representations of was it was to be Indigenous were not necessarily the same as the way Indigenous women defined themselves. However, these Indigenous women had neither the right to appeal nor the means to seek justice when governments sanctioned their exploitation and abuse through legislation. The difference between slavery in America and indentured labour in Australia was that government, not free enterprise, controlled the terms and conditions of the trade. Ella Simon tells the story of her cousin who was sent to work by the Aborigines Protection Board in New South Wales:

Finally the Board sent her to work in a home where she wasn't paid wages for nine years! The money — 1 s 6d a week and 5s a week after four years! — was supposed to be paid into the Board which 'minded' it for her. That was a laugh. So I went in with her to the Board to get the money that she had worked for all those years. Not only did they refuse to give her any, they also told me I was too light-skinned for them to help. I got that bit of information for nothing! (Simon 1987:101)

Marnie Kennedy says "[w]e Aboriginals are a good example of white exploitation. We were the slaves, to be worked long hours and as long as we could stand for little pay and most times with no time off. White man would work his eight hours and no more" (Kennedy 1990:56). Indigenous women and men were not legally entitled to be paid award wages until the mid 1960s. This change came about partly as a result of European and Indigenous action during and immediately after World War II, which had helped to publicise Indigenous exploitation and impoverishment (Howard 1982:85). In addition, the introduction of the welfare state and an increase in government intervention into the economy characterised this period in Australia's history. Indigenous people were entitled to some social services, but this money was handled by the manager of the reserve, the cattle station, the mission or the relevant government department handling "native affairs". Governments across Australia appeared to be consistent in restricting indentured domestic service to single or unmarried Indigenous women. Some women literally escaped, as Glenyse Ward recounts:

> In her usual manner, Mrs Bigelow dropped me off at the bus station and left me to get my own ticket. There were two buses, one to Bunbury and one to Busselton. I went on board the bus to Bunbury, which would connect with the train to Armadale and so take me back to Wandering mission. I sat there looking out the window. I waited for her car to disappear. Then I jumped up from my seat, went down the aisle, collected my case and changed buses. I then bought my ticket — to Busselton. I was very nervous and confused and felt frightened, as I didn't think I had the nerve to do it. Deep down inside me I was happy — a lot. I felt a load lift off my shoulders as the bus I was on pulled out (Ward 1988:153).

For others, marriage and children replaced formalised indentured labour, although women such as Alice Nannup, Della Walker, Ruby Langford, Marnie Kennedy, Eileen Morgan and Rita Huggins often worked for the white missus to obtain extra income for their families. While motherhood became a basis for self-actualisation and status, Indigenous women lived life under a vague but real sense of threat that their children would be taken from them. Evelyn Crawford says that "[a]fter the mission time, we were always afraid there were people waitin' to grab us and take us away" (1993:99). Their experiences told them that their lives could be disrupted at any moment by government officials, and, of course, that the closest relationships were often the ones most at risk.

Racial oppression is evident in the narratives of Indigenous women in the descriptions of personal interaction with white people which form part of the "social processes which allow such differentiation to flourish as a set of practices and an ideology" (Cowlishaw 1988:248). The control and subordination of Indigenous women and their families was legally sanctioned and enforced through policies of assimilation which utilised biological criteria and cultural inferiority to separate and displace children from their mothers, families and land. Scientific discourses in the white public domain provided certain knowledge about the biological and cultural inferiority of Indigenous women, this knowledge informed the action and decisions of government and served as a rhetoric of rationalisation for the implementation of its policies by agents who legitimately sought to impose it. Acts of white supremacy were commonplace in the lives of Indigenous women.

In 1967, the Australian people passed a referendum amending the Constitution. As a result of the amendments, Indigenous people were counted in the census and the Commonwealth government was given the power to legislate on behalf of people of any race (Howard 1982:173). This meant that state governments no longer had complete control over the lives of Indigenous people. The Commonwealth Liberal–National coalition government advocated a change in policy from assimilation to integration, but their new policy was not implemented. In 1973 the newly elected Labor government developed and implemented instead a policy of self-determination. Racial discriminatory legislation began to be repealed and government-funded Indigenous community controlled organisations were established to deliver services. Changes in policy are reflected in the life writings of Indigenous women whose experiences are testimony to the fact that racism was legally sanctioned until 1976. Greater degrees of freedom and control over their own lives came about for these women in the 1960s and 1970s, when many became involved in Indigenous community life and politics. This occurred during a period when rights were demanded and won by the civil rights, gay and lesbian rights and women's rights movements throughout the western world.

In the 1960s and 1970s Molly Kelly and Daisy Kadibil returned to their beloved Jigalong from where they had been taken as children. Sally Morgan and her mother made the trip to Port

Headland and Corunna station. Alice Nannup returned to Roebourne, Rita Huggins was reunited with Carnarvon, her place of birth. Della Walker and Elsie Roughsey taught the old ways to children and Ruby Langford became immersed in community life. Glenyse Ward became a young mother, married and settled in Broome, Western Australia. Margaret Tucker was appointed to the Advisory Council of the Ministry for Aboriginal Affairs in New South Wales and Aboriginal community organisations. Monica Clare became the Secretary of the Aborigines Committee of the South Coast at Woollongong in New South Wales. Eileen Morgan and Evelyn Crawford became educators teaching Indigenous culture. Ida West became President of the Tasmanian Aboriginal Centre. Mabel Edmund took up art, and her paintings are held in private collections throughout the world as well as the Queensland Museum. Since the 1970s Indigenous women continue to write books about their lives and their families, their kin and community who helped shape each herstory.

The manufacturing of a distinctive subjectivity through the experiences and knowledges exposed in the life writings by Indigenous women is both an expression of different cultural forms and resistance to white domination (Morris 1989:219). Different ethics, behaviour and values repudiate the moral and intellectual hegemony that effects such domination and oppression. The lives of Indigenous women discussed in this chapter are part of the collective history of Indigenous people's political and cultural struggle, which forms part of the conscious and unconscious social practices of everyday life in both Indigenous and white cultural domains (Larbalestier 1991: 91). The cultural specificities of these Indigenous women's lives are enmeshed in historically constructed relations with white people that continue to inform processes of inter-subjectivity in Indigenous and white cultural domains.

Government intervention into Indigenous women's lives was part of the social processes that shaped the nature of these relations. Through a change in government policies since the 1970s, many of these women obtained a tertiary education after they raised their families, and they acknowledge that they are now freer than when they were young. However, their life writings show that they know that such freedom has not come without cost nor has it changed in any fundamental way the nature of their sociality, which is still predominantly maintained by and intimately connected to Indigenous cultural domains. Kin, extended family and community are important to Indigenous women because they are where social memory becomes activated through shared experiences, knowledges and remembering. The life writings are testimony to how bodies are enacted and experienced in very different ways depending on the cultural and historical position of different subjects. The body for Indigenous women is the link to people, country, spirits, herstory and the future, and is a positive site of value and affirmation as well as a site of resistance.

Relationality and spirituality: Indigenous women's subjugated knowledges

Indigenous women's life writings point to the fundamental incommensurability within our nation: "what for white Australia has been the fortuitous 'settlement' of the country, for indigenous people can only be seen as a tragic 'invasion' " (Ang 1997:62). Another incommensurability is that what for White Australia was cheap labour and a civilising mission, for Indigenous women constituted stolen children and slavery. Protection and then assimilation were government policies under which the Indigenous women grew up. Under these policies, Ella Simon (1987), Alice Nannup (1992), Daisy Corunna (Morgan 1987), Molly Kelly and Daisy Kadibil (Pilkington 1996) are defined by government and church officials, on the basis of biological criteria, as half-castes. However, such labelling tells us little about the way in which Indigenous women's subjectivity is shaped and reshaped by the subjects themselves through their experiences.

Although every voice is distinctive and the life writing of each Indigenous woman has its own form, they share common elements of a worldview (Hooton 1990:314).The content of the life writings gives priority to different subject matter than white women's autobiographical texts. It is no mere coincidence that Indigenous and white men are not mentioned or featured as main characters in the texts; it is Indigenous women's relations with other Indigenous women that are given significance. Marriage is talked about as companionship rather than a western romantic epic; sometimes finding a partner is barely raised in discussion. Nor is business or career success a measure of self worth in these life writings. There is also little or no emphasis on sex. Some argue that such a silence could be a response to dominant representations of Indigenous women's sexuality as being excessive, promiscuous and animalistic (Clough 1994:101). However, it is more likely that sexuality is kept private or accorded little attention because this is where Indigenous women have drawn the boundary between themselves and their audience. A boundary that is related to the way in which cultural processes have shaped their subjectivity.

Relationality

Through the use of oral histories and collective memories Indigenous women's narratives make visible and affirm the continuity and persistence of Indigenous subjugated knowledges in spheres of interdependent cultural domains which are peopled by both spiritual beings and human beings. Spirituality permeates life in that the universe is not blind or mechanical but aware and organic (Gunn Allen 1992:80). Unlike most white women's autobiographies, these narratives express collective relations between a number of Indigenous people transcending several generations. These relations are underpinned by connections with their country and the spirit world. In each of the life writings all the Indigenous people are related by descent, country, place or shared experiences. Such relationality means that in their relationships with other Indigenous women, men and children they are inclusive rather than exclusive. That is, personal and intimate relations are extended beyond immediate kin and the boundaries between Indigenous women and other Indigenous people are negotiated on this basis. In Indigenous cultural domains relationality means that one experiences the self as part of others and that others are part of the self; this is learnt through reciprocity, obligation, shared experiences, coexistence, cooperation and social memory.

Ruby Langford, Della Walker, Alice Nannup, Connie McDonald,

Elsie Roughsey, Ella Simon, Rita Huggins, Margaret Tucker, Eileen Morgan, Evelyn Crawford, Daisy Corunna and Glenyse Ward reveal experiences of learning by relationships of reciprocity and obligation through stories, and through observation and mimicking of adults and other children. They acquired these knowledges through their experiences in Indigenous cultural domains located on missions, reserves or cattle stations or with their families in Indigenous communities. The most important relationships for Indigenous women in their life writings are with their immediate, surrogate and extended families. In the texts Indigenous women, mothers and grandmothers demonstrate a spirit of generosity to their families and communities, as the following quote from Monica Clare illustrates:

> One day, Dave and his children were lucky. Wandering along not knowing what to do, they ran into a blacks' camp and were welcomed to a feast of porcupine and emu. Isabelle and Morris had other children to talk to and play with. The women there cared for them both, while some of the older men took Dave aside, and talked to him (Clare 1978:18).

Eileen Morgan recollects:

> Each house at Wallaga Lake only had one small tank for a family of fifteen or twenty, because you didn't just have your own children — you'd have your whole family, the nannas and pops and everyone. This is how we've always lived. That's our culture of sharing and living together (Morgan 1994:25–26).

Children who were taken as babies from their mothers and lived in the mission dormitories had no recollection of their families. They learnt from the older children about the principles of relationality. Glenyse Ward recollects:

> All I could see was a smiling face, very close to mine, with blue cloth draped over her head. I came to know her as Sister Gertrude. She passed me over to a big girl from the group, who soaked my dress with tears and squeezed me nearly to death. Then the big girl knelt down with me so that the smaller girl who had been pushing and shoving with the desert blonde, could give me a big slopping kiss on the cheek. Little did I know that the big girl who was crying and the little girl who kissed me were my natural sisters. They were Nita and Sally — Nita was considered a working girl at the age of fourteen. She left the mission to work for white people when I was seven. Sally, who was eight years old, spent a lot longer with me, growing up with all

the other girls round about the same age as us. We all considered one another sisters (Ward 1991:2).

Indigenous women's relationality encompasses principles of generosity, empathy and care that connote ideals of respect, consideration, understanding, politeness and nurturing. All of the Indigenous women sought to impart such principles to their own children and grandchildren in later life.

Spirituality

Social relationships are important in all cultural domains, but their nature differs and the moral universe, which informs these relationships in Indigenous cultural domains, is outside the experience of white women. Relationality is one dimension of this moral universe that is spiritually interconnected. Indigenous women perceive the world as organic and populated by spirits, which connect places and people. Sally Morgan's grandmother and mother hear the corroboree in the swamp when Sally's father is ill and understand this as the spirit's recognition of the father's mental turmoil. After his death the corroboree is no longer heard. When Daisy Corunna dies, it is the call of the bird that tells Sally about the end of her grandmother's life. Glenyse Ward learns from the older girls of the spiritual beings, the mumaries, in the caves near Wandering mission. The older girls tell her that if she and the other children are naughty the mumaries will come and take them away. Alice Nannup returns to make peace with her country with the snake that lives in the waterhole at Mallina by performing a water-based ritual. Ruby Langford receives a sign of bad news when late at night there are three knocks at her door but no one is in sight. The next morning Ruby's friend Harold Leslie is told his father has died.

Ella Simon recalls stories told to her by her grandmother which were "to make us keep the law or just be better people" (Simon 1987:106). One story concerned the muckarung (lizard) who was once a young Indigenous woman who disobeyed the law by going near the men's bora ground. She was punished by being turned into the muckarung that sits on a log waving its front legs as if to signal 'go back, go back'. As a child Ella was told the story of the goi-on, which was something like a ghost, and was used to stop Indigenous children from wandering off and getting lost. Della Walker tells of how the red waratah tree grew on the rock near the sea on the mid north coast of New South Wales. A young Indigenous woman sitting by the sea pined for her lover who had been killed in war. She died of a broken heart and when her family arrived to take her body home they found a waterfall had formed from her tears and a red waratah tree was growing in the place where she had died. The tree is still there today (Walker & Coutts 1989:8–9).

Such stories and experiences illustrate the way in which the spiritual nature of the world is incorporated into the socialisation of Indigenous children. Unlike white constructions of Christian spirituality, Indigenous spirituality encompasses the intersubstantiation of ancestral beings, humans and physiography. The spiritual world is immediately experienced because it is synonymous with the physiography of the land. In the life writings the reality of spirituality is a physical fact because it is experienced as part of one's life. As Brewster comments, "such knowledge is incommensurate with a rational belief system and as such it is tacit resistance to western ways of thinking" (Brewster 1996:9).

Indigenous women do not just perceive events and objects differently from white women; we also understand ourselves as persons in quite different ways. In the life writings of Indigenous women, white women are represented as being impersonal, individualistic and egocentric with interests to protect. Indigenous women self-present a construction of the subject that is holistic and collective in nature. In these life writings, differences among Indigenous women tend to be articulated in terms of country, mission or kinship rather than ego, race or class. The life writings are not based on psychological deconstructions that seek to explain why things happened in terms of actors' motivations and intentions. Rather, descriptions are given of how things happened, because Indigenous women perceive themselves as being an extension of the earth, which is alive and unpredictable. Hence their understandings of themselves, the world and other people as being interconnected also reflect this view. In the life writings Indigenous women perceive their experiences and others' experiences as extensions of themselves. As Morris argues, this is a construction of self that extends beyond the immediate family:

> The interconnectedness of self to others is related to those with whom one is familiar: those with whom one is related, one grows up with or, more specifically, those with whom one engages in relations of mutuality — where notions of generalised reciprocity shape and inform daily interactions (Morris 1989: 215).

The life writings of Indigenous women show a moral ordering of sociality which emphasises mutual support and concern for those with whom they are interconnected, and reveal much about how relationality and spirituality constitute Indigenous women's subjectivity. Knowledges about one's spirituality and relationality are subjugated; that is, they are disguised and hidden but are present in inter-subjective relations between Indigenous women and white women.

As keepers of the family, Indigenous women are the bearers of subjugated knowledges, and their experiences speak of inter-subjectivity between white women and themselves in white cultural domains where incommensurabilities operate in communicative exchange. Lois McNay, drawing on Habermas, argues that "an individual's actions are always subject to an interpretative indeterminacy in so far as a subject never simply acts through desires and potentialities, but rather the definition of his/her actions/desires are always subject to the interpretations of others" (1992:175). And Foucault tells us that at the level of the subject, oppression and domination can be minimised by being a reflexive subject (1988:18). Questions raised by Indigenous women's life writings include: How does one know when subjugated knowledges are operating in a particular cultural context where two subjects may speak the same language but position the world in distinctively different ways? How can one be reflexive about knowledge that one does not know? And what is the extent of the indeterminacy?

The common discursive worlds we construct through dialogue are partial and incommensurabilities will exist in communicative exchanges (Ang 1997:59). Indigenous women's life writings reveal that they have no choice but to be conscious of white knowledges and behaviour. Indigenous women are the ones who have to negotiate subjectivity and deploy different subject positions in processes of inter-subjectivity with white women irrespective of their class. There is no such imperative for white women in their relationships with Indigenous people. The marginal position of Indigenous people in Australian society means that white knowledges and cultural practices always circumscribe our subjectivity. Therefore incommensurabilities will accompany communicative exchanges between differently positioned subjects.

Indigenous and white women's inter-subjective relations

The subject position "Indigenous servant"

Government policies implemented on missions and reserves and by employers were aimed at producing disciplined servants, who would comply with the requirements of being in service, by alienating them from Indigenous culture and their country. Indigenous women received punishment for contravening rules and learnt discipline but were not convinced that white ways of doing things were just and proper, because they drew on their experiences and knowledge of another standard of being human. Alice Nannup recalled the beatings she received for minor breaches of rules that she perceived as unfair. Elsie Roughsey writes that rules controlled all aspects of life on the mission and Indigenous people were beaten for minor breaches. Ella Simon, Ruby Langford, Rita Huggins, Della Walker and Daisy Corunna all worked hard under harsh conditions and routines devised by the white missus. In these white cultural domains Indigenous women were given authoritative direction and instructions which they learnt in order to function in their roles as domestic servants. It was training in subservience and basic domestic skills, not social etiquette, which was transferred by white managers, women bosses and missionaries. In white cultural domains the inter-subjectivity of relationships was not based on mutual understanding and relationships of reciprocal recognition.

The deployment of different subject positions is evident within the life writings. Indigenous women were confronted with having to define the boundaries between themselves and white people because of the impersonal extrinsic nature of the power relations

involved. The subject position "servant" was deployed by Indigenous women in an alien white domain where the disciplinary
process was directed at them with both moral and physical force.
In white cultural domains, Indigenous women became subjects
to be taught, while white women and men assumed the role of
the knowing subject. In their life writings Indigenous women
reveal that they were treated as though they had no knowledge,
feelings or emotional attachments. They were perceived as being
a tabula rasa — a blank slate to be written on. The dehumanised
position of Indigenous women is exemplified repeatedly in the
narratives. Daisy Corunna recalls when her daughter Gladdie was
taken from her by white Alice Brockman:

> When Gladdie was 'bout three years old, they took her from me. I'd
> been 'spectin' it. Alice told me Gladdie needed an education, so they
> put her in Parkerville Children's Home. What could I do? I was too
> frightened to say anythin'. I wanted to keep her with me, she was all
> I had, but they didn't want her there. Alice said she cost too much to
> feed, said I was ungrateful. She was wantin' me to give up my own
> flesh and blood and still be grateful. Aren't black people allowed to
> have feelin's? (Morgan 1987:332).

Mr and Mrs Campbell arranged for Alice Nannup to be taken
from her mother on the pretence of giving her an education
(Nannup et al. 1992:39), and the missionaries kept Elsie Roughsey from her family in the mission on Mornington Island. Rita
Huggins was separated from her mother and father on the
Cherbourg reserve to be trained for domestic service, and Alice
Nannup talks about the deliberate removal of northerners to the
south in Western Australia. Indigenous women were objects to
be moved around. In some of the narratives there are examples
of personal relationships with white people and acts of kindness.
Ella Simon and Alice Nannup's white fathers were part of their
world, but on the fathers' deaths there was no further contact
with their white relatives. Glenyse Ward found a friend in the old
man who worked in the orchard; Alice Nannup's family received
Christmas presents from a former employer; Della Walker's
mother received any leftover food from Craigmore Guest House
where she worked. Molly, Daisy and Gracie received food and
clothes from Mrs Flanagan after their escape from Moore River

Mission, only to have her telephone the Superintendent of the Mission to tell him where her young visitors were heading.

Despite these isolated experiences of white people's generosity, most of the time Indigenous women were treated as though they had no feelings or opinions about themselves or the world in which they lived. Glenyse Ward recollects her white missus informing her that she was the white missus's black slave. Alice Nannup recalls her experiences with her white missus, Mrs Larsen, who talks to Alice about her life, but never asks Alice about her family. Alice recalls what Mrs Larsen wrote in a letter to her brother in Sydney about the fact that one of the white girls she employed had left:

> "My little black girl has been with me for such a long time and she's worth a hundred of those others that I can't trust so I've decided to keep her on for awhile". You know, I think it's terrible that she called me that, her "little black girl". I mean, she wasn't thinking about my feelings to say that (Nannup et al. 1992:101).

These experiences of oppressive inter-subjective relations with white women outlined in the life writings do not disrupt the resilience and importance of Indigenous sociality. Throughout their lives Ruby Langford, Della Walker, Alice Nannup, Connie McDonald, Elsie Roughsey, Ella Simon, Molly Kelly, Gracie Cross, Daisy Kadibul and Glenyse Ward socialise and operate in predominantly Indigenous cultural domains. It is the knowledge, values and behaviour patterns of early childhood and life in Indigenous cultural domains circumscribed by mission dormitories and reserve managers that these women hold onto and cherish. They understood that they had to conform to acceptable and appropriate behaviour in specific situations as defined by white cultural norms. Different subject positions are apparent in Indigenous women's narratives. Glenyse Ward is the obedient servant to her white missus on the farm and a "troublemaker" in the company of other girls on the mission. Connie McDonald is the shy, reflective daughter in the company of her half-caste father but an articulate and outspoken young girl when she deals with the missionaries.

The denial of Indigenous women's social context and subjectivity by white women and men is in contrast to experiences in the Indigenous domain. Indigenous women learnt as children that they were not seen as individuals but as someone's sister or brother, daughter or grandaughter and that they belonged to a certain group of people. In their life writings the women grew up to marry and have children of their own, and as Indigenous policies changed in the 1970s they gained more freedom and control over their lives, and asserted themselves more in the white domain.

Margaret Jolly argues that white women in colonial Australia displayed a maternalism, which allowed them to maintain their superordinate position as mother in their relationships with Indigenous women (1993:114–15). Jolly's use of the image of mother, which implies affective and emotional and personal relations, is not borne out in Indigenous women's life writings. Impersonal extrinsic relations form the basis of communicative interchanges between Indigenous women and white women, which links the subject position middle-class white woman to white race privilege derived from colonisation.

The personal, emotional and affective aspects of existence in the private realm are also undermined by the subject position "Indigenous servant", whose presence reveals that not all women do the work that maintains the relations of ruling while being excluded as a group from ruling. The subject position "Indigenous servant" disrupts the feminist assertion that all women are against domination because of their feminine psychic orientation. Indigenous women's perceptions of the white missus are that she was not a sister, just as she was not a mother. White women participated in gendered racial oppression by deploying the subject position middle-class white woman both unconsciously and consciously, informed by an ideology of true white womanhood, which positioned Indigenous women as less feminine, less human and less spiritual than themselves. Although the morphology of colonialism has changed, it persists in discursive and cultural practices.

The subject position middle-class white woman

Political and legislative control by the state, informed by racist ideology, influenced public discourse, which in turn impacted on the private convictions and personal beliefs of white middle-class women about true womanhood and the biological and cultural inferiority of Indigenous women. Doris Pilkington tells us how a Mrs Chellow from Murra Munda Station wrote to the Chief Protector in Perth in December 1930 about Molly and Gracie:

> There are two half-caste girls at Jigalong — Molly 15 years, Crissy (also called Gracie) 11 years; in my opinion I think you should see about them as they are running wild with the whites (Pilkington 1996:41).

Constable Riggs, Protector of Aborigines, soon arrives to take the girls to the Moore River Native Settlement on the pretence that they will be going to school. Mrs Chellow's use of the words "running wild" implies that Molly and Gracie are animals who could not control their behaviour. They needed to be civilised and their sexuality controlled. As hooks (1997) and others have argued, throughout history the black female body has been an icon for sexual deviance. Chellow's actions also reveal the way in which white race privilege allows her to assume the superordinate position of the white woman who has the right to judge and make recommendations about Molly and Gracie.

Such maternalism and white race privilege are also evident in the actions of Alice Brockman, who tells Daisy Corunna that because she cannot afford to keep Daisy's daughter Gladys, the girl must be sent away (Morgan 1987). Towards the end of her life, Daisy implies that Alice Brockman knew who fathered Daisy and Gladys. Alice can live with the product of her father's sexual indiscretion, namely Daisy, but seeks to remove the product of his incestuous rape, Gladys, without any consideration of the feelings of Daisy and Gladys. Through her actions Alice protects the family name and social status of her father by positioning Daisy and Gladys as less than human by denying aspects of their subjectivity. Alice denies their emotional relationship as mother and daughter. She is able to do so because what underpins her actions is a belief in the less than human status of Daisy and Gladys. Alice also knows that the state will support her request to remove Gladys for "economic reasons" because its policies are predicated on the same belief.

Alice Nannup is told she is to be taken away for an "education", a plan that appears to have been instigated by Mrs Campbell. Mr and Mrs Campbell take Alice to Perth to work for them as their servant before being placed in the Moore River Native Settlement (Nannup et al. 1992: 58–60). Mr and Mrs Campbell collude to deceive Alice's mother about her education. They believe it would be in Alice's best interests to remove her from her family and country so that she can be trained as a domestic servant for white women. Again it is no accident that the pre-pubescent Alice is taken away before she reaches the stage of sexual promiscuity. White women's fear of Indigenous women's sexuality was connected to preserving their social status as white men's possessions, a status connected to an ideology of true womanhood which encompassed Christian morality, virtue and reproduction of the white race (Riddett 1993:89). The presence of Indigenous women allowed white women to sexualise their world "by projecting onto the black body a narrative of sexualisation" which was disconnected from the virtue and purity of subject position middle-class white woman (hooks 1997:114).

White race privilege and the oppression of Indigenous women, men and children were legitimated by the state and were connected to property and power. In New South Wales Della Walker's father and mother keep the Protector of Aborigines at bay until they are forced to moved onto the Tabulum Indigenous mission because most of the land where they lived was being resumed by Council for its white residents (Walker and Coutts 1989:19–29). Due to poor conditions in the camp on the edge of town, Ella Simon's grandparents move onto land donated by the McClennans (Simon 1987:5). This land was later appropriated by the state and became the Purfleet Indigenous Reserve. As more and more white people moved into the area, appropriating land through government grants and, later, purchases, Indigenous people became displaced, dispossessed and forced into dependency on government; socially and economically they were systematically being excluded from the new society.

The exercising of white race privilege and the oppression of Indigenous people encompassed not only exclusion but also a deliberate attempt to fragment family bonds. In Queensland Elsie Roughsey says it was the missionaries who desired to place her in a sex-segregated dormitory to go to school with the other

children on Mornington Island (Roughsey 1984:7). Elsie is given
no explanation for her removal from her parents and is later sent
out to work on stations. Rita Huggins' family is rounded up by
troopers and escorted to Cherbourg Indigenous reserve. Like
Elsie, Rita is separated from her parents on the reserve, placed
in a sex-segregated dormitory and sent out to work as a domestic
servant. The separation from families on reserves and missions,
such as that experienced by Glenyse Ward and Doris Pilkington,
was common in Queensland and Western Australia. However, in
New South Wales both Ella Simon and Della Walker spend their
childhood with their respective grandparents and parents on
Indigenous missions and reserves until they are sent away to work.
Life on Tabulum and Purfleet was still subject to discipline,
punishment and control. Both Della and Ella work as domestic
servants for white people under the regulations of the Aborigines
Protection Board.

Expressions of racism at institutional and individual levels
"were not premised on a random pattern of intolerant behaviour
but rather inscribed into a systematic pattern of inclusion and
exclusion" (Morris 1989:188). The systematic separation and
exclusion of these Indigenous women from the wider society, due
to perceived biological and cultural inferiority, was reproduced
in communicative exchanges. Relations were underpinned by
ideas associated with biological inferiority, impurity and pollu-
tion. A doctor, who will not touch Indigenous people, refuses
Della Walker's husband treatment (Walker & Coutts 1989:60).
The Sister in Charge refuses Mabel Edmund's father hospitalisa-
tion because he is black. When Mabel questions whether the
Sister is prejudiced, she replies "Oh no, I am not, dear, but some
of the other patients might say something to upset him" (Edmund 1992:70). Glenyse Ward is made to eat and drink out of a
tin mug and plate instead of the china plates and cups used by
the white missus and her family which she cleans every day. Alice
Nannup is not allowed to eat in the dining room with white guests
in the boarding house where she is staying. Despite the fact that
Alice's board and lodgings are paid for, she is made to assist the
white women who own the boarding house in the kitchen without
pay. Indigenous women's physical contact or presence in relation

to certain contexts and items were deemed to be polluting and purifying. The contradiction between these two positionings is clear. Indigenous women were allowed to be in contact with material items and operate in certain contexts as servants (that is, as objects), but to allow them the same service or use of the same material items meant recognising them as equal subjects. Such recognition would have disrupted the ontological basis for hierarchy and discrimination.

White women are represented everywhere in Indigenous women's life writings as disembodied, disembedded and dominant subjects in their relations with Indigenous women. Distance, unease, racial superiority and often cruelty pervade these relations. Riddet's analysis of white settler women's relationships with Indigenous women in the Northern Territory links such behaviour to the fact that white women were caught up in the imperatives of survival. It was "circumstances, including those of their conditioning and their acceptance of their task, their role [which] were not conducive to the setting up and keeping of friendship ties with Indigenous women" (Riddett 1993:89).

Resistance

Denying white representations

Acts of humiliation and cruelty by white women pervade Indigenous women's life writings. Most Indigenous women experienced the lack of an adequate diet, which at times almost resulted in starvation. Partial wages were rarely paid and beatings were meted out frequently. Margaret Tucker recalls the outcome when her mistress discovers the dirty nappies she has been hiding in order to protect the white woman's youngest son:

> I was expected to wash the dirty nappies, some of which I had hidden from my mistress in case the little fellow would be spanked. I know now how wrong it was. On this particular day she found the pile of messy napkins. I was horrified inside and prayed the little fellow was not near. I knew she loved him in some sort of way of course. She grabbed me by the hair and threw all those dirty nappies over me. I fought like mad. I don't know where I got the strength from. She was trying to rub them on my face (Tucker 1983:111).

Indigenous women were locked into pervasive and entrenched relations of power through which racial, sexual, economic, political and cultural oppressions were part of public discourse sanctioned by the state. However, despite the enveloping of Indigenous women in these relations, they were not passive victims; they participated in forms of resistance that were at times overt, but usually discreet and indirect. Forms of resistance are also contradictory; for example, oppression often induces feelings of inferiority and servility in the oppressed, which can result in a conscious disavowal of being a member of the stigmatised group. Ella Simon often separates herself from the category "Aborigine" [Indigenous] in her text, and Daisy and Gladys Corunna both deny to Sally Morgan that they are Indigenous women, preferring instead to identify as Indian or white. The overt denial of Indigeneity by these Indigenous women in certain contexts, however, does not disrupt their socio-cultural practices in other contexts. Daisy, Gladys and Ella resisted the representations of the dominant culture in particular contexts by denying Indigeneity, but that did not stop white and Indigenous people from placing them within the category "Indigenous". Nor were their family history, socio-cultural practices and subjugated knowledges representative of the subject position middle-class white woman. They deployed different subject positions depending on who they were engaged with, and when and where they were engaged. Indigenous women's subjectivity has been shaped by historically imbued representations of Indigeneity developed in anthropological and legal discourses as much as by an Indigenous discourse of self-presentation.

In the life writings of Indigenous women there are numerous examples of overt acts of resistance occurring on a daily basis. All these women break the rules of the mission or reserve and receive punishment, but that does not deter them. Stealing, lying, making use of white property, mimicking and outright wilfulness, escape and sometimes violence find expression in white cultural domains outside the mission or reserve, in public spaces and households where these Indigenous women are enmeshed in relations of domination and oppression. Doris Pilkington's mother and aunties defy their captors when as young girls they escape from the Moore River Native Settlement and, on foot, follow the rabbit-proof fence back to their homeland some thousands of kilometres away. Working for her first white employer, Glenyse Ward uses her white missus's good china and consumes food denied to her when the white missus leaves the house. Alice Nannup lies to the Indigenous trooper in order to protect her boyfriend whom she hides in the teacher's house on the mission. Ella Simon makes demands for better living conditions on Purfleet and Rita Huggins spends time in the Cherbourg gaol for seeing boys in defiance of the rules.

Christianity played an important part in the containment of Indigenous women on reserves and missions. While it was supposed to assure their compliance and docility, it also exposed to them the hypocrisy of its own teaching through the gap between white practice and beliefs. Christianity served as a tool of resistance in some contexts by contributing to the moral grounds for projecting Indigenous women's rights and value as human beings. Glenyse Ward draws on Christianity to make the decision finally to leave her employer who treats her as a black slave:

> I just couldn't keep on working for her after meeting people like the nuns and their friends and dear old Bill, who I was going to miss a lot. I felt in myself that I could not continue on anymore, no matter what the circumstances were (Ward 1988:151).

In Indigenous cultural domains subjectivity is the site of resistance. The existence of subjugated knowledges of relationality and spirituality in Indigenous women's discourse denotes a rejection of the impersonal contractual relations of the dominant society, where "social patterns of individuation and atomisation are consistent with constructions of a self-possessing and self-appropriating individual" (Morris 1989:219). These knowledges also provide a basis for resistance in that the meanings they contain allow for a different positioning than that represented in dominant white discourses.

The self-presentation by Indigenous women in their life writings provides evidence that "we have never totally lost ourselves within the other's reality. We have never fallen into the hypnosis of believing that those representations were our essence" (Dodson 1994:9). Indigenous women's life writings provide evidence of incommensurabilities and the complex ways subject positions are socially constructed and deployed. The self-presentation disclosed in Indigenous women's life writings unmasks the resilience, creativity and strength of Indigenous women and the continuity of colonisation in discursive and cultural practices.

CHAPTER TWO

Look Out White Woman: Representations of "The White Woman" in Feminist Theory[1]

The colonial object is furthered not only by the canonical literature of the West, as Spivak suggests, but also by a would-be oppositional feminist criticism whose practitioners continue to see whiteness as so natural, normative, and unproblematic that racial identity is a property only of the nonwhite. Unless the object of study happens to be Other, race is placed under erasure as something outside immediate consideration, at once extratextual and extraterrestrial (duCille 1997:35).

White western feminisms are predicated on sex and gender differences; they are part of the ontological basis of feminism that informs theory making. An effect of theorising about sex and gender differences is the creation of the universal woman: white, middle-class and heterosexual, whose life is oppressed under patriarchy. Since all women are positioned as being oppressed in society based on this model, white women's race privilege, conferred by association with white men, remains invisible in analyses. In the 1960s, women of colour, African American women and lesbian women challenged the universal white heterosexual woman by claiming that she did not reflect their lived experiences. They argued that age, sexuality, race, ethnicity and class meant that their experiences of oppression were different from those of white middle-class heterosexual women. The intellectual activity of women of colour, African American women and lesbian women facilitated the development of new theories about multiple and interlocking oppressions. However, these new theories were then critiqued on the basis that they had become additive in an attempt to be more inclusive of women's differences. Since the mid 1980s a transition has been taking place in thinking and writing about what constitutes difference. However, the new theories of difference rarely include naming and interrogating representations of whiteness in both theory and practice.

In this chapter an evaluation of some feminist literature will show that representations of whiteness as dominance, subject position, standpoint and privilege are present but remain invisible in feminist theories of difference. The feminist project has been concerned with theorising oppressions, signified by differences embedded in power relations, which conceal white race privilege. An effect of such theorising is that the privileged subject position and standpoint from which white feminists conceptualise and write is not made visible in their work. This invisibility often leads white feminists to reinscribe racial dominance in theorising, and dealing with, differences in practice. In the words of Toni Morrison, "[m]y project is an effort to avert the critical gaze from the racial object to the racial subject; from the described and imagined to the describers and imaginers; from the serving to the served" (Morrison 1993:90).

Locating the white woman in feminist theory

Whiteness is often invisible to white women as a marker of racial identity and is not perceived as problematic because one's identity is thought to be "natural" (Hurtado and Stewart 1997:299). The degree to which this naturalness is embedded in white consciousness is reflected in the work of white feminists, whose theories parody the patterns most visible to them from their privileged subject position. White women's privilege in theory has become normalised because it is grounded in the assumption that the womanness of all women was the same version of womanness experienced by white middle-class women (Spelman 1990:165). Such an assumption is found in the work of first wave feminists Mary Wollstonecraft and Harriet Taylor.

Wollstonecraft exposed contradictions in Enlightenment thinking on gender and sexual difference. She examined the differences between men and women by focusing on the female condition. Her work showed that the Enlightenment's ideal of a universal human nature meant in practice two codes: one code constituted the feminine and the other the masculine. Arguing against this separation, she asserted:

> If women are by nature inferior to men, their virtues must be the same in quality, if not in degree, or virtue is a relative idea; consequently their conduct should be founded on the same principles and have the same aim (Wollstonecraft 1971:36).

Taylor argued similarly for equity between white men and white women in marriage. The men referred to by both Wollstonecraft and Taylor were not black men or working-class men but middle-class white men. They wrote as though gender could be isolated from other aspects of identity and by doing so they made race and class invisible. Gender oppression was the universal oppression of all women because all men oppressed all women.

Wollstonecraft and Taylor were able to speak from such a privileged subject position because of their white middle-class location, which provided the context and resources for their scholarly activity. Wollstonecraft and Taylor were not writing about the black or Indigenous women in Britain's colonies or the working-class women who serviced the homes of their middle-class sisters, or the relations between themselves and those women who had limited access to education and different experiences of married life. Wollstonecraft and Taylor, by making invisible race and class in their representation of gender oppression, were by omission centring the life experiences of middle-class white women. To represent middle-class white women as all women was a political act, because it meant that shared oppression could be the basis for political mobilisation. The articulation of gender as the primary form of identity and oppression became the basis of white feminist epistemology and political action.

Theorising gender/sex/class differences between white women and white men

The work of Wollstonecraft and Taylor influenced the thinking of subsequent generations of feminists who theorised on the basis of the sex/gender oppression thesis. One of the most popular articulations of sex and gender oppression is liberal feminism, which continues to influence the political practice of many women. Liberal feminists such as Betty Friedan (1963) argue that sex is biologically based while gender is culturally constructed. In other words, men and women are biologically different but equal in their capacities; they are alike but not identical. Liberal feminists state that unequal treatment of women in relation to men has occurred because their biological differences have been used as the basis of discrimination. Women are equal with men in capacities but not opportunities in society, and it is stereotypical beliefs about women that mask the claim of equal capacities.

Liberal feminists assert that women's incorporation into labour markets in society should be based on merit and "domestic necessities may be fulfilled through the market; supplemented via the welfare state; shared between partners and minimised by technology (washing machines, microwave ovens, etc.)" (Coole 1988:235). Evans argues that liberal feminists do not deny gender difference; instead they seek to reduce or eliminate it (1995:13). Liberal feminists seek structural reform to reduce inequalities. They do not seek to change the structure that gives men power over women, and implicitly acknowledge that they are in an asymmetrical relation of power with men. What liberal feminists accept as part of their doctrine is all women are equal; there are no systemic or patterned differences between groups of women. There are advantaged and disadvantaged women but the liberal feminist goal is to remove barriers to equality of opportunity wherever these exist, although it is acknowledged that some women face more barriers than others.

According to the logic of the liberal feminist argument, disadvantaged women are not represented in social locations in society because they are unable to compete on the basis of merit with men or other women. Because it centres white middle-class women as the normative position from which to judge the oppression of women, liberal feminism dehistoricises women and lacks an understanding of the different historical and material conditions that enable certain women to compete on the basis of merit. The invisibility of white race privilege and racial and class oppression is an outcome of giving primacy to gender oppression and sex difference. Belonging to a privileged group means that liberal feminists can centre themselves as the subject of their theory while excluding other women.

Socialist and marxist feminists start from the assumption that the world is not equal. Nonetheless, whiteness remains invisible but central to their analyses. Unlike liberal feminists, they see the differences between men and women as being the outcome of both patriarchy and capitalism. Marxist feminists view female oppression as the outcome of class, while socialist feminists argue that the gendered division of labour is the product of patriarchy operating in a capitalist system. Differences between men and women are not biologically determined but class and gender based (Armstrong et al. 1986:208). Equality for marxist and socialist feminists is linked to outcomes: they argue for equality of conditions for men and women so that people will be treated identically and receive equal rewards irrespective of gender. In this literature, gender oppression by men of women is given primary focus, and class oppression treated as an additive. The experiences and life chances of white middle-class women in terms of class, capitalism and patriarchy are presented as if they constitute the norm. The relations under interrogation are those between white women and white men rather than between different classes or races of white women, women of colour, Indigenous women, African American women or lesbian women.

Similar criticisms can be made about the work of Michele Barrett (1980:252), who argues that the oppression of women in capitalist society cannot be explained by simple materialist or ideological explanations. Barrett points out that the ideology of gender is fluid and operates within different historical class contexts and has some material basis. The ideology of gender is tied to the relations of production through the family and its division of labour:

> The relations of production and reproduction of contemporary capitalism may operate in general according to exploitative capital accumulation processes that are technically "sex-blind", but they take the form of a division of labour in which ideology is deeply embedded (Barrett 1980:252).

The ideology of gender cannot be separated from economic

relations, she argues, and feminists should join with socialist men to develop a strategy to overcome their common oppression. Barrett's positioning of the relations of production and reproduction as "sex-blind" fails to account for the fact that they are also "race blind". Race privilege and oppression do contribute to who participates, and to what degree, in exploitative capital accumulation processes. As the work of Rose Brewer (1993) reveals, black women's labour is marginalised within the United States economy. A similar study conducted in Australia shows that Indigenous women's labour is also marginalised within the economy (Runciman 1994).

An Australian study of gender and class analysis by Janeen Baxter complements the work of Barrett. She argues against the proposition that the class position of the family should be determined by the occupational status of the male (1988:106), on the grounds that this fails to provide us with an understanding of the sex-inequalities that exist within families. Utilising data from a Brisbane-based study, conducted by the Sociology Department at the University of Queensland, which examined the existence of cross-class families, Baxter argues that "women's position in the class structure is determined by both class exploitation and gender domination" (1988:121). Baxter's analysis was organised and based on the assumption that the researched population would be white heterosexual families. Both Baxter's and Barrett's white subject position influences their work to the degree that whiteness is accepted as the norm. Their respective analyses mask the importance of the way in which race and cultural difference shape family structures, sexuality and class.

"Race" is also not consciously incorporated into the work of another Australian feminist, Lois Bryson (1994:179), who asks the question, "Is gender equality increasing" in Australia? She sets out to answer this question by examining the development of the position of women in paid employment and their relationship to social policy. Although she positions the category "women" to subsume all women in her analysis, Bryson is in effect talking only about white women in Australia. Bryson argues that since colonisation the poverty of families has ensured the economic activity of all its members, but around the turn of the century women's "invisible and visible labour" became concealed by the legal recognition of the family wage secured by male unionists. Bryson perceives the invisibility and visibility of labour, but is unable to make race visible in her analysis. She claims further that in 1901 women constituted 20 per cent of the official workforce and by 1991 this had risen to 41.8 per cent. The increased participation of women in the workforce is acknowledged in government policy, which defines women as workers. Welfare policy positioned women as dependent and provided support for them if they required assistance up until the 1980s. Bryson points out that "the widow's pension is an entitlement for which there has never been a male equivalent" (1994:190). She argues that the gendering of welfare policy in the mid 1980s changed this positioning: labour market programs were specifically designed to incorporate single female parents into the workforce, and only mothers with dependent children were entitled to a widow's pension. White women thus redefined social policy as workers rather than dependants. In Bryson's analysis white women's problems are centred and normalised. "Race" is integral to the analysis, but made invisible. Bryson does not mention that the benefits accrued to white women from the State did not automatically flow on to Indigenous women (McGrath 1993) and that the conditions under which white and Indigenous women laboured were not the same (Kidd 1996). Nor does she recognise that the unpaid or minimally paid labour of Indigenous women and men for years supported white families and government programs (Kidd 1996). Whiteness is centred, naturalised and normative within Bryson's text. Bryson concludes that the changing position of women in society has resulted in their inclusion in the class structure as workers independent of men, and that this change in status has been reflected in social policy. However, she believes that these changes are the outcome of "the demands of the economic system or where they serve state purposes" (1994:192). Although she acknowledges that structural inequalities still remain, she points out that women's financial independence in the public sphere as independent workers in the class structure "is highly significant to the question of gender equality" because it reduces one form of inequality and therefore one form of oppression (1994:193).

Bryson's analysis conforms to a marxist feminist position because it sees equalising the opportunities between white men and white women through the marketplace as reducing some of the oppression of women. Unlike Barrett and Baxter, Bryson is primarily concerned with the relations of production outside the home and positions white women's economic independence as a liberating force. Earning equal pay with white men does not necessarily reduce the oppression experienced by white or other women. What it offers is financial independence from white men and a range of choices and options. It does not fundamentally change the power relations between white men and white women. All three analyses are concerned with the relations between white men and white women in the gendered division of labour, but the relations between different women are not addressed. None of the authors illuminates the different impact of change on different groups of women, because the focus of their studies is the gender and class oppression of white women. They reduce the nature of oppression to whether or not white women's unpaid or paid work is valued within capitalist patriarchal societies. Class and gender are visible in these accounts, while race as whiteness and "Other" remains invisible. An element of white superiority comes through in their analyses, in that there is an assumption that what white women desire is exactly what other women desire.

Marxist and socialist feminists position power as being structurally determinate and linked to property ownership. Whelehan argues that the main problem for marxist feminists is dealing with two social mechanisms that oppress women: "the operation of a patriarchal ideology of immutable sexual difference within the family and a sexual division of labour in the workplace" (1995:47). What is also problematic in their work is the lack of concern with unpacking the relations between differently racialised women from different classes. Nor is there an understanding of the way in which white women derive power from their race privilege through association with white men; instead all men are perceived to have power over all women.

Unlike socialist and marxist feminists, radical feminists argue that it is patriarchy, not capitalism, which oppresses women. They position the differences between men and women as a patriarchal construction that values the masculine over the feminine. In doing so, they too make invisible white race privilege. According to writers such as Adrienne Rich, white men privilege male values and use biological difference, violence and aggression as a means to oppress women in society. In their analyses, radical feminists have tended to focus on reproductive technology and the institution of motherhood as ways of demonstrating that men control women through controlling their bodies. Again power in society is perceived as being systematically controlled and exercised by all men over all women. What is left uninterrogated in radical feminist analyses is the way in which patriarchy privileges whiteness as a social category.

Radical feminists accept that there are both sex and gender differences between men and women. Adrienne Rich (1977) has argued that because men fear women's reproductive capacities they need to control women's bodies. She asserts that motherhood as an institution underpins social and political systems, but she does not explicate which racialised forms of motherhood underpin which social and political systems. For her the normative form of motherhood is white motherhood. She states that motherhood "has withheld over one-half of the human species from the decisions affecting their lives; it exonerates men from fatherhood in any authentic sense; it creates the dangerous schism between 'private' and 'public' life; it calcifies human choices and potentialities" (Rich 1977:13). Motherhood as an institution has made some classes of white women prisoners of their bodies. Radical feminists have failed to take account of is that for other women, such as Indigenous women in Australia, motherhood meant having their children forcibly removed from their care (Wilson 1997). Rich's theorising does not include African American women and Indigenous women in the United States who have experienced similar fates. The assumption for Rich is that white motherhood is the normative centre from which to begin the analysis of marriage as an institution.

Rich influenced the work of Australian feminists such as

Robyn Rowland (1987), who argues that male scientists have appropriated the female body in their research to reproduce and reconstruct human beings. Rowland argues that male technological control over female reproduction may on the one hand alleviate the biological burden of women, but it places them in a position where women are disempowered in reproduction. In Australia, the United Kingdom and the United States the appropriation of the female body by reproductive technology is in the hands of white male scientists who are producing a product for clients who are wealthy enough to afford it, such as white middle-class and upper-class heterosexual couples. Rowland is remiss in not recognising the degree to which reproductive technology positions the white female body as being accessible and acceptable, unlike the black body which was accessed for enforced sterilisation and experimentation (Carby 1997:49). In the world of reproductive technology the white female body is objectified; it signifies womanhood and the continuation of the white race.

The work of radical feminists has influenced both poststructural and postmodern feminists, who are concerned with theorising the body, based on sexual differences. Genevieve Lloyd (1989) argues that there are different opinions about the relationship between gender and sex. She asserts that it is not sufficient to assume that the differences between the sexes are biologically driven. The body is socially constructed and our minds reflect the socialisation of our bodies. She argues that "with gender there are no facts of the matter, other than those produced through the shifting play of the powers and pleasures of socialised, embodied, sexed human beings" (1989:21). While Lloyd acknowledges that the body is socially constructed, she does not take her analysis further to show that within different cultures female bodies are read and valued differently. Socially constructed biological differences between white and black female bodies means living with different experiences of racism, race privilege and sexism. The erasure of race denies other women's experiences and by implication it is the white female body that is centred in the analysis. The societal norm of the white female body is centred in such a way that its privilege is rendered invisible. According to Lloyd's analysis, gender is not racialised. Her race blindness reveals what Rich calls "white solipsism" at work, "the tendency to think imagine, and speak as if whiteness described the world" (Rich 1979:299)

Moira Gatens, an Australian feminist, argues that the separation of sex and gender results in disembodiment. The mind (gender) / body (sex) dualism developed through masculine discourse remains intact through the work by feminist theorists. Drawing on the work of Spinoza, Gatens asserts that the body is not passive, but an active site where "thought is dependent for its activity on the character of the body and the manner in which, and the context in which, it recreates itself" (1988:68). Like Gatens, Threadgold asserts that there are many different stories of the body and of sexual difference which

> ... compete and struggle to construct (and sometimes silence) different and heterogeneous and multiple realities, meanings, knowledges, biologies, bodies and subjectivities as they are in turn constructed and silenced or articulated by them (Threadgold 1990:33).

Gatens and Threadgold have shifted the gender and sex oppression to focus on the body; they centre sex/gender difference and then talk about the multiplicity of ways in which the body is constructed. Although they recognise that the body is diverse and multiple in the way it is read and constructed, it is the white body that remains centred. The invisibility of this racialised body is an effective means of denying the presence of other racialised bodies. Focusing on the multiple ways of reading and interpreting the body negates the power relations between different bodies and ignores the way in which some are privileged while others are oppressed in structural hierarchies.

Whiteness remains invisible in these analyses because these women have a consciousness that they live in gendered bodies, but they do not have a consciousness that they live in racialised bodies. Fundamentally this is because they construct their oppression in opposition to white men on the basis of gender. White middle-class feminists utilise race privilege to write about their gendered oppression, but whiteness remains invisible, unnamed and unmarked in their work. The values and assumptions that make whiteness invisible, unnamed and unmarked to white people in society are enmeshed in the epistemology and knowledges with which white feminists work.

Theorising sexual differences between women

Difference based on sexuality became part of feminist discourse in the 1960s. Whelehan states that lesbian women became enmeshed in the politics of identity in the 1960s as part of the militant political gay and civil rights movements (1995:88–89). Despite their participation in both the first and second waves of feminism, lesbian feminists argue that the concerns of heterosexual feminists have dominated the feminist agenda, whereas "[f]or lesbian feminists the problems of female sexuality and sexualised images of women were crucial to their analysis of women's oppression" (Whelehan 1995:90).

Charlotte Bunch argues that heterosexuality is the means by which men dominate women in society: "[t]he original imperialist assumption of the right of men to the bodies and services of women has been translated into a whole variety of forms of domination throughout this society" (Bunch 1991:321). If women do not accept this assumption then they are queer. Women who do accept it participate in receiving the privileges that go with being heterosexual, thereby reinforcing the maintenance of male supremacy. Bunch goes on further to argue that lesbian feminists are outside patriarchy because "our existence challenges its life" (1991:324). In this sense Bunch reduces patriarchy to male-female sexual relationships, and assumes that all lesbians are the same. Such an assumption centres white lesbians, because race and cultural differences of lesbians who are women of colour, African American and Indigenous women are not given significant attention in her work. White lesbians may live outside society through their self-presentation and a culture of sexual difference, but they are also located in, and circumscribed by, a society where heterosexual whiteness is the institutionally embedded societal norm.

Biddy Martin argues that feminists such as Bunch essentialise the lesbian woman. Martin states that "whatever the intent of these efforts to render lesbianism internally coherent and stable, discipline and control are the effects" (Martin 1992:99). Martin refers to the works of Susie Bright, Judith Butler, Eve Sedgwick and others to show that ambiguities exist within the lesbian position and that lesbianism has been constructed through an analogy with male sexuality. Feminism has been caught up with unifying sex, gender and desire and relegating them back to a gendered core which reduces lesbian acts, desires and features to being secondary and accidental (Martin 1992:102). The importance for Martin is that other differences, such as race, class and sexual roles, impact on the position of lesbian. She asserts that "[s]uch layerings — demonstrate that we confront not just the restricting frame of masculinist domination and compulsory heterosexuality, rather a much more complex set of social performances and regulations, in which gender is never stable or unified" (Martin 1992:117). Although Martin's critique of Bunch's theory of heterosexual oppression includes race, this is discussed as racial oppression rather than as white race privilege. A conscious recognition of the racialisation of "Others" within theory does not mean the same as theorising the racialisation of the white self.

Barbara Creed, an Australian feminist, shares Martin's concerns about the essentialising tendency of lesbian feminists. She finds an alternative in queer theory:

> Queer theory challenges identity politics, opting instead for diversity, plurality. Questions of class, colour, race and ethnicity are crucial. Another equally important area relates to questions of sexual desire. Queer theory addresses a range of practices, including bisexuality, sado-masochism, cross-dressing, transexuality and transvestism (Creed 1994:153).

Some queer theorists include other desires within this framework, such as fetishism, coprophilia and bestiality, while others reject such inclusion. Creed argues that this shift in identity politics to recognise multiple subject positions that are not fixed has come about because of the impact of the work of Foucault, Lacan and Lyotard on academia in the last 20 years. She argues that "there is no single, acceptable, normal lesbian or gay male identity" (Creed 1994:157). Although Martin's work and Creed's work illuminate the differences that exist within primarily nonheterosexual practices, they maintain that the main point of lesbian and gay oppression is sexual orientation/desire. What is

informative about this literature is that it points to the importance of preferences, lifestyle factors and behaviours that may or
may not be a matter of choice. Most white heterosexual men and
women will interpret the white female body as heterosexual
because it is the norm in society, and such readings allow for
"passing" by white lesbians in some contexts. Hence, they are not
excluded from exercising their class or race privileges. White
lesbian women can draw on privileges that they have been made
to feel are theirs by birth and by citizenship because they are white
(McIntosh 1992). They can participate in society without "race"
ever being a visible, salient condition of their lives. Women of
colour, African American women and Indigenous women who
are lesbians do not invoke the same readings, nor do they exercise
the same race privilege. Belonging to a visible and marked
racialised group plays an important part in determining life
chances, opportunities and outcomes for different women.

"Race" is erased in the dialogue between white heterosexual
and white lesbian feminists because sexuality is the primary
oppression and difference for white lesbian feminists, while white
heterosexual women give primacy to oppression based on gender
and sex. White heterosexual women's relations with white lesbian
women will be different from their respective relations with
African American women, women of colour or Indigenous
women regardless of whether those women are heterosexual or
lesbian. White lesbian women do not give up all their race
privilege because of their sexuality, although this depends on the
context in which they are located. In certain contexts white
lesbian women are able to exercise their race privilege by passing
as white heterosexual women; this form of strategic intervention
allows them access to opportunities that may otherwise be denied
on the basis of their sexuality. An emulation of such strategic
intervention by lesbian African American women, Indigenous
women and women of colour would be difficult to sustain.

Theorising culture as difference: white women and women of colour

Women's culture as difference finds its expression in feminism
as shared values, popular practices or artistic products. Radical

feminists assert that there is a separate women's culture, although there is no agreement on what women's culture is or could become. However, there is agreement on some universal principles. In the work of Mary Daly and Hester Eisenstein culture is deployed as shared values. They argue that women's values and virtues should be paramount in any commitment to social change. Eisenstein argues that socially constructed virtues of women such as their "capacities to nurture, to affiliate with others, to work collectively" are all "crucial characteristics" (Eisenstein 1984: xix) of this culture. Eisenstein specifies certain cultural values that she argues all women share irrespective of their race or cultural context: she utilises sameness as a way of evading power relations and consequently reinscribes colour blindness. Nurturing and affiliating with "Others" differs in different cultures and contexts, because these capacities are tied to other cultural values and obligations. Eisenstein centres the capacities associated with her social experiences of being a white woman.

For Mary Daly the work of radical feminists is to break through the patriarchal maze that positions women as evil and inferior: "[i]t is women ourselves who will have to expel the Father from ourselves, becoming our own exorcists" (Daly 1978:2). Women must build female culture to be free of patriarchy and empower themselves through appropriating and revaluing language — for example the epithets crone, hag and spinster — which has been used to negate women. Daly seeks a separate world for men and women based on their cultural differences, but which women's cultural difference is she speaking about? Lorde (1983:95) argues that to imply that all women experience the same oppression is to ignore the multiple tools of patriarchy and how women against women wield them. Cultural differences of other women are cited and evidenced in Daly's book, but she tends to portray women of colour and African American feminists as victims. Cultural differences between women become erased as Daly centres white female values as the norm from which to construct her version of women's culture to which we should all subscribe.

A different understanding of culture is operationalised by feminists in cultural politics, who are concerned with the "feminist insistence that narratives about women should be written by them and for them" (Waring 1994:11). The substance of these narratives is an expression of difference that challenges dominant white narratives in the cultural production of literature. Fine art, poetry, fiction, film and oral history are different forms of representation, which carry ideological investments. Women telling their stories is empowering:

> What is crucial is to enable writers, artists, filmmakers in communities that have been and are marginalised to take up the space they need to bear witness. To match up the "by" with the "about" is not an attempt to emulate some tokenistic purity, it is to acknowledge functions of cultural producers and products, specifically for dominated cultures (Waring 1994:15).

To give space to and acknowledge both cultural producers and their products presents us with a benign concept of cultural difference that reinforces the "exotic" and the "primitive". Cultural difference is included not on the terms of the marginalised culture, but on those of the dominant group. Accessing professional advancement and economic support means having to adhere to the central values of white culture. Implying that white women of the dominant culture can alleviate the oppression of women from other cultures by providing them with the space to have a voice expresses a naivety about why white women have the power to be able to be inclusive. White women's need to be inclusive must be matched

> ... by an awareness of how the legacies of our privilege appear in the ways we may try to satisfy that need: in our confusing imagining women with knowing them; in priding ourselves on tolerance; and in appropriating others' identities through our desperate rush to find similarity (Spelman 1990:185).

A similar conception of culture exists within the poststructural discussion of Gayatri Spivak (1992) on translation. She argues that the act of translation itself is a cultural enterprise that requires an extension of the self beyond one's cultural borders. Translation, the art of learning another language, can provide women with some consciousness of the knowledge acquired by other women during their lifetime. One becomes closer to the subjectivity of the "Other" (1992:177). Spivak provides us with a strategy for getting beyond cultural blindness; the nuances of cultural differences are negotiated through both language and praxis. However, people may speak the same language but not share the same meanings and this may not be conscious to those involved in speaking to each other. Communication between Indigenous women, African American women, women of colour and white feminists using the English language has not resulted in shared meanings, goals or politics. Learning the language of another does not necessarily result in changing the subjectivity of the person who carries the baggage of a different culture, but it does make dialogue possible, as Spivak's work demonstrates.

Valentine Moghadam (1994) argues that the proliferation of postmodern and poststructural academic work in cultural analysis has led to "culture" being given "a unique role for the appraisal of social reality" (Moghadam 1994:5). "Culture" is located in such work as a process in which identities are discursively and historically constructed. The work of Radha Kumar (1994: 274–92) on feminism and identity politics in India reveals the degree to which Muslim culture has reinforced men's power over women by the use and construction of "traditions" that position women as subservient and inferior. These "traditions", she argues, are a manifestation of Muslim men's need to assert their cultural dominance after British colonisation, rather than being orthodoxy. Kumar's work shows indirectly the legacy of white colonialism where whiteness shapes the lives of Muslim men. The invention of a tradition that did not exist prior to colonisation is a strategy to reclaim the colonised Muslim male self through the subjugation of Muslim women. Whiteness is salient in shaping the lives of people of colour through its ideological presence in former British colonies.

Theorising race difference: non-white and white women

In feminism, "race" as difference has been an issue of concern primarily to African American women and women of colour. Rarely has the racialisation of white women been an issue for white feminists, although there are a few exceptions, such as Adrienne Rich (1979), Elizabeth Spelman (1990) and Ruth Frankenberg (1993). Most feminist analyses have been concerned with the effects of the reproduction of white domination (that is racial oppression) rather than an examination of white race privilege. The foci of analyses of racial oppression are usually non-white women. The reproduction of white domination is evident in the work of Rose Brewer (1993), who has conceptual- ised African American women's oppression in the United States by theorising a gender/race division of labour. Brewer argues that African American women's labour is marginalised within the economy. African American women are usually found in the service sector working as skilled or semi-skilled employees for low wages or they are not working at all. She claims that the degree to which they are incorporated into the division of labour de- pends on the level of "economic restructuring and capital mobil- ity, racial formation and gender inequality" (1993:26–27). Power for Brewer is located structurally and is tied to property relations. Race and gender oppressions are the explanations given for African American women's class position. Brewer's work implic- itly reveals that white domination confers, for those who are white, systemic advantage. As Daniels (1997) argues, "whiteness as a racial category is predicated on economic inequality as a key feature and mechanism in the perpetuation of the color line" (1997:13).

Floya Anthias and Nira Yuval-Davis (1993), analysing "race" as difference in Britain, offer a different theoretical perspective from Brewer. They argue that "race" and "racism" need to be separated, because the latter is not an extraction of "race" but rather has "to be understood with reference to the discourses and practices by which ethnic groups are inferiorized, excluded and subordinated" (1993:viii). Anthias and Yuval-Davis argue that the concept "race" is embedded in the "constructs of collectivity and belongingness ... postulated through notions of common origin or destiny, not in terms of cultures of difference but ... the specific positing of boundaries" (1993:2). For Anthias and Yuval- Davis "racism" is the process of inferiorisation, while "race" is the boundary marker of difference. In their theorising Anthias and Yuval-Davis have not focused on whiteness as an ethnic or racial category. To include whiteness as a racial or ethnic category would mean that the analysis of racism would have to include discourses and practices of white supremacy. The shift in focus would then involve deconstructing processes involving both race privilege and racial oppression.

In her early work in feminism, bell hooks (1981) critiqued the political agenda of white feminists. She argued that white women have produced a movement that is racist and exclusionary of many non-white women. The focus of white feminists on equal rights for women will not result in exploding "the ideology of domination that permeates Western culture on various levels — sex, race, and class, to name a few " (hooks 1981:194). For hooks, oppression exists in many forms, but her concern is to raise the consciousness of feminists about racism. She argues that white women have more power than Black women do because they are part of the dominant oppressive group; they have power over Black women (see also hooks 1989, 1991, 1992, 1993, 1996a, 1996b). Despite the fact that hooks sees feminism as being fundamentally racist, she believes it has something to offer Black women in America. What is required is a redefinition of feminism: "to be feminist in any authentic sense of the term is to want for all people, female and male, liberation from sexist role patterns, domination and oppression" (hooks 1981:195). hooks' work returns the gaze on racism in feminism from the standpoint of an African American woman and in doing so she makes white supremacy visible. Her work gives insights about the different racialised social locations of African American women and white feminists.

Unlike hooks, Patricia Hill Collins (1991) does not explicitly engage with white feminists about their racism. Instead she is interested in theorising the interconnectedness of race, class and gender in African American women's lives from an African American woman's standpoint. Collins argues that Black feminist thought is the product of a dialectic between their oppression and political activism (1991:5–6). She analyses the way in which African American women have been constructed and represented in dominant discourses and their resistance to this through activism, which she argues, produced Black feminist thought. In a later work, Collins expands on her analysis of Black feminist thought:

Restated, Black feminist thought consists of theories or specialised thought produced by Afro-American women intellectuals designed to express Black women's standpoint. The dimensions of this standpoint include the presence of characteristic core themes, the diversity of Black women's experiences in encountering these core themes, the varying expressions of Black women's Afrocentric feminist consciousness regarding the core themes and their experiences with them and the interdependence of Black women's experiences, consciousness, and actions (Collins 1997:252).

Collins utilises the concepts of race, class and gender to articulate a position from a different standpoint that provides critical insight about the condition of Black oppression and resistance to white dominance. Theorising the interdependence of Black women's experiences and thought Collins maps out Black feminism "as a process of self-conscious struggle that empowers women and men to actualize a humanist vision of community" (Collins 1997:258). Collins shows how Black women's epistemology can be forged out of a historically constituted dialectic of Black women's oppression and resistance to white hegemony.

Kimberley Christensen (1997) argues that some white feminists in the United States have responded to critiques by African American and women of colour of racism within feminism. Women's Studies programs are now more inclusive of race and cultural diversity. However, Christensen asserts that the majority white feminist movement has been politically unsuccessful in dealing with racism because its analyses focus on "individualistic racism" which, while important, has led to a failure to challenge the wealth and power differentials that perpetuate racism (1997:617). White feminists, according to Christensen, need to analyse and challenge the institutional location of racism. Christensen's refocusing on the structural location of racism is commendable, but it is based on two flawed assumptions. The first being that racism at the level of subjectivity is not connected to power relations that are structurally located; and second that Women's Studies programs, which are more inclusive, have led to a conscious racialisation of the white self. Both assumptions are spurious. White women's conscious racialisation of "Others" does not necessarily lead to a conscious racialisation of the white self (Frankenberg: 1993). As argued in Chapter 5, there is a direct relationship between the ability of white women to exercise white race privilege and its institutionalised location.

Denise Thompson (1994), an Australian feminist, argues that criticisms of the white middle-class bias of feminism by women of colour and African American women are unfounded in general. She claims that feminism has always provided a forum for the voices of African American women, women of colour and Indigenous women because it is women who speak in feminism, not men. Thompson argues that the anti-racist debate in feminism has failed to understand and recognise that the main enemy of feminism is male domination. Racism is a form of male domination which, like other differences, is "a function of the invidious hierarchical divisions among categories of people which are required for the maintenance and continuation of male supremacy" (Thompson 1994:2). Thompson positions women who are not white feminists in the anti-racist debate as being usurpers who have temporarily deprived white women of the centre. In order to steal back the centre, Thompson equates racism and sexism through positioning male domination as the common enemy of all women. In doing so she obscures and marginalises the role of white race privilege in her analysis (Grillo & Wildman 1995:172).

Susan Stanford Friedman (1995) offers a slightly different way of positioning racism. She argues that feminists need to go beyond the fixity of the white/other binary through cultural narratives of relational positionality, which involve shifting identities that have dependent points of reference in different contexts. Identities are therefore situational and fluid; they allow us to go beyond binaries and can enhance feminist multiculturalism by showing the complexity of "thick descriptions and local histories of racial and ethnic difference" (Friedman 1995:40). Despite Friedman's appeals to go beyond fixity, whiteness as an identity is difficult to separate from racial dominance. In fact, relational positionality works to obscure the power differences between individuals, groups, communities and institutions by ignoring racism as a system of categorisation and identity formation. White race privilege, in Australia and elsewhere, is structurally located and it determines the life chances of white and non-white people every day.

Engaging a feminist politics of difference

From the mid 1980s there has been a change in focus on what constitutes difference and what needs to be interrogated. The task for feminist critical theory in the 1990s was to develop political theory that was inclusive of differences and was emancipatory and reflective. In Australia, Susan Sheridan (1988) asserts that with the development of feminist cultural studies there has been a conceptual shift from examining "the cultural meanings of gender difference and the positioning of women in culture" to exposing the cultural production of meaning through critical analysis (Sheridan 1988:2). Through the use of discourse and deconstruction analysis, heterogeneity is revealed, similarities and differences dealt with. However, as the subsequent literature shows, the shift to include differences does not include identifying whiteness as a difference that warrants interrogation.

White feminists theorise the politics of difference

The additive approach, which still gave primacy to gender oppression, is embedded in the dominant political strategy offered by Shulamith Firestone, who in 1970 advocated the following:

1. Never compromise basic principles for political expediency.
2. Agitation for specific freedoms is worthless without the preliminary raising of consciousness necessary to utilise these freedoms fully.
3. Put your own interests first, then proceed to make alliances with other oppressed groups. Demand a piece of that revolutionary pie before you put your life on the line (Firestone 1970:443).

Firestone makes gender oppression the primary oppression by telling women to put their interests first and then consider an alliance with other oppressed groups. What Firestone does is assume that gender can be isolated from other aspects of identity such as race, class, sexuality and ethnicity. Such an assumption underpins a dominant white heterosexual feminist location, because priority must be given to overcoming gender oppression at the expense of other oppressions. Marilyn Frye, writing some 13 years later in *The Politics of Reality* (1983), although recognising that race and class play an important part in oppression, supports Firestone's strategy. Frye concludes that women are oppressed primarily because they are women and that their alliances should be built on this basis. The privileging of white gender oppression by Firestone and Frye complies with a universalist and essentialist construction of woman based on the premise that because all women are oppressed as women, this oppression must be the same. Frye's and Firestone's focusing on power relations between white men and white women means that their gaze is averted from analysing the power relations between different women which prevent political alliances. They focus on the lives of some women rather than others; the white heterosexual middle-class woman is centred in their work.

Roberta Hamilton and Michele Barrett in *The Politics of Diversity* (1986) offer another way of politicising differences, from a Canadian perspective, in response to the fragmentation of feminism due to the recognition of difference in the United States and Britain. The collection of papers deals with nationalism, ethnicity, racism, motherhood, sexuality and subjectivity, as well as the social reproduction of gender and the gendered division of labour. Unfortunately this book is primarily concerned with analysing diverse issues from within a socialist/marxist feminist framework which is primarily aimed at unpacking gender and class power relations between men and women. The politics of diversity here fails to include race as salient in shaping women's lives and affecting the development of political strategies. For Barrett and Hamilton the political solution to fragmentation in Britain and the United States is to convince women to analyse diverse issues from a particular theoretical perspective. These early theories of dealing with differences in practice were developed by white middle-class women whose theorising tended to reflect the patterns most visible to them. What remain invisible and uninterrogated in their work are their racial identity and the way in which white race privilege is salient in shaping power relations between women.

The 1990s marked the emergence of, and engagement with, a politics of difference in feminism. Iris Young, in *Justice and the Politics of Difference* (1990), argues that to seek liberation on the basis of the transcendence of group differences is assimilationist, in that it equalises differences. She asserts that the self-definition of group difference is liberalistic as a politics of difference. Young tells us that both the assimilationist and group difference models are expressed in the women's movement. She argues that humanist feminism that seeks sexual equality is assimilationist, whereas separatist feminists who argue for gynocentrism are self-defining. In the politics of difference, groups who assert a positive identity "seize the power of naming difference itself, and explode the implicit definition of difference as deviance in relation to a norm, which freezes some groups into a self enclosed nature" (1990:171). This in turn undermines the essentialising of difference by those who wish to defend privilege. Difference is not based on fixed attributes but is an outcome of the relations between groups and their interactions with institutions. Young argues that groups form not on the basis of a common identity, but through the "social process of interaction and differentiation in which some people come to have a particular *affinity*". It is affinity that "names the manner of sharing assumptions, affective bonding, and networking that recognizably differentiates groups from one another, but not according to some common nature" (1990:172). On the basis of this affinity people have a common identity, which is the defining attribute of a social group.

Young's concern is to show how groups can articulate processes of governing to achieve a form of democratic pluralism based on multiple differences that are not fixed. However, if social groups exist, there must be boundaries that mark out the differences between groups; therefore there has to be some fixity in play. Why is it a consistent pattern historically in Australia that governments are made up of groups of white, predominantly heterosexual males? Some attributes are certainly valued more than others in securing power within society. Young's politics of difference does not include the advantages that white men gain from women's disadvantages, nor does it explain why this social group is able to maintain such privilege. In effect, the non-recognition of white male privilege protects it from being made visible, and there is no connection made between how groups of white women by association with these men also benefit from this privilege in relation to other women.

Engaging with a politics of difference, the Australian feminist

Elaine Jeffreys states in "What Is 'Difference' in Feminist Theory and Practice?" (1991) that the meaning of difference has evolved since the second-wave of feminism:

> ... the (re)consideration of difference suggests a shift from the search for, or construction of, totalising explanations of women's oppression, to an exploration of the mechanisms of oppression, and thus the workings of power at the most strategic and local level including that of the body (1991:10).

This (re)consideration means that we must examine how our identity and positioning is negotiated within the parameters of the discourses we use. Jeffreys argues that a claim to identity is a political strategy and is not based on fixed attributes, but "the assertion of difference must remain a strategic one, rather than become an end-point in itself" (1991:10). Jeffreys implicitly acknowledges that some groups have a greater range of options than others do when claiming identity and developing strategies. She argues that if we refuse to order our differences hierarchically they can be used to form alliances. The logic of Jeffreys' political strategy is based on white liberal individualism: we each have control over how our multiple differences are ordered within feminism. This is a political strategy that neutralises differences and conceals the exercising of white race privilege and other relations of domination between women in feminism. It is both power evasive and colour blind.

Meekosha and Pettman (1991), two Australian feminists, argue against the politics of identity on the grounds that the closure of identity politics does not allow for fluid and multiple identities. They also assert that "class perspectives on power and on the complexity of the dominant group have been lost in the process" (1991:79). They state that "in broader terms, women, Aborigines or Asians are often represented as if those categories are unproblematic and as if the members and their characteristics are in some way natural" (1991:78). Here the category "woman" is implicitly designated as white, whereas Aborigines and Asians are genderless. Whiteness is not named as part of identity formation in Meekosha and Pettman's critique of identity politics. In identity politics the process of white "Othering" itself produces closed boundaries and limits that are beyond the control of those

categorised as such. Meekosha and Pettman's political strategy
for feminists to create a more inclusive sisterhood is to gender
other struggles. To speak of gendering other struggles is to centre
the subject position middle-class white woman. Whiteness as
difference, privilege and identity is not marked, named or challenged in Meekosha and Pettman's work. Perhaps this is because
it is perceived as being natural and normal and is therefore
invisible to the writers.

In "Power, Bodies and Difference" (1992), the Australian
feminist Moira Gatens argues that difference is not about biological facts but about the way that "culture marks bodies and creates
specific conditions in which they live and recreate themselves"
(1992:133). Differences are therefore multiple. The problem
with Gaten's theory of difference is that she does not provide us
with an explanation of how bodies are enacted and experienced
in very different ways depending on the cultural and historical
position of different subjects (Kirby 1994). As bell hooks argues,
"[r]epresentations of black female bodies in contemporary popular culture rarely subvert or critique images of black female
sexuality which were part of the cultural apparatus of nineteenth-
century racism and which still shape perceptions today" (hooks
1997:114). The Black presence in North America "allowed whites
to sexualize their world by projecting onto black bodies a narrative of sexualization disassociated from whiteness" (hooks
1997:114). Gatens' theory appears to be a narrative about all
bodies, but by commission she centres the body most familiar to
her — the white female body — as she has not theorised the
subjective enactment or experiences of other bodies with different histories in different cultures.

Sandra Harding engages with a politics of difference in *Reinventing Ourselves as Other: More New Agents of History and Knowledge*
(1993). Harding argues that the complex ways differences have
been used to construct gender and the many different forms of
feminism require white feminists to rethink their conceptualisations of theorising about difference. She states that standpoint
female feminists advocate that only women can theorise about
women because of their respective experiences. However, she
believes that, in order to create a broader understanding of the

differing social locations in society, men must be allowed to write from a male feminist perspective about women. Similarly she advocates that white women can learn from the insights of marginalised women to generate analyses:

> The self-understanding I seek is to emerge as a result of my locating myself as a European American person in the analyses originally generated by thinkers of Third World descent and then continuing in the analyses by thinking about my world with the help of the accounts they have provided — yet still out of my own different social location. I can be only a white person who intends to take responsibility for her racial location; I cannot be a person of Third World descent, seeking to take responsibility for that social location (1993:151–52).

Harding provides us with an understanding of difference which acknowledges that there are multiple social locations from which to speak, theorise and write, and by implication they are all equally valued. However, she fails to account for why some social locations are more privileged than others and why the responsibility for some racial locations has not been by made by choice but rather by coercion. Harding may take responsibility for her race location, but her lack of interrogation of power relations between different social and racial locations means that she does not acknowledge the white race privilege that she is able to exercise.

Candace West and Sarah Fenstermaker theorise difference as "an ongoing interactional accomplishment" (1995:9). How class, race and gender are accomplished depends on their specific interaction, but the categorical diversity of the participants is not necessary to their accomplishment and those who participate in it may not share the same meanings. What is interesting in West and Fenstermaker's analysis is that, although white women are identified as such, they are not racialised; instead class or gender masks their race privilege. "Race" refers to all those who are non-white. Failing to racialise white women, as such means that white race privilege remains uninterrogated as a source of oppression and inequality.

Christine Sylvester (1995) asserts that the current focus on difference needs to be turned into a politics. We must all become world travellers who have mobile multiple subjectivities which can allow us to use empathetic methods and politics to sustain contradictions:

> We might think of mobile subjectivities as the borderlands all of us inhabit, even those of us who think we are at home and safe in the West, in the Self, in one corner of the feminist parade with one's mates — in contradistinction to some Third World woman who is never entirely at home in a world of colonial "othering" power, who is always playing the borders (Sylvester 1995:959).

Sylvester's construction of the world traveller rests primarily on the experiences of women of colour, African women and African American women who have consciously to manage their subjectivities within dominant domains. The logic of Sylvester's argument is that if these women can do it then so can white women in the West. However, the use of analogy suggests that the circumstances of white western women are the same as women of colour, African women and African American women. The unintended result is that sameness erases differences. Sylvester's analysis privileges the subject by unpacking women's intra-subjective relations but not inter-subjective relations, and fails to see the disjuncture between deploying multiple subjectivities as choice rather than compulsion. Unacknowledged white privilege confers dominance and choice for white women in the West in relation to other groups of non-white women. White race privilege also conditions its practitioners into being comfortable, confident and oblivious to the way in which they are trained to inflict daily doses of hostility, violence and distress on non-white women (McIntosh 1992:101). A lack of consciousness about the unearned white race privilege of multiple subjectivities means race would play a different role in the lives of white women as opposed to women of colour, African women and African American women.

Marilyn Frye (1996) argues for a more inclusive feminism by constructing the category "women" as structure, which involves the necessity for differences:

> ... if the category of women is constructed as a positive self-supporting category not constituted by universal exclusive relation to the absence-of-it but by self-reliant structures of differentiation and relation, the identity or subjectivity associated with it has no built-in exclusivity or closure against other identity categories, no analytically

built-in hostility to multiple category memberships and subjectivities. Self-constructive involvement in one category does not preclude self-constructive involvement in others as well. Social-political identity is not species membership and is not set membership, nor is it a hybrid of the two (Frye 1996:1004–5).

Although Frye's theory attempts to provide a way to understand concrete situations, she concludes by stating that theory "does not settle practical and specific questions of what is best for whom" (1996:1009). Yet Frye's theory is telling us what is best for whom: it is in the best interests of feminism to embrace such a theory so that white women are not positioned as the dominant group who own and control it. A question arises from Frye's work: who has the power in feminism to determine who will decide and ensure that the category of women is constructed as a positive self-supporting category? Frye's attempt to erase the generic woman only results in creating a new white version "who is all and only woman, who by some miracle of abstraction has no particular identity in terms of race, class, ethnicity, sexual orientation, language, religion, nationality" (Spelman 1990:187).

Susan Hekman argues that accommodating difference and maintaining the political and analytical force of feminism requires us to recast feminist standpoint theory by defining it as situated and engaged knowledge, a place from which to develop a counter hegemonic discourse and argue for reducing repression. "Women speak from multiple standpoints, producing multiple knowledges. But this does not prevent women from coming together to work for specific political goals" (Hekman 1997:363). Hekman equalises and fragments standpoints, which is different from the position taken by Collins (1997:371) who argues that black women's "standpoint refers to historically shared, group-based experiences. Groups have a degree of permanence over time, such that the group realities transcend individual experiences". Recasting standpoint theory does little to change the power relations between women in feminism; some standpoints are more privileged than others. White race privilege forms part of white women's standpoint in feminism and it confers unearned power.

The first Australian book to address a politics of difference, entitled *Feminism and the Politics of Difference* (1993), was edited by

Sneja Gunew and Anna Yeatman. The book introduces the reader to a number of areas identified by difference, which are interrogated by feminists within the text. Race and ethnicity, appropriation, authenticity, legitimation, identity politics and non-exclusive cultural and gendered representations mark the areas of difference. The assumptions that underpin the book are that there are multiple differences that are not fixed and require analysis. Most of the articles are dedicated to interrogating specific differences, although Anna Yeatman offers a theory of accommodating difference within feminism through arguing that multiple oppressions occur simultaneously. Yeatman argues that it is the specifics of the context that will determine which oppression is dominant and the subject should identify this. In recognition of the fact that some women will experience different forms of oppression because of their race, ethnicity, age, disability or sexuality, she states that an emancipatory project is one whereby the custodians of feminism make space available for marginalised women to have a voice. "This means that our vision for change for this polity and the larger national polity within which it is situated has to take up this relationship and work with it" (Yeatman 1993:243). Yeatman acknowledges the imbalance in power between the custodians of feminism and marginalised women and the need for marginalised women to self-present about their different oppressions. However, the custodians of feminism remain anonymous, and how they got to be in such a position is not disclosed in Yeatman's theory of multiple and interlocking oppressions. While the focus is on systemic racial oppression, in theory white race privilege will remain uninterrogated as a site of domination, because whiteness is not positioned as racial location and identity.

Alison Jaggar, in *Living with Contradictions: Controversies in Feminist Ethics* (1994), argues that feminism is connected to issues such as economic justice, environmental damage and racial bias in such a way that it cannot be single-minded:

> Our commitment to ending women's subordination inevitably leads us to confront complex, multidimensional problems that require us to balance a variety of values and to evaluate the claims and interests of a variety of groups or even species including a variety of groups of women (1994:11).

Jaggar calls for the feminist movement to be sensitive to the voices of women who have been muted by the dominant culture: "we must respond to those voices by giving special attention and weight to the concerns they express" (1994:12). Jaggar, like Yeatman, explicitly recognises the differences in power, but she too does not interrogate how some white women have more power than others. Both Yeatman and Jaggar's theoretical positions tell us that in order for them to be able to offer to include those who are excluded they must be speaking from a position of white privilege. Offering to include is a sign of ownership and control, and inclusion of "Other" on white women's terms will not decentre white women's dominant status in Australian feminism.

In an article entitled "Specificity: Beyond Equality and Difference", Shane Phelan (1991) argues for specificity which recognises our multiple identifications and locations in power. She argues that white middle-class theoretical engagement with difference has often been about unified differences, not the acceptance that there are differences between women. Phelan asserts that within feminism

> We need to hold together structural analyses of inequalities with a recognition of the unique, multiple embodiments of those without expecting that these mesh completely. A worthwhile politics requires both that we recognise differences and that we share a community; that we value both relationality and individuality (Phelan 1991:140).

Phelan's argument for specificity implies that each part of our identities is separate from every other part and that they are situated in different locations of power. It is only at the level of abstraction that such separation can occur. The application of such theory in practice leaves us with investigating multiple identifications in individual subjects and tells us nothing about the way in which similarities exist in the context of differences between us, and how some women's identities are more privileged than others. As Hurtado and Stewart (1997) argue,

> ... mechanisms of power employed in the exercise of whiteness ... are geared to the maintenance of structural power for white people as a whole. Whether individual whites use these mechanisms or not is irrelevant to the outcome of the white group's superiority (1997:303).

An engagement with a politics of difference as multiple standpoints, oppressions, subjectivities, subject positions, identities and locations provides us with a way of understanding the heterogeneous and heteronomous representations of gender, sexuality, ethnicity, race, class and nationality. However, the effect of such theorising is to make a politics of difference in practice colour blind in terms of whiteness and power evasive in that all differences are rendered equally significant. There appears to be no scope for fixity in power relations between women, yet feminists argue that statistically and corporeally men have more power than women do in the world. For white feminists there appear to be no limits to differences that constitute subjectivity and no limits to the degree to which they can be invented and overcome.

Non-white feminists engage with the politics of difference

African American women, women of colour and Indigenous women have also engaged with a politics of difference from different perspectives. Unlike white feminist theorising on difference, women of colour, African American women and Indigenous women do include within their respective positions the idea that there is some fixity to difference in power relations which places limits on inter-subjective relations. Women of colour, African American women and Indigenous women's knowledges are situated differently from those of the white feminists discussed above. The respective positionings on power relations of African American, Indigenous women and women of colour are based on their lived experiences of being located within them. They speak not from a position of race privilege but from one of racial oppression.

Bernice Johnson Reagon, in *Coalition Politics: Turning the Century* (1983), argues that to accommodate differences we, as women must do coalition work. This means that we must recognise that we have to respect differences and work with them even if they are dangerous and painful. Coalition work will mean operating in different contexts because people's differences and commonalities shift depending on where they are located. Reagon provides an insight into the intersecting ways that various differences can produce alliances based on commonalities and dissimilarities. She also acknowledges that this will be dangerous and painful work, but to respect differences and work with them requires a consciousness of what those differences are. Whiteness in feminism is not identified as a difference. Many white feminists want to form alliances with women of colour, African American women and Indigenous women but they remain unconscious and ignorant of their white race privilege.

A collection of essays, edited by Lisa Albrecht and Rose M. Brewer, entitled *Bridges of Power: Women's Multicultural Alliances* (1990), attempts to provide a framework for forming alliances and bringing about social change. Albrecht and Brewer argue that what is important in alliance forming is a "model of leadership that will account for differences and the re-visioning of traditional conceptions of power" (1990:4). They acknowledge that contemporary feminist perspectives see power as a process by which people change themselves at the personal level or collectively, and that there are power differences between women. However, they argue that all women should be treated as equal when forming alliances and that "it is critical that women who have privilege come to terms with the implications of it" (1990:9). Albrecht and Brewer acknowledge here that women have power over other women and request that those with power understand that in order for all to be equal in alliances the powerful must give up some of their power.

Mohanty et al., in *Third World Women and the Politics of Feminism* (1991), state that a history of third-world women's engagement with feminism is lacking, noting that there is no simple way of writing about their diverse struggles and histories. Mohanty et al. propose that despite the differences in location, conflict and histories of these women we can still locate them as an imagined community where women are committed to "horizontal comradeship" (1991:4):

> Thus, potentially all women (including white women) can align themselves with and participate in these imagined communities. However, clearly our relation to and centrality in particular struggles depend on our different, often conflictual, locations and histories (1991:4).

Mohanty et al. argue that the category "Third World Women" or "women of colour" is not biological or sociological but a political constituency. It is the commonality of the context of struggle that determines possible political alliances. Mohanty et al. recognise the partiality involved in politics through the idea of the imagined community, and acknowledge the different relationships that different women will have to particular struggles due to their different locations and histories. Conflict is perceived as a necessary part of these relations and is also evidenced in the work of Nellie Mackay in *Acknowledging Differences* (1993). Mackay argues that for women:

> The social transformation to which we aspire unites differences and diversity without erasing the specificities of the histories and the cultures that give each group of American citizens its own identity. Coming to terms with some differences will always present great difficulties for us, difficulties that may appear almost insurmountable at times. Yet, we must face them honestly (Mackay 1993:280).

Mackay shares with Reagon, Mohanty et al. and Albrecht and Brewer an acknowledgment of the difficulties of doing what Reagon calls coalition work due to an imbalance in power relations. Audre Lorde argues that differences between women should be a source of strength and part of the "necessary polarities between which our creativity can spark like a dialectic" (1983:99). Lorde perceives difference as a source of productive outcomes, but also states that "ignoring the differences of race between women and the implications of those differences presents the most serious threat to the mobilization of women's joint power" (Lorde 1992:49).

Marnia Lazreg asks: "What is the nature of the feminist project? What is its relation to women in other places? Is there something at the heart of academic feminism that is inescapably Western gynocentric?"(1988:96). Lazreg is concerned at the way in which difference is treated in discourse and deconstruction analyses, which she argues essentialises difference and renders us unable to discern the relationship between a variety of modes of being different in the world. This form of analysis does not deal with inter-subjectivity, which ties men and women of different cultures together. For Lazreg inter-subjectivity acts to prevent objectification of the "Other" and reminds us of our entitlement to our culturally specific mode of being human:

> The question is to define a critical writing space within which women who are not making their careers in Western Universities, but who are the subjects of our writing, can identify. This requires resisting the temptation of seeing in US or French women's present needs our ideals. It also calls for a comprehensive exploring and understanding of the body of knowledge produced by the Indigenous peoples of these areas of the world (1988:102).

Lazreg seeks to decentre the knowledges of western white women by recognising the validity of Indigenous knowledges. Lazreg believes that by recognising the subjectivity of "Other" objectification can be prevented, but although recognising the subjectivity of "Other" may reduce objectification it does not erase the power relations that exist in inter-subjective relations between different subject positions that have an unequal structural location.

Indigenous women such as Rayner Green, a Native American woman, and Haunani-Kay Trask, a Native Hawaiian, offer their perspectives on difference in feminism. Green believes that "it is now time for feminist scholars to ask Native American women — indeed, all groups of women they study — what their agendas are and how feminist scholars might lend themselves to the task" (1980:267). Acknowledged within Green's statement are the discrepancies in power between Native American women and feminists. She seeks to subvert the relation by stating that white feminist scholars should consult first with the women they intend to write about, as white feminists do not have the right to write about the lives and experiences of these women without their permission. Trask takes issue with feminism by arguing that there are vast differences in culture and heritage between haole (whites) and Hawaiians; culture is larger than women's rights:

> For most haole, feminist or otherwise, my stance appears to end any potential coalition work or even a meagre understanding across our barriers of culture and history. In reality, however, the opposite is true. We confront each other, warily, carefully, every day. Occasionally, we work together. But struggle is what we do, not what we meditate on in some quiet remove from the heat of political and cultural battle. In a life of Indigenous struggle, questions regarding relationships between theory and praxis recede into the clouds. I

work with haole, and fight with them, all the time. How can I not since haole and haole institutions determine so much of Hawaiian life? (Trask 1996:915)

Trask highlights incommensurable differences between white feminist individual rights and the collective rights of a people to practise their culture. Trask's position shows that incommensurabilities exist and difficulties are experienced daily in being and asserting difference as an Indigenous woman in a colonised white-dominated society. Trask resists the power that haole have over her, while understanding that she is always compromised by the persistence of that relationship.

Similar perspectives on engaging with difference in feminism have been offered in Australia by women of colour and Indigenous women. Perera argues that Australian feminism deals with issues relevant to "middle-class Anglo/Celtic women who have their own (invisible because dominant) ethnicity" (1985:14). White feminism in Australia will have to do more than "offer good intentions and a haphazard willingness to accommodate minorities within their already defined boundaries" (Perera 1985:14). She asserts that white feminism needs to give priority to non-white women's needs and accept as legitimate the specificity of non-white experience. Perera, like Green, acknowledges the power imbalance between non-white and white feminists by highlighting the fact that the prioritising within feminism is in the hands of white feminists. She recognises that they hold a privileged position and there is a certain fixity to the power relation — hence her appeal to them that non-white women's needs be given priority and that they accept the legitimacy of non-white experience.

Ganguly, writing some ten years later in Australia, echoes similar statements about the lack of inclusion of non-white women in Australian feminism. She argues that, although women of colour in Australia have mobilised themselves to highlight their issues and concerns, they have been left out of women's studies:

Women's Studies in Australia is overwhelmingly monocultural or, at best, Eurocentric. Where differences are recognised, they are largely discussed in terms of dialogues between "First World" and "Third World" women. Dialogues between women from the dominant culture and women from the various NESB communities have yet to make their mark in mainstream feminist circles (Ganguly 1995:47).

Ganguly recognises white ownership of women's studies and the lack of engagement between women from "non-English-speaking backgrounds" (NESB) and mainstream — meaning white — feminism. Australian feminism is a white middle-class movement, according to Adele Murdolo (1996:79–82), who argues that it is the embodied experiences of Anglo women that are represented in texts. She argues that Australian feminism has treated difference as benign diversity in order to contain Indigenous and NESB immigrant women. Murdolo asserts that white feminists' recognition of diversity results in a "unity of diversity" which is positioned as being unproblematic. The recognition by white middle-class feminists of the differences of NESB immigrant women and Indigenous women often results in the appropriation of their concerns, which renders their subjectivities invisible.

Ien Ang (1995) argues that feminism in Australia sees itself as existing in a multicultural nation that is inclusive of all women. Differences are to be dealt with through "recognition", "understanding" and "dialogue". Ang argues that:

> The problem with such terms is first of all they reveal an overconfident faith in the power and possibility of open and honest communication to "overcome" or "settle" differences, of a power-free speech situation without interference by entrenched presumptions, sensitivities and preconceived ideas (1995: 59).

For Ang, dealing with difference in feminism as a multicultural nation is utopian. Instead, white feminists should see the necessity of a politics of partiality where the field of its political intervention is limited. Feminism must accept that it is not the political home for all women all the time. Ang's argument reveals that white feminists are able to believe in a power-free speech situation because they speak from a position of white race privilege that remains undisclosed, unmarked and invisible to those who possess it.

Jackie Huggins, the only Australian Indigenous woman who has consistently engaged with feminism, argues:

Despite the predominance of patriarchal rule in Australian society, Australia was colonized on a racially imperialistic base and not on a sexually imperialistic base. No degree of patriarchal bonding between white male colonizers and Aboriginal men overshadowed white racial imperialism. In fact, white racial imperialism granted to all white women, however victimized by sexist oppression, the right to assume the role of oppressor in relationship to black women and black men (Huggins 1991b:7).

Huggins believes that white feminists need to come to terms with their racism before there can be dialogue between Indigenous and white women. She positions white women in the role of oppressor because of the power they share by association with white males. The theft of Indigenous people's land and subsequent dispossession, rape, massacres, forced incarceration on reserves and forced use of our labour provided the basis for white race privilege in this country. White feminists benefit today from the historical events that shaped and continue to shape the nature of power relations between them and Indigenous women. The work of Perera, Ganguly, Murdolo, Ang and Huggins demonstrates, that, from the perspective of the "Other", Australian feminism is dominated and controlled by white women.

Signposts and points of departure

The representation of "difference" in feminism was first articulated as gender, culture and class differences between white women and white men. The shift to examining differences between women began with specific differences and then moved to positioning differences as multiplicity. As the foregoing literature review shows, whiteness as subject position, "race", privilege and dominance are not marked as a difference in the early literature, which focuses instead on the differences between white women and white men. Nor is whiteness made visible in the later literature, which focuses on differences between white women and women who are "Other". The implicit representation of whiteness in the work of women of colour, African American feminists and Indigenous women provides signposts. Their work gives direction for creating feminisms that through theory and practice do not just tolerate racial differences, but understand that they are constituted through and implicated in complex power relations between all women.

A small but growing number of feminists have made whiteness visible in their work and provide signposts for further research. Adrienne Rich (1979:306) states that white feminists utilise white solipsism through a tunnel vision that centres their experiences at the expense of other women. Elizabeth Spelman (1990) argues that, although white women need to know about women who are different from them, they should

> be aware of how the legacies of our privilege appear in the ways we may try to satisfy that need: in our confusing imagining women with knowing them; in priding ourselves on tolerance; and in appropriating others' identities through our desperate rush to find similarity (Spelman 1990:185).

Ruth Frankenberg's (1993) work on the social construction of whiteness demonstrates that "race", while invisible, is salient in shaping the lives of white women, who deploy a number of race difference discourses in their everyday practices. Philipa Rothfield (1994), a white Australian feminist, argues that there is tension born out of the way in which white feminist theory, developed by theorists whose race privilege is derived from a network of relations of domination, tends to blanket political practices and concerns. African American feminist Toni Morrison demonstrates in *Playing in the Dark: Whiteness and the Literary Imagination* (1993a) how whiteness in the American literary imagination is predicated on a real or fabricated African presence, where:

> ... the subject of the dream is the dreamer. The fabrication of an Africanist persona is reflexive; an extraordinary meditation on the self; a powerful exploration of the fears and desires that reside in the writerly conscious. It is an astonishing revelation of longing, of terror, of perplexity, of shame, of magnanimity. It requires hard work not to see this (Morrison 1993a:17).

While the African presence is in the imagination of white writers, bell hooks (1992:168) argues that whiteness is also represented in the black imagination and it too is often associated with terror through a collective memory of historically asserted white power. The work of Rich, Spelman, Frankenberg, Rothfield, Morrison and hooks reveals that whiteness is represented in texts yet it remains invisible. As subjects and socially situated knowers, all women are enmeshed in racialised power relations that have been historically constituted through discourses and the material conditions that furnished and sustain them.

CHAPTER THREE

Puttem "Indigenous Woman": Representations of the "Indigenous Woman" in White Women's Ethnographic Writings

> I did not know then that to embrace the "authentic" Indian produced by the Western science of anthropology would be to adopt a Western construct — a textbook or domesticated Indian ... Western historicizing posits Indigenous peoples as illusory; historically, they are inscribed to stand as the West's opposite, imaged and constructed so as to stress their great need to be saved through colonization and civilization (Crosby 1994:87–88).

The key role of social anthropology is to identify, interpret and explain cultural difference (Moore 1988:189). Knowledges about cultural difference produced in social anthropological discourse through ethnography provide understandings about human diversity and can be used to counter culture-bound ways of looking at the world. However, this view of anthropology has been challenged. In North America, the publication of the anthology *Writing Culture: The Poetics and Politics of Ethnography*, edited by James Clifford, inspired debates in anthropology that questioned the "realist" tradition of ethnographic writing. Clifford and others argue that the production of anthropological knowledges requires interpretation, cultural translation and the writing of cultures; consequently anthropologists are involved in the process of cultural representation (Clifford 1986). Feminist anthropologists Deborah Gordon and Ruth Behar agree that anthropology is an interpretive quest involved in the process of cultural representation. They acknowledge that the new experimental ethnography proposed by Clifford requires anthropologists to "reflect a more profound self-consciousness of the workings of power and the partialness of all truth, both in the text and in the world" (Behar & Gordon 1995:4). However, they argue that this new ethnography is grounded in male subjectivity that excludes women.

The debates on writing culture did cross the ocean, but they have had little impact on Australian anthropology.[1] Perhaps this is because Australian anthropology is the child of British social anthropology and remains loyal to its parent. Australia as a former British colony provided fertile ground for the anthropological enterprise that began in this country in the late 19th century. The school of evolutionary thought in both Britain and America influenced the direction of research in Australian anthropology and was in turn influenced by such research. Darwin used data from Australia to support his theory of evolution, arguing that the Aboriginal [Indigenous] female was the living example of the difference in degree between humans and apes (Cowlishaw 1986a: 3). Others, such as Durkheim (1961), found the elementary forms of religion, and Freud (1983) the origins of totem and taboo, in early Australian ethnographic writings. Evolutionary theory provided the framework for anthropological analyses that were primarily concerned with racial differences.

Evolutionary theory was superseded after the First World War; British and Australian functionalist anthropology emerged through the efforts of white male anthropologists such as Radcliffe-Brown and Malinowski. This change in theory shifted the focus from racial difference to cultural difference in anthropological discourse (Asad 1973:9). Male anthropologists dominated anthropology in Australia, although there were a few women anthropologists carrying out fieldwork. Phyllis Kaberry, Olive Pink and Ursula McConnel were some of the early white women anthropologists — exceptions in this otherwise male-dominated discipline — whose primary objects of study were Indigenous people. Australian "Aboriginalist" anthropology dominated the discipline in academic circles and its practitioners were, and still are, positioned as experts on Indigenous culture, and it is predominantly they who teach and control Indigenous Studies in Australian universities.

Anthropological representations of "cultural difference" are utilised within popular and other discourses. Anthropological data and research has been an important resource base for American, Canadian and British feminist theorising about the universality of women's oppression and the cultural construction of gender. Adrienne Rich (1977), Mary Daly (1978), Juliet Mitchell and Anne Oakley (1986) and others have used ethnographic texts to argue their respective positions on women's culture by drawing on the representations in these texts. The written work of women anthropologists is also an important resource base for feminists theorising about Indigenous women in Australia. The work of a number of women anthropologists is cited in Australian feminist texts, for example Grieve and Grimshaw (1981), Bottomley et al. (1991), Saunders and Evans (1992), Grieve and Burns (1994), Caine and Pringle (1995), Pettman (1992) and Bulbeck (1997). While feminists have sought to write about Indigenous women, their work draws on women anthropologists' representations of Indigenous women, which are accepted without interrogation.

Feminist discourse has in turn impacted on anthropology. In the 1970s women anthropologists began to "confront the problem of how women were represented in anthropological writings" (Moore 1988:1) by male anthropologists, and anthropological writings about Australian Indigenous women by white middle-class women proliferated during this period. Since the work of Phyllis Kaberry in the 1930s, many women anthropologists continue to be influenced by the women's movement in their writings. Representations of Indigenous women, in the work of women anthropologists, are centred on the role and status of Indigenous women. The majority of ethnographic research was carried out on cattle stations, church missions or government reserves. They were located in remote areas such as the Kimberley region of Western Australia, Cape York Peninsula in Queensland, Arnhem Land and the Western Desert in the Northern Territory and the north-west of South Australia.

White middle-class women anthropologists' representations

of the "Indigenous woman" are problematical. The concern in this chapter is not to position white women anthropologists as ethnographic liars, nor is it to provide a definitive statement on who is and who is not an Indigenous woman. Instead it is to argue that white middle-class women anthropologists' representations create a binary opposition of "traditional" versus "contemporary" Indigenous women which privileges certain groups of Indigenous women as culturally and racially authentic and positions the rest as racially and culturally contaminated. The "contemporary" and "traditional" Indigenous woman binary has salience because women anthropologists utilise a distorted methodology, which relies on a particular ideological construction of culture and race (Asad 1979; Cowlishaw 1986b). The methodology denies the historical construction of racialised power relations that shaped the subject positions of both women anthropologists and Indigenous women. Anthropological representations of the "Indigenous woman" are reinterpretations of our lived experiences and they erase our subjectivity because fieldwork is premised on many exclusions, silences and absences. As Cowlishaw notes, "those things which [anthropologists] do not name are rendered passive, indeterminant, irrelevant" (Cowlishaw 1993:183). Indigenous women are represented as objects within texts, etic representations that have become truth in public and academic discourses.

Anthropological representations of the "traditional" and "contemporary" Indigenous woman were played out and contested in public and academic discourses in 1989 in what has become known as the Bell–Huggins debate.[2] The key women involved were Professor Diane Bell, a white feminist anthropologist, and a number of Indigenous women: Topsy Napurrula Nelson, Jackie Huggins, Isabel Tarrago, Jo Willmot, Kathy Willets, Liz Bond, Lillian Holt, Eleanor Bourke, Mary Ann Bin-Sallik, Pat Fowell, Joann Schmider, Valerie Craigie and Linda McBride-Levi. The controversy arose over an article written by Diane Bell and Topsy Napurrula Nelson. The article, "Speaking About Rape Is Everyone's Business" was published in *Women's Studies International Forum*, Volume 12, No. 4, 1989.

The Bell–Huggins debate highlighted the way in which the

white feminist anthropologist used the "traditional" versus "contemporary" binary to authenticate some Indigenous women at the expense of others. The support given to Bell by the white feminists involved illustrated the social authority and legitimacy of anthropology in its representations of the "Indigenous woman". It also illuminated how white women involved in feminism and anthropology centre their agenda on rape as the rightful and legitimate position from which to speak and write. Bell's deployment of the "traditional" versus "contemporary" Indigenous woman binary to defend her position was neither deliberate nor a coincidence. It is part of the legacy of Australian Indigenous anthropology and its representations.

The "traditional" versus "contemporary" Indigenous woman binary

In 1988 Francesca Merlan published an overview of the Australian anthropological literature on gender in Indigenous society written between 1961 and 1986 by women anthropologists. Merlan argues that most of this literature is concerned with the position of Indigenous women in their societies, and is organised around sexuality, reproduction, bestowal, marriage and religion. She identifies three main theories in the literature about the relationship between Indigenous women and Indigenous men: men are dominant and women subordinate; men and women have interdependent roles in society; men and women have separate but complementary relations. Merlan states the questions that have guided research on gender have, however, arisen from European women's concerns about the nature of their involvement in Australian society rather than "from an appraisal of the problems confronting Indigenous societies today" (Merlan 1988:63). She argues that the literature focuses on traditional socio-cultural systems rather than specifying the continuity and change of the current situation. She asserts that the external internal relationship of contemporary Indigenous social life and non-Indigenous social life has to be built into any social analysis (1988:63).

Merlan's overview of this literature makes an important point about the need to move beyond the traditional frame of reference to deal with social change. Her advice is commendable, but it is based on an assumption that all that needs to be done is to insert history. For Merlan, change comes from including more data rather than from interrogating the epistemological assumptions and methodology used in the anthropological representations of Indigenous women. Merlan's critique is problematic because it is underpinned by particular ideological constructs of "race" and "culture" which are outcomes of the methodology employed by her and the women anthropologists she critiques.

The greater part of the published work of women anthropologists is concerned with specific groups of Indigenous women who are identified as "traditional" or "traditionally oriented".[3] Although the term "traditionally oriented" is used as a way of letting go of the pretence that it is possible to study a pristine pre-colonial culture, analyses proceed as if such a culture exists. This is because the ideological construct of "culture" that informs the texts is based on "seeing authoritative meanings as the *a priori* totality which defines and reproduces the essential integrity of a given social order" (Asad 1979:607). Authentic culture is an *a priori* system of essential meanings embedded in traditions named, defined and represented by Australian Indigenous anthropology.

A few published works by women anthropologists are concerned with Indigenous women who are identified and categorised as being half-caste, part Aborigine or of mixed descent.[4] These texts are informed by an ideological construction of "race" which constitutes an *a priori* essential biologism based on skin colour. The deployment of the two ideological constructs of "culture" and "race" results in the establishment of a traditional versus contemporary binary within the texts. These texts relate both directly and indirectly to specific aspects of the role and status of Indigenous women who are represented as "traditional" or "contemporary".

What is evident from the texts by women anthropologists is that their analyses are underpinned by particular ideological constructions of "culture" and "race" which establish a "traditional" versus "contemporary" binary. In constructing the "traditional", the theoretical deployment of "culture" and "race" denies everyday practice as the stuff of culture and refers to the anthropologically constructed, dehistoricised, *a priori* authoritative meanings which preserve and capture within the text the exotic and the biologically pure. This is particularly evident in the work of Catherine Berndt (1964; 1978; 1979; 1981; 1982; 1983), who argued that the role and status of women in traditional society is one of interdependent independence. In the domestic sphere men exercised formal authority and/or dominance, and women had informal authority and/or dominance over men. These relations depended on links through marriage and descent (Berndt 1978:80). In the economic sphere both men and women had formal authority and/or dominance, and women had informal authority and/or dominance over men. In the religious sphere men had formal authority and/or dominance over women, and both sexes exercised informal authority and/or dominance over each other. What is represented within Berndt's text is Indigenous women's role and status in a pristine precolonial culture that by implication is biologically and culturally pure. What is and what is not "traditional" Indigenous women's role and status is defined and reproduced within a framework that is an essential part of the methodology of Indigenous anthropology.

The methodology allows for an illusory absence of colonisation which is preserved and felt in the presence of its absence, as is also evident in the work of Phyllis Kaberry, the first white woman anthropologist to represent Indigenous women. Writing in 1935 on the importance of women and men in mourning ceremonies and their role in identifying spirit children and spirit centres connecting people to country, Kaberry notes:

> [W]ith the exception of those living on the missions, most natives in this region are concentrated about the station homesteads, and are employed in stock work, gardening, and domestic duties. They wear European clothes and receive rations of flour, tea, beef, and tobacco. It is only during the "wet" season, when work slackens off between September and March, that they go "walkabout" in the bush to hold their inter-tribal meetings for initiation and mourning ceremonies (1935:x).

Kaberry also noted that the Indigenous population in the

Kimberley was declining. She attributed the decrease to the "breakdown of their old life", the effect of gonorrhoea, and abortion (1935/36b: 399). Indigenous women living on remote government reserves or Christian missions under welfare conditions not of their own making, and over which they had little control, were not seen to compromise their status as anthropological informants because they spoke language, did some ceremonies and were biologically uncontaminated (Cowlishaw 1986b: 227).

Kaberry's focus on "traditional" Indigenous women was part of her commitment to refuting the prevailing view of male anthropologists that "traditional" Indigenous women "were no more than domesticated cows" (Kaberry 1939:9). She believed that "from the outset one is disposed to envisage her [Indigenous woman] as an active social personality: as a human being with all the wants, desires, and needs that flesh is heir to" (1939:9). Kaberry argued against the proposition that Indigenous women were subservient to Indigenous men. In 1939 she argued that "traditional" Indigenous women had their own ceremonies, participated in some collectively with men, had rights in land, and that their labour was crucial to gathering food, socialising children and domestic production in general. Throughout the text, Kaberry implicitly contrasts the role of white women with that of "traditional" Indigenous women, arguing that the latter had more autonomy and independence in their society. In both texts Kaberry separates Indigenous women's lived experience into two domains because her search is for essential meanings which can only be found in the domain of traditional culture. What occurs when these Aboriginal women are not in the bush but living on stations is excluded from the analysis.

When white women anthropologists such as Marie Reay and Dianne Barwick are confronted by colonial history through their fieldwork among "contemporary" Indigenous women, the search for *a priori* authoritative meanings that can only be found in traditional culture becomes problematic:

> The use of the terms half-caste, mixed bloods and part-Aborigine without the relevance of "caste" and "blood" to what were supposedly studies of culture being spelt out, imply a causal connexion between the dilution of the blood and the loss of Indigenous, that is, tradi-

tional practices. In some cases there were references to these matters but no systematic analysis was attempted (Cowlishaw 1986b: 226).

What becomes operationalised and takes precedence in analysis is an *a priori* essential biologism, which is used to explain social change. Racial purity becomes the measure of both unauthentic and authentic traditional Indigenous culture. In an article about seeking to demonstrate the degree of assimilation, Reay wrote about the marriage patterns of 264 "Indigenous and Mixed-Blood Women" (Reay 1951/52:116). The Indigenous women were categorised according to caste: "12 are full-blood, 26 are three-quarter caste, 129 are half-caste, 77 quadroon and 20 octoroon or lighter" (Reay 1951/52:119). She concludes that of the women "76 have married men of darker castes than themselves, 114 married men of their own caste, and 11 have married lighter men" (Reay 1951/52:116). She notes that the population is getting lighter, and, by implication, becoming assimilated. Reay utilises an essential biologism to define marriage patterns, which are then used to measure the degree of assimilation.

Barwick uses historical records of the Protection Board in Victoria to explore changing gender relations. She utilises the anthropological construction of the "traditional" Indigenous women and representations of the white woman to measure the degree of transformation occurring for Indigenous women on station communities between the 1860s and 1886. While her analysis locates the Indigenous women on the station communities in terms of the experiences and activities of their daily lives, Barwick offers an assimilationist model as explanation of cultural transformation. This is because Barwick utilises "culture" as *a priori* essential meanings to separate what she perceives as Indigenous women engaging in white women's cultural practices and "traditional" Indigenous cultural practices. Her concluding quote illuminates her representation and positioning of the Indigenous women in the texts under her gaze. Barwick states that "the families here live like English workingmen and the lubras are ladies now" (1978:62). The anthropological methodology works to centre both traditional Indigenous women and white western women. In the work of both Reay and Barwick the "contemporary" Indigenous women's racial purity and culture are positioned as ambiguous and oscillate between how they are like or unlike their "traditional" sisters or how they are like or unlike white women in their behaviour and practices. They are similar to their "traditional" sisters in relation to the specific cultural remnants and like their white sisters in relation to specific acquired behaviours, but they are also unlike both because of perceived racial differences.

The "traditional" versus "contemporary" binary is utilised in the work of Jane Goodale who began fieldwork in the 1950s on Melville and Bathurst Islands, home of the Tiwi people. She wrote about the social organisation of the Tiwi with reference to the life cycle of the Tiwi women because she believed it could be analysed systematically (Goodale 1971). Her work shows that Tiwi men and Tiwi women have shared and complementary roles in the sexual division of labour and in ritual and ceremonial life. This argument is followed through in another paper where she contests the proposition that meat is symbolically valued above vegetable foods because it is appropriated by men. Goodale shows how the power of a particular poisonous yam that is prepared by men over three days integrates the entire world of the Tiwi. "It is a world in which one part is considered masculine, but exploited and maintained by the women, and in which the yam represents all life-sustaining food, integrated with a part of the world which is considered feminine, but exploited and maintained by men, in which the Kulama yam represents all human life itself" (1982:207–8). Goodale acknowledges that "the data on which this discussion is based are derived from studies made during a period when nearly all Tiwi had been drawn into either mission or government settlements, where a majority of time was spent in non-traditional activities concerning settled life" (1982:198). Despite this acknowledgment, Goodale's concern in her analysis with the ideational order of the Tiwi (that is, with the *a priori* essential meanings embedded within "traditional" beliefs) results in her negating the way in which "settled" or "contemporary" life also shapes the ideational order.

A slightly different use of the "traditional" versus "contemporary" binary is evident in the work of Isobel White (1978). White conducted her fieldwork in South Australia among the Pitjantjatjara, Janggundjara and Andigirinja women (1978:36). White makes no explicit reference to colonisation nor does she explicitly contrast "traditional" Indigenous women with white women in her text, but she is influenced by the women's movement. What is clear from White's work is that she is opposed to the view that "traditional" Indigenous women are chattels of their men. She acknowledges that there is variation among Indigenous societies, but feels that some generalisations can be made about "traditional" Indigenous women's status. White's theory of the status of "traditional" Indigenous women is based on an examination of their participation in the spiritual dimension of life. She argues that "traditional" Indigenous women's status is that of junior partner to traditional Indigenous men in all aspects of their lives and that Indigenous women accept this status because they know they reproduce human life while men reproduce spiritual life. White's text gives the impression that "traditional" Indigenous women have escaped colonisation. White's concern with identifying the authentic cultural practices of "traditional" Indigenous women reveals that she too works with an ideological construction of "culture" as *a priori* essential meanings.

Annette Hamilton, drawing on her fieldwork in Northern Arnhem Land in 1967–68 and the desert regions of north-west South Australia among the Janggundjara and Bidjandjara speakers in 1970–71, writes of gendered power in these societies. Hamilton investigates gender and power through marriage, ritual, kinship and the sexual division of labour, and, unlike most of her contemporaries, recognised that questions dealing with oppression, subordination and asymmetry are fundamentally concerned with power relations (Hamilton 1971; 1975; 1978; 1980). She notes that, in comparison with western white women and because of their social worth and economic freedom, "traditional" Indigenous women in Australia have captured the interest of feminist anthropologists.

Hamilton (1981) argues that regional variation in Indigenous Australia provides different models of gender relations. In Central Australia Indigenous men and women "constituted themselves into exclusively homosocial associations" (1981:84) which allowed for autonomy and independence. In Arnhem Land,

Indigenous women's sociality was confined to economic and domestic spheres of life. Female deference to men was reproduced through gerontocratic polygyny and compulsory remarriage and Indigenous women were included in some ceremonies but on Indigenous men's terms. Hamilton argues that, although each sex is powerful to itself, men can dominate women by force. She states that the two arguments about violence — that colonisation may have increased the incidence of violence for Indigenous women and the reverse that violence has decreased because of colonisation — cannot be supported. Hamilton concedes that neither proposition can be substantiated because the data is lacking from pre-colonial times and it is unlikely that living informants can contribute to resolving this problem. Hamilton uses the "traditional" versus "contemporary" binary in an interesting way. Her analysis of Indigenous women's sociality is located within the "traditional" sphere, but in her discussion of violence she juxtaposes the "traditional" and the "contemporary" to highlight the dilemma of finding "truths". However, this dilemma seems to occur only in her work on violence; her representation of Indigenous women's sociality masks colonisation because Hamilton's work is premised on a construct of culture that positions authoritative meanings as the *a priori* totality that defines and reproduces the essential integrity of Indigenous women's sociality.

Gillian Cowlishaw's early work examines the role and status of Indigenous women through infanticide, fertility and socialisation. Cowlishaw argues that "traditional" Indigenous women practised infanticide because of "physical, psychological and social conditions" (Cowlishaw 1978:267). In reviewing the literature on infanticide she rejects the proposition that women disposed of children because the population was increasing or because they were unable to feed and carry more than one infant while serving their husbands. Drawing primarily on her work among the Goinjimbe in South Arnhem Land, she argues that infanticide was a response to both the brother–sister avoidance relationship and the mother–male child relationship. Brothers expect their sisters to control their sexual and emotional behaviour; it is taboo for men to hear other men swearing in front of their sisters and by law they can physically punish their sisters for such outbursts. Women are socialised into fearing men and accepting that men have the right to make demands on women's labour. Cowlishaw argues that by killing her infant, the woman either denies her brother a niece to use in bestowal or her husband a son to participate in ceremonies, which in effect circumscribes male control over her reproductive powers.

Cowlishaw's argument on infanticide is further supported in her work on fertility and socialisation (Cowlishaw 1981; 1982). Cowlishaw argues that, although Indigenous women do have a degree of dissenting interest in relation to men's control and power over them in the areas of abortion, infanticide, ritual life and marriage arrangements, they are socialised into "the ideological message of male hegemony" (1982:505). Indigenous women are not subservient or powerless even though they are in a subordinate position to Indigenous men. Cowlishaw draws on other disciplines including psychology and sociology to give theoretical sophistication to her analysis of the role and status of Indigenous women in southern Arnhem land. However, this does not result in her moving beyond anthropological discourse, because she is still positioned within the "traditional" versus "contemporary" binary. Cowlishaw positions infanticide as a practice that disrupts but does not transform "traditional" male hegemony: her explanation is predicated on authentic culture as an *a priori* system of essential meanings embedded in traditions defined and represented by anthropology that serve to exclude colonisation.[5]

The "traditional" versus "contemporary" Indigenous woman binary is pervasive in more recent work by white women anthropologists. Drawing on her work among the women at the Warrabri settlement in the Northern Territory, Diane Bell argues for the recognition of "traditional" Indigenous women's role and status as autonomous and independent, based on the law of the Dreaming. The evidence for this independence and autonomy prior to colonisation can be found in women's ritual domain. She argues that "in acting out the responsibilities conferred upon them as women by this law, women engage in work which is distinctively theirs. In the past this ensured that they would be recognised as full members of their society" (1993:337). However, Bell acknowledges that the sexual division of labour has changed for these women because of colonisation and white patriarchal practices. Traditional Indigenous women are excluded from politics and community decisions; white men talk only to Indigenous men; and alcohol and domestic violence are a part of their everyday lives. Bell asserts that the relations between the sexes are now based on sexual asymmetry, replacing complementarity and interdependence (1987:115).

On the surface, Bell's work offers what seems to be a departure from the "traditional" versus "contemporary" Indigenous woman binary. Her attempt to overcome the binary division lies in Bell's provision of an historical context for the Warrabri settlement and her acknowledgment of change in the sexual division of labour. However, these observations are disconnected from her analysis of the ritual domain. Bell manages to keep the binary intact by creating two domains, one being ritual and the other being whatever is going on or whatever has happened in these women's lives outside of this context. In other words, it is the ritual domain that she positions as the "traditional", while the other domain becomes the "contemporary". According to Bell, the ritual domain yields the true tradition and women's power base, whereas in other facets of their lives Indigenous women share the same sort of oppression as their white sisters under patriarchy. The "traditional" Indigenous woman has a different role and status from the white woman, but according to Bell she does share the same oppression.

Victoria Burbank carried out fieldwork in Numbulwar, Northern Territory on Mirriri as ritualised aggression. Burbank (1985:47) states that Mirriri is a "ceremonial or ritual expressive of a social relation consistent with the larger system of etiquette" concerning brother–sister avoidance. She argues that, although it is a ritual expressive of a social relation, it operates to create psychological and physical distance that reduces the occurrence of shame and incest. "The accepted motive behind an attack on a woman by her brother is a culturally expected dislike of sisters and 'shame' in the relationship that is intensified by a violation of the etiquette that surrounds it" (1985:53). Burbank's analysis provides an explanation of certain forms of aggressive behaviour in this community, but she notes that there were only three examples of Mirriri during the period of study. Burbank fails to identify whether other forms of aggression or display occurred during her study or to explain other forms of aggression. The location of her analysis within the traditional framework, where culture is a system of *a priori* essential meanings, does not allow her to study aggressive behaviours that occur outside a tradition that can be traced to the pre-colonial era.

Culture as *a priori* essential meanings and biological essentialism underpins the work of Rozanna Lilley (1989) who examined the text of the Finnis Land Claim that involved the Gungarakayn, the Warray and the Maranunggu people of the top end of the Northern Territory. Lilley demonstrates how gender shapes inter-group and intra-group arrangements of power and how these arrangements shape gender. She used the text of the Finnis Land Claim to illuminate these relations. Justice Toohey granted all these groups a share of the land, which was once Gungarakayn country. Lilley states that the history of the Gungarakayn reveals that they "left" their country due to invasion and settlement by Chinese and Europeans in the area, so many of their ties to the land under claim were tenuous or utterly destroyed. Gungarakayn people who "left" their country intermarried with Europeans or other Aborigines not of the area and the majority of the claimants were Indigenous women of mixed descent. These facts led to three conceptual problems which dominated the proceedings of the land claim: whether or not ownership of land can be lost due to a lack of occupancy or responsibility; what constitutes a real Indigenous person; and the role of women in relation to land.

The Gungarakayn women's authenticity as "Indigenous women" was interrogated by both white people and other Indigenous people involved in the claim, who positioned the women as not being "real Indigenous women" on the basis of their mixed descent and education. Some of the women had tertiary qualifications and others were employed in the public service. Racial impurity and the acquisition of white knowledge were used to reduce the authenticity and legitimacy of the Gungarakayn women's claims. The spuriousness of their claims was also linked to the way in which they articulated their relations to land, which Lilley argues is inconsistent with the pre-contact role and status of women in this area. Lilley argues that these women reinvented themselves by asserting that it had always been women's role to take care of country, but she does so based on the anthropological argument that only men were responsible for the social reproduction of society. Lilley asserts they did this in order to comply with requirements of the *Northern Territory Land Rights Act* (1975). Lilley seems to be ignorant of the anthropological definition of "traditional owner" in the Act, which is based on patrilineal descent and primary spiritual ties to particular sites. The definition privileges male ownership because the anthropological knowledge that informed the development of the Act was based on work carried out by male anthropologists whose informants were Indigenous men.

Lilley supports her thesis about the role and status of pre-contact Gungarakayn women by reference to anthropological work carried out by men in the 1930s and the more recent work of Hamilton (1978; 1981) and White (1978). The knowledge of these anthropologists is used to substantiate the view that the Gungarakayn women claimants were acting fraudulently. What Lilley's text reveals is the connection between whose representation is perceived as being legitimate and whose knowledge gets privileged over the Gungarakayn. It is the anthropological knowledge and representation that Lilley privileges by positioning anthropologists as the experts on pre-contact women's role and status. Although Lilley concludes by stating that anthropologists should be concerned not with cultural continuities but "the conscious use of cultural constructions of the 'has always been' as part of a process whereby people give meaning to their world and actions in it" (1989:95), she contradicts herself. She fails to consider the role of anthropology in the construction of "traditional" Indigenous culture and how she draws on this knowledge to expose the supposed spurious meaning that the Gungarakayn women have given to their world. Her text illuminates the way in which the "traditional" versus "contemporary" Indigenous woman binary is operationalised as the measure of cultural authenticity and racial purity.

Problematising anthropological representations of Indigenous women

The use of culture as *a priori* essential meanings to construct the traditional Indigenous woman in the anthropological literature raises questions about the representation of such a woman. If she exists, she does only what anthropology decides for her and she has completely escaped colonisation. Her lack of subjectivity means she is an object, whom anthropologists have constructed in their imagination and on paper. The traditional woman is the woman against whom all Indigenous women are measured, yet in her pristine state she does not exist. What do exist are different Indigenous women who have different cultures that do not mirror anthropological representations.

The use of an *a priori* essential biologism by white women anthropologists as the basis of interpreting and explaining the cultural differences between Indigenous women is also a problem. It produces a contradiction; biologically and culturally the contemporary Indigenous woman is liminal, but is on a trajectory of assimilation towards the white woman. In other words, the contemporary Indigenous woman is becoming more like a white woman in practice because she does not look "Indigenous" and lacks traditional culture. The problem with this proposition is that assimilation is a superficial explanation of Indigenous women's cultures. How can Indigenous women be assimilated when we do not have access to the same resources and opportunities as white women? Indigenous women do not share the same history, socialisation patterns, knowledges and experiences as white women. In society our biological characteristics are read, and have been legislated, as signifiers of "Other". Indigenous women have different experiences based on such a positioning in our social interaction with white women, men and institutions. What anthropology fails to theorise is the idea that there are multiple Indigenous women's cultures that exist outside the parameters of the "traditional" versus "contemporary" Indigenous woman it has constructed. Indigenous women have forged and continue to forge cultural practices under conditions and in contexts not of our choosing; and we do so creatively. The cultures that we create do not mirror those represented by anthropologists.

Learning to speak English and mimicking the customs of the coloniser does not fundamentally transform subjectivities that have been socialised within Indigenous social domains. Individuals learn to acquire new knowledges in order to act and function in contexts not of their choosing or control within the dominant culture. Indigenous women have had to gather knowledge about white people and use it in order to survive in the white Australian society. The accumulation of such knowledges does not mean that we have become assimilated. Instead, what it points to is that Indigenous subjectivity is multiple because of the conditions under which it has been and is shaped. However, multiple subjectivities do not preclude the existence of a core subject position that has the ability to acquire, interpret and create different subject positions in order to participate in society. What women anthropologists have failed to understand in their desire to represent Indigenous women are the complexities Indigenous women face in a world under conditions not of their choosing, where they must translate and interpret whiteness, while being "Other". For Indigenous women, survival demands expertise in translation, performance and self-presentation.

The intended audience for the work of white women anthropologists consists of other anthropologists, and their desire to explain is symptomatic of the desire to create a gendered self in a world of other that can be controlled and known. The "traditional" versus "contemporary" Indigenous woman binary is intrinsically linked to the subject position middle-class white woman. This subject position represents the standard against which the "traditional" Indigenous woman is measured to determine what she is not. Indigenous women who are identified as "contemporary" are also measured against this subject position to show similarity with white women and difference from the "traditional" Indigenous woman. The "contemporary" Indigenous woman is represented as though she is never white enough, but some of her practices are interpreted as being consistent with those of her white sisters.

The subject position middle-class white woman is located structurally and is embodied in the subjectivity of the white women anthropologists. As Merlan (1988) identified, the concern of white women anthropologists was the nature of white women's oppression in a white-male-dominated society. The subject position middle-class white woman is embedded in the texts of white women anthropologists because the subtext is their concern with questioning the universality of women's oppression and its cultural construction.[6] The universality of women's oppression is addressed through examining the role and status of "traditional" and "contemporary" Indigenous women. All the texts reveal that "traditional" and "contemporary" Indigenous women are oppressed; where the analyses differ is in the context and the degree of oppression.

This book contends that the context and degree of oppression relate to the location under scrutiny, whether it be Arnhem Land in the Northern Territory, a cattle station in the Kimberley or the town of Walgett in New South Wales. The existence of Indigenous women's oppression in different locations works to support the universal that all women are oppressed. Focusing on Indigenous women who are positioned as "Other" and of a different culture from white women gives salience to this universal in feminist and other academic discourses. The centring of the subject position middle-class white woman in these texts also occurs in contradictory ways through the examination of "traditional" versus "contemporary" Indigenous women's cultural difference. In seeking to analyse and explain the role and status of Indigenous women, women anthropologists have sought to investigate how their cultural spheres are in substance unlike or like those of their white sisters, through the centring of their analyses on the areas of concern to white feminist discourse. That is, the sites analysed reflect or symbolise those sites under interrogation in western society by the women's movement, such as marriage, kinship, women's economic activity, sexuality, reproduction, ritual and socialisation. This is not to say that the Indigenous women who are written about by white feminists are not concerned with these aspects of their lives; but Indigenous women do not set the terms of reference for investigation nor are they the intended audience of this literature. The literature is written about Indigenous women, not by us, for us or with us.

The status of Indigenous women as objects within the text relates to the methodology employed by women anthropologists. Although the objects of the analyses are Indigenous women, this has not meant that a feminist methodology has been employed. Instead the literature falls under what Henrietta Moore (1988:1) calls an "anthropology of women", in that the guiding principle for white middle-class women anthropologists was challenging male representations of the role and status of Indigenous women. However, these white women anthropologists mounted their challenge within a methodological framework that does not allow for the theorisation of Indigenous women as socially situated subjects of knowledge. Even Bell, who is explicit about her feminist politics and method, is constrained by this framework, which reproduces particular ideological constructions of culture and race that are accepted as truth.

All the fieldwork undertaken by women anthropologists occurs in contexts shaped by colonialism. As victims of their methodology, white women anthropologists suppress the experiences of Indigenous women and provide a distorted representation of Indigenous women's gender, a representation that is explicitly linked to the ethnocentric notions embedded in anthropology's methodology and their political positions on gender. This representation is acted upon and serves to disempower Indigenous women because it has become "truth" in feminist discourse and white culture.[7]

The anthropology of Indigenous women is premised on authentic culture as an *a priori* system of essential meanings embedded in traditions and an *a priori* essential biologism based on skin colour, which privileges some Indigenous women over others. The Bell–Huggins debate is an example of the use of the "traditional" versus "contemporary" Indigenous woman binary in public discourse and illuminates its continuing relationship to the subject position middle-class white woman. Bell and other white women anthropologists, by conceptualising the "authentic"

culture and "Other" in this way, circumscribe the possibility of
theorising cultural and social change brought about by colonisation (Asad 1979:609). Their work utilises and reinforces a distorted methodology:

> ... instead of taking the production of "essential meanings" (in the
> form of authoritative discourse) in given historical societies as the
> problem to be explained, anthropology takes the existence of essen-
> tial meanings (in the form of authentic discourse) as the basic
> concept for defining and explaining historical societies (Asad
> 1979:623).

The use of this methodology, which is based on a system of
closures that define what is the object of study and what methods
will be used to obtain the data, produces a distorted representation of Indigenous women's gender and the colonised conditions under which it has been manufactured. The ideological
constructions of "race" and "culture" are a part of the epistemology that informs the methodology employed by white women
anthropologists who have constructed particular knowledges and
representations of Indigenous women. One effect of such knowledges for Indigenous women in making claims for land is that
they can become victims of anthropological knowledges that
devalue their interpretations of their lives and contexts in their
own terms.

The power to define and represent reveals inequalities in the
relationship between white women anthropologists and the Indigenous women they write about. Anthropological discourse
operates within academia where knowledge production is supported and valued. In this discourse self definition by Indigenous
women is not accorded the same value. To what degree Indigenous women in their specific and different cultural contexts are
oppressed and how gender is culturally constructed in these
contexts are questions that require further interrogation and
research. The answering of these questions also requires the
deployment of a feminist methodology that utilises Indigenous
women's experiences as empirical and theoretical resources to
move beyond the "traditional" versus "contemporary" Indigenous woman binary.

Feminists who rely on ethnographic texts to utilise knowledges
about Indigenous women are also implicated in "the ideological

process whereby Aborigines are defined, delineated and controlled" (Cowlishaw 1986b: 234). White women anthropologists and feminists need to "search for new ways of representing and understanding discourse within the context of social life" of Indigenous women, including interrogating the subject position middle-class white woman in racialised power relations (Asad 1979:609). This should involve

> a sustained analysis of the epistemological assumptions that inform and privilege Western thought and its cultural representations, and a deconstruction of our desire to render the space of alterity into a generalised equivalence, whether between women or between cultures (Kirby 1991:400).

Knowledge is never innocent or neutral. It is a key to power and meaning. It is used to dominate and control. When white women anthropologists write about Indigenous women, they do so in the conventions of representation bounded by their discipline, university and politics and white Australian culture (Asad 1986:159). Such representations are based on interpretation and translation and, as such, offer partial truths about Indigenous women.

CHAPTER FOUR

Little Bit Woman:
Representations of Indigenous Women
in White Australian Feminism[1]

> White women ... are extraordinarily reluctant to see themselves in
> the situation of being oppressors, as they feel that this will be at the
> expense of concentrating upon being oppressed. Consequently the
> involvement of British women in imperialism and colonialism is
> repressed and the benefits that they — as whites — gained from the
> oppression of black people ignored. Forms of imperialism are simply
> identified as aspects of an all embracing patriarchy rather than as sets
> of social relations in which white women hold positions of power by
> virtue of their "race" (Carby 1997:49).

As part of the colonising process, white women in Australian
society exercised their race privilege and were compliant, to
different degrees, in the gendered racial oppression of Indigenous women in a variety of contexts. Many white women continue
to be well intended in their actions towards Indigenous women,
but their behaviour and intentions have not always been interpreted in the same way by Indigenous women. In white cultural
domains Indigenous women's subject positions were and are sites
of both oppression and resistance. The domestic and other white
cultural domains provided context for processes of inter-subjectivity between Indigenous and white women which were not
based on shared knowledges, common experiences and mutual
reciprocity. Instead inter-subjective relations were based on a
form of interpretative indeterminacy arising from the juxtaposition of different knowledges, herstories, experiences, material
conditions and social locations. The impersonal extrinsic rela-

tions disclosed in communicative exchanges between Indigenous women and white women are linked to the exercising of white race privilege derived from colonisation.

White Australian feminists are perhaps the first group of white women who took an interest in issues to do with Indigenous women and they documented their actions. However, the majority of white feminists were, and are, often oblivious to Indigenous women's perceptions of relations with white women. Colonised material relations between Indigenous women and white women occurred in different cultural domains contextualised by historically specific discourses. The subject position middle-class white woman has been and is enmeshed in an historically specific feminist discourse where it constitutes the norm and remains invisible, unnamed and unmarked. It is at the intersection of race, gender and middle-classness that white feminists embody and deploy the subject position middle-class white woman in their relations with Indigenous women. This chapter begins by locating this subject position in an overview of the historical interconnected relations between white feminists and Indigenous women in the first wave of feminism. The subject position middle-class white woman is then made visible in an examination of the second wave of feminism (the Women's Liberation Movement), the establishment of Women's Studies and the theoretical positioning of Indigenous women by white feminists since the 1970s. The subject position middle-class white woman is disclosed in a politics of difference encounter between Indigenous women and white feminists in the 1990s. The chapter concludes with a discussion on the invisibility of this subject position in feminist discourse.

First-wave feminism: white women's rights through state protection

In 1894 women in South Australia received the right to vote. Although some feminists argue that suffrage was a victory for all women in South Australia, only some Indigenous women had their names placed on the electoral roll; others could not exercise their right to vote because of racialised bureaucratic intervention (Crowley 1996:2–3). The formal right to vote did not empower

Indigenous women, nor could they participate in the first wave of Australian feminism, because they were not free. Their legal status as wards of the state empowered white protectors to circumscribe their movements, cultural practices and behaviour. The removal of Indigenous girls from their families and the subsequent compulsory exploitation of their labour as domestic servants became official policy in South Australia some 17 years after the first-wave of feminists campaigned for and won the right to vote.

Marilyn Lake argues that Australian feminists perceived themselves as the upholders of civilisation and the custodians of race (1996:13). Unwanted male behaviour such as drinking, gambling and predatory sexuality undermined civilisation and jeopardised the welfare of women and children. Lake asserts that "in response to perceptions of women's special vulnerability in a masculinist society, there was a heavy emphasis in Australian feminist campaigns on the need to provide 'protection' rather than, say, 'emancipation' for women and girls" (1996:13).

In 1894 Maybanke Wolstenholme, President of the New South Wales Womanhood Suffrage League, called for women to be pioneers in their advancement (Spearritt 1992:325). Wolstenholme and others, such as Dora Montefiores, were radicalised by their personal experiences in a masculinist society of divorce, separation or the death of their husbands. Other women, such as Catherine Helen Spence and Rose Scott, came from privileged backgrounds and chose to remain single in order to pursue the improvement of conditions for white women. Spearitt attributes the capacity of these women to be activists to a number of factors, such as the change to a family wage economy, the increase in educational opportunities for middle-class women, the expansion of urban bourgeoisie, and intellectual debate on nationalism and socialism in the 1890s.

White middle-class women, who were predominantly Anglo-Celtic, established various organisations advocating women's advancement that focused on improving their sexual and social status and politicising their cause through such means as direct action, newspapers and feminist journals (Spearitt 1992:326). Kay Saunders (1991:64) argues that organisations such as the

Women's Christian Temperance Union and the Australian Women's Suffrage Society spoke for and on behalf of middle-class white women and saw the demands of working-class white women as secondary. The subject position white woman was deployed strategically to represent the experience of all women irrespective of class and race. This subject position embodied certain characteristics that reflected a combination of middle-class ideals such as "temperance, industriousness, thrift, refined manners, and Victorian sexual morals" (Davy 1997:216). They were characteristics that correlated white womanhood with respectability.

Spearritt argues that, after World War I, Australian feminists became involved in more issues of concern but not all had the same priority. Eugenics, sex education, sexology and women's rights within marriage, as well as an improvement in the economic conditions of working-class women and families dominated the feminist agenda (Spearritt 1992:366). Some feminists advocated birth control and increased sexual expression for women in marriages, whereas others argued against birth control on the grounds that the white population of Australia needed to be increased. Those who advocated birth control and greater sexual expression believed that the quality of the white population was more important than its quantity. A poor family environment meant unfit children. Some feminists argued for eugenics and proposed a form of scientific motherhood whereby white women would be fertilised by artificial insemination with sperm from donors of good stock (Spearritt 1992:369).

Reproductive matters were not the only concern of feminists. Feminists turned their attention to the productive relations and conditions of white women workers. Increased wages and better working conditions were advocated for white women workers and feminists wanted Indigenous women to be paid some form of wage directly instead of employers giving their wages to the state. Equality of wages and working conditions with white women was not part of the feminist agenda for Indigenous women. Despite feminist agitation for improved working conditions, a backlash occurred. During the Depression white women were blamed for taking white men's jobs and public discourse elevated maternity and marriage as the proper role and function of women.

Women's intervention into the public sphere became limited by such a discourse, but their concerns with production and reproduction continued to be expressed in both private and public domains.

Federation of the nation state in 1901 gave white women and white men, irrespective of class, the right to vote as federal citizens. Race was very much an issue in the development of the new constitution and the establishment of Federation. The newly elected parliament acted on its constitutional mandate and passed the *Immigration Restriction Act*, which was the legislative base of the so-called White Australia Policy (McGrath 1993:104). Restricting immigration to "Whites" resulted in a reduction in the number of migrants, and concerns were raised about low population figures. In 1904 a Royal Commission into the Decline of the Birthrate called on white women to exercise their citizenship by reproducing. The new enfranchisement for white women tied them to increasing the white population, which resulted in feminists demanding that white women be granted a maternity bonus for their reproductive services. This bonus was granted to married white women in 1912. Feminists supported both the White Australia Policy and the need to increase the population: whiteness became the unifying symbol of Australian nationalism. In these early years, in contrast to the situation in which American women's rights movements developed, race was "so pervasive that it was not divisive" (Saunders 1991:64). Susan Sheridan concurs with Saunders: in her review of white Australian women's writings, she argues that the exclusion of Indigenous women from their texts was tied to a white Australian identity that required the discursive dislocation of "Others" (1988b: 76). Australian feminists supported a national identity of white womanhood reproduced in their image: white, respectable and middle-class.

The engagement by feminists in the late 1800s and early 1900s with the state supports Bulbeck's argument that Australian feminism consists of two types: official feminism and clearing-house feminism. "Official feminism" refers to feminist engagement with, and participation in, the state and its bureaucracies; "clearing-house feminism" refers to theorising and teaching of women's studies (Bulbeck 1994:115–16). Bulbeck states of the former:

> Between the 1920s and the 1940s, Australian feminism used the welfare state to improve the position of women as mothers. The Maternity Allowance Act in 1912 granted five pounds for the birth of every child to mothers of European background. From the 1920s, women won widow endowment and the widow's child allowance, and focused their attention on better education and health care for families (1994:115–16).

Unlike white women, Indigenous women were not encouraged to produce offspring, nor were they directly entitled to receive maternity allowance until after 1941. Some Indigenous women, including my grandmother Lavinia Moreton, contested this decision though to no avail (Walker 1997:13) Child endowment was granted to some Indigenous women only if they were exempted from the status of "Indigenous Ward" (McGrath 1993:105). Exemption was determined by a state official on the basis of the perceived degree of whiteness of the skin, living conditions, evidence of intelligence and display of social behaviour akin to white people. The majority of Indigenous women did not fit into such categories and few were exempt from the status of Aboriginal Ward of the State. They were not eligible for allowances and their education and health care was poor. Missions were entitled to the child endowment for Indigenous children under the age of 16 years if they "fed, clothed, housed and maintained them" (McGrath 1993:105). Indigenous women could not inhabit the subject position middle-class white woman whose privileged positioning by the state was reserved for white women.

The impoverished conditions of Indigenous people did not go unnoticed by feminists. In the 1920s Women's Service Guilds were concerned about the sexual abuse of Indigenous women and over the next twenty years they became interested in other aspects of Indigenous affairs (Davidson 1997:140–42). The Chief Protector of Aborigines in Western Australia sought an alliance with the Women's Guilds in order to put pressure on the government to fund his civilising mission for Indigenous people. His mission was consistent with the Guild's belief that "it was the duty of highly evolved civilizations to treat more primitive people

kindly and assist in their development" (Davidson 1997:140).
This belief was informed by a premise of the dominant ideology
of white male imperialism: "it was only through contact with
Western civilization that the 'natives' had any chance of being
delivered from their own tyrannical customs" (Ware 1992:147).
White feminists were able to deploy the subject position middle-
class white woman to signify and enact aspects of white male
ideology without having to inhabit the subject position "white
male" (Davidson 1997:212).

In 1926 middle-class white women representatives from the
Women's Services Guilds accompanied Protector Neville to the
Moore River settlement, and Davidson states that, in their news-
letter *The Dawn*:

> the settlement was described as a "model village" containing a "bon-
> nie set of young people" who were bright and healthy. Married
> couples in camps were perceived as providing "happy pictures of
> domestic life", and elderly Aborigines were described as "perfectly
> content" although living in primitive conditions (Davidson
> 1997:145).

In *When the Pelican Laughed*, Alice Nannup recalls that when
Mr Neville visited Moore River Mission in the 1920s it resulted in
more work for the Indigenous children and a series of performances being enacted to enhance the image of the "model village".
According to Nannup, "Whenever Mr Neville came everything
had to be spit and polish — the best thing about someone from
the outside coming was we would get better food, something
special, just in case whoever it was came into the dining room and
had a look around" (Nannup et al. 1992:70). Neville had sold the
idea of educating the natives to the Women's Guild as part of the
civilizing project, but his idea of education meant very little.
Nannup recalls a conversation about education that she over-
heard between Neville and the sewing mistress. "They were talking about education and other things, and I heard him say, 'Ohh,'
it's all right, as long as they can write their name and count money
— that's all the education they need' " (Nannup et al. 1992:71).
The juxtaposition of the different readings of Neville's visits to
Moore River by white feminists and Alice Nannup reveals the
complicity of the subject position middle-class white woman with

institutionalised forms of whiteness that justified feminist motives for a greater good while reinscribing white dominance.

In the 1930s white feminists extended their agenda in Western Australia, largely due to the work of a white woman, Mary Montgomerie Bennett, who had worked with the United Aborigines Mission at Gnowangerup and later the Forrest River Mission (Davidson 1997:151–61). Bennett, through her work, was appalled by the conditions under which Indigenous people were forced to live. In her address to members of the Women's Services Guild of Western Australia Bennett argued that Indigenous women were not depraved but deprived. Bennett's address provided a catalyst for the actions of Australian women delegates to the conference of the British Commonwealth League, an international forum in which the treatment of Aborigines under state and federal legislation was criticised (Paisley 1993a: 139).[2] The Women's Services Guild of Western Australia was one group of women activists who promoted themselves as experts on reforming Indigenous policy and were committed to advocacy on behalf of Indigenous women. They articulated their maternal project in terms of a "sisterhood" across racial lines and they influenced government policy on Indigenous affairs. They opposed the removal of "half caste" children from their mothers and families to be educated and trained, and they lobbied for the direct payment of wages to Indigenous women to enable them to achieve economic independence from Indigenous and white men (Paisley 1997:121).

The Women's Services Guild of Western Australia and the British Commonwealth League insisted that white female representation was a necessity on "Royal Commissions and special boards of inquiry and as doctors and protectors" of Indigenous people (Paisley 1993a: 141). The desire of feminists to be a part of state intervention and their need to civilise Indigenous women through training, education and paid work was tied to their contradictory positioning of Indigenous women's sexuality as the source of the "half caste" problem. Edith Jones, a representative of the Australian Women Voters in 1929 at the Conference of Representative Missions, Societies and Associations Interested in the Welfare of Aborigines, stated:

The question of the half-caste is a big problem because the Aboriginal woman is behind all the troubles which have been mentioned today. We want to help that woman, and I believe that help can only be achieved by the direct application of the mind of women to this problem (Jones in Paisley 1993a: 148).

In 1933, in a letter to the *West Australian* newspaper, Bessie Rischbieth, President of the Western Australian Services Guild, wrote on behalf of twelve other organisations outlining the need for the involvement of white women on a proposed commission of inquiry into Indigenous conditions:

... the importance of this is apparent from the very nature of one of the main problems which must be solved viz. the half-caste problem. The solution of this undoubtedly rests with the Aboriginal woman, and psychologically it is only women who can measure up the needs of native women (Paisley 1993a: 148).

As agents of civilisation and custodians of the white race, feminists sought to preserve white racial purity by civilising Indigenous women and reforming their sexuality. The appeal for government intervention on the basis of such agency reveals the sexism and racism embedded in their project. Their contradictory positioning of Indigenous women's subject position was more than a maternal gaze. Here the construction of gendered identity and sexuality is predicated on the subject position white woman who is summoned and strategically employed to re-present and remake the Indigenous "Other". Sexual propriety authorised by the subject position middle-class white woman operated to deconstruct and reconstruct Indigenous women in the image of true white (middle-class) woman. Feminism operated within an institutionalised whiteness constituted by a framework of order, rationality, rigidity, gentility, reason, propriety, stability and the capacity to set boundaries (Dyer 1988:47–9). Within this framework, civility, combined with a variety of morals and values, informed the sexual propriety and respectability located in the subject position middle-class white woman.

White women and white men without consultation with Indigenous people had, up until the 1930s, directed white feminist involvement in Indigenous issues. However, Indigenous advocacy in the 1930s seems to have impacted on the work of the Guilds. A resolution put forward at the Australian Federation of Women

Voters Fifth Triennial Conference in September 1936 in Adelaide proposed:

> ... the setting up of a National Commission composed of anthropologists, full-blood and half-caste Aborigines including women, to enquire into, and advise the Prime Minister on, Aboriginal issues. It recommended that a federal Department of Native Affairs be set up, with a full-time Minister and Advisory Council to administer Aboriginal Affairs in federal territories and "to assist State Aboriginal Departments along certain specified lines" — Hereafter the Guilds would concentrate on lobbying to move Aboriginal affairs into the federal sphere, although at the same time the groundwork was being laid for the beginnings of cooperation with Aboriginal groups (Davidson 1997:163).

The Australian Federation of Women Voters lent its voice to the Aborigines Progress Association in New South Wales by calling on the prime minister, Joe Lyons, to convene a joint federal and state conference on issues of Indigenous citizenship rights. World War II intervened in the work of Women's Guilds and the advocacy of Indigenous citizenship was not taken up again until the late 1940s. An outcome of the impact of World War II was an increase in women's intervention in the public domain. Unlike the United States, the Australian nation state in 1941 supported female participation in the public domain by formalising industrial conscription for women into the armed services. Indigenous women such as Oodgeroo Noonuccal joined the Australian Women's Armed Services, but she did not receive the same pay as her white sisters. Feminist concerns were focused on motherhood, childcare, contraception, sexual freedom and equality within heterosexual marriages, and improved economic conditions for women (Saunders & Bolton 1992: 388–89).

Feminist concerns with sexual freedom within marriage did not transfer to supporting sexual liaisons between American servicemen and young Australian women. In fact:

> Historians such as Gail Reekie, Marilyn Lake, Kay Saunders and Helen Taylor, and Kate Darian-Smith all comment that feminists, although supporting equal treatment for males and females on all moral matters, ultimately endorsed conservative concepts of true womanhood (Saunders & Bolton 1992:392).

World War II impacted on race relations and feminist concerns with racial purity. Kohn argues that racism was a causative factor in the advent of the war and that between 1939 and 1949 there was a decisive shift in western countries in relation to race (1996:48). "In the shadow of the extermination camps, world leaders met to consider what policies should be adopted to prevent once and for all the excesses of race theory" (Hannaford 1996:385). Prevention took the form of the Universal Declaration on Human Rights, passed by the United Nations General Assembly in 1948 without dissent (Humana 1992:382).

In late 1943 the first Australian Women's Conference for Victory in War and Victory in Peace was held in Sydney. The conference adopted the Australian Women's Charter, which endorsed "women's rights to paid work, the necessity for adequate child-care, the provision of housing, social security, access to adequate education, the particular needs of rural women and, notably, Indigenous women" (Saunders & Bolton 1992:394). However, the intent of the Charter was not carried through, due to political fracturing within the women's movement: "Australian women, like Australian men, held their politics along a conservative, liberal, left continuum and no real cohesion could be achieved under the single category of gender" (Saunders & Bolton 1992:394).

The Australian Women's Charter represented a shift in feminist politics in that white feminists were no longer seeking to define the particular needs of Indigenous women, but the needs of white women remained centred within the Charter. From the 1950s to the 1970s Women's Guilds supported some of the political endeavours of Indigenous people. Davidson argues that as Indigenous people became more politically active Women's Guilds left Indigenous issues to Indigenous activists (1997:244). The shift in Guild politics did not disrupt the subject position middle-class white woman because she was not the primary focus of Indigenous issues and activism; and Australian feminism continued to be predominantly a white middle-class women's movement. The social and material distance between white women and Indigenous women in the Women's Guilds meant that white feminists could rely on the respectability and credibility embodied within the subject position middle-class white woman to work for justice although concurrently affirming their loyalty to whiteness.

The second wave: women's liberation, femocrats and women's studies

The history of the first wave of feminism reveals that for white feminists the Australian state was positioned as an ally "able to provide the protection that would make possible women's independence from men" (Lake 1996:19). The principle of equal pay was generally accepted and discrimination was removed in a number of areas (Davidson 1997:250). The outcomes achieved through the state by the first wave of feminism by implication show that the state supported and endorsed the subject position middle-class white woman as the legitimate representation of womanhood.[3]

In the 1960s feminist politics changed under the influence of both the civil and anti-war movements. Middle-class white women, inspired and led by women such as Anne Summers and Germaine Greer, became more militant and confrontational in demanding their rights, in particular the right to sexual freedom outside marriage. Lake argues that it was precisely during this time, when Indigenous women were absent from the feminist gaze, that white women reclaimed their sexuality by throwing off the Victorian shackles of sexual repression (Lake 1996:13). The new feminist politics was a radical departure from the "civilized, courteous methods of persuasion used by the earlier women's movement" (Davidson 1997:274). Curthoys (1994) argues:

> There were many sources for this widespread female rebellion. There had for at least a decade been growing contradictions: between the increasing numbers of women with higher education, and the restricted range of, and low pay for, the jobs those women could enter; between the need for female labour in the expanding tertiary sector of the economy, and the social stigma against married women working; between ideals of sexual permissiveness and the "sexual revolution", and a sharply defined "double standard" of sexual morality; and between the demographic trend to shorter periods of childbearing and rearing within a woman's life cycle, and the continuing social assumption that a woman's role was indeed "in the home". All this laid the basis for an enormous groundswell of discontent (1994:16).

In 1972 the establishment of the Women's Electoral Lobby and its participation in the federal election that year placed feminist demands on the political agenda. In 1973 Elizabeth Reid was appointed Women's Adviser to the newly elected Labor prime minister, Gough Whitlam, and "several hundred Australian Feminists entered the government in the following decade" (Curthoys 1994:16). The "femocrat" had become a force in public life (Bulbeck 1994:117). Not all white feminists agreed with the new relationship with the state; some radical, lesbian and socialist feminists saw the move as a sell-out to patriarchy (Simms 1981). However, their concerns did not disrupt the establishment of the Office of Women's Affairs (OWA), within the Department of Prime Minister and Cabinet, which provided a mechanism whereby feminists influenced, and continue to influence, government policy.

Women's community-based services were introduced; rape crisis centres, refuges for women and children who were victims of domestic violence, and women's health services were established for, and controlled by, predominantly white women. The Women's Liberation Movement saw doors open for white women, including radical and socialist feminists, and the rights of women being advocated within both conservative and liberal political circles (Curthoys 1994:18). Although overtures were made to include Indigenous women, immigrant women and women with English as a second language within the women's movement — particularly on consultative committees and in the use and delivery of services — whiteness remained centred and dominant (Perera 1985; Ganguly 1995; Murdolo 1996; Kaplan 1996). White women continue to constitute the majority of women elected to parliament and they are the women who are appointed to government, business and women's committees and boards. Since the 1970s, equal pay, equal employment opportunity, the right to abortion, maternity leave, child-care and equality before the law have been and remain issues that dominate the white feminist agenda.[4] Equal employment opportunity for women in the private sector is monitored by the Affirmative Action Agency under the *Affirmative Action (Equal Opportunity for Women) Act 1986*. However, the Affirmative Action Agency does not keep separate statistics on women who have English as a second language or Indigenous women. The policy outcomes of the second wave of feminism are also connected to the state recognising the subject position middle-class white woman as the embodiment of true womanhood.

Women's studies: feminist theory

Feminist theorising in Australia also developed during the 1970s. Magarey et al. (1994:285) argue that the Australian women's movement has been educationalist. Informal discussion groups among women led to collective research papers, and, later, national conferences on topics such as feminism, socialism and labour provided the impetus for the establishment of Women's Studies within various academic institutions. National conferences provided the opportunity for Indigenous and immigrant women not of Anglo-Celtic origins to discuss and raise racial and cultural issues of concern to them as women. Murdolo (1996:78) argues that white feminists deferred racial and cultural issues raised at the conference in the name of unity until the 1984 Women and Labour conference, where race and ethnicity were to be placed on the Australian feminist agenda. However, the next Women and Labour national conference was not held until 1995. At this conference white feminists took action over the Hindmarsh Island Royal Commission. Doreen Kartinyeri, a Ngarrindjeri, told the conference about the contested claims concerning Indigenous women's business at Hindmarsh Island in South Australia. After her speech "the legendary Zelda D'Aprano leapt up waving a fifty dollar bill to start a fund-raising drive; fax numbers were swapped; letter-writing campaigns launched; and an ad-hoc interstate coordinating committee was set up" (Zetlein & Brook 1995:158). Although some white feminists have continued to give support to the Hindmarsh Island issue, the questions raised at the 1984 conference by Indigenous and immigrant women "have not yet been fully worked through in Women's Studies, nor indeed in many other areas of feminist endeavour in Australia" (Magarey 1994:292).

By 1989 Women's Studies programs were located in at least 13 universities and Australian feminist theorists had achieved international recognition. White women had successfully manipulated the symbolism of the middle-class subject position white woman and its embodiment of respectability to achieve their ends. In many ways white feminist investment in institutional credibility took precedence over an action agenda. The institutionalisation of women's programs, although being projected as an achievement for all women, was also a reinvestment in whiteness, because feminists were not challenging white race privilege; they were exercising it. Bulbeck (1994) identifies a shift in feminist theorising in the 1980s and 1990s:

> In the 1970s, feminists were generally described as either liberal (believing that equality with men could be achieved by destroying formal barriers), or as Marxist/socialist (believing that women's liberation must by accompanied by class revolution), or radical (believing there were oppressions intrinsic to women and built on the female body and its alienation from ownership and control by women). In the 1980s feminist theory turned away from "things" to "words", and from material events to their discursive meanings. This was accompanied by a turn away from the simple politics of intervention advocated by earlier femocrats. A grafting of feminism and postcolonialism superseded the rational female subject, the heroine of 1970s feminism, with the "postcolonial" subject, fractured along contradictory lines of race, gender, and class. A grafting of psychoanalysis and feminism fractured the female interior to explore the ways women desire and collude in their subordination. No longer is women's oppression obvious and external; no longer are women a universal and pre-given category with a clear political agenda (1994:119).

Although Bulbeck's overview of "clearing-house feminism" portrays theoretical shifts in Australian feminism in which there has been a grafting of feminism and postcolonialism, such a grafting reflects only a marginal location within Australian feminist theorising. Where is the "postcolonial" subject fractured along contradictory lines of race, class and gender in the most influential works of Australia's internationally recognised theorists such as Elizabeth Grosz's *Sexual Subversions* (1989), Carole Pateman's *The Sexual Contract* (1988), Moira Gatens *Feminism and Philosophy* (1991) or Meaghan Morris's *The Pirate's Fiancee* (1988)? The speaking position of these white feminists is contextualised by a complex global system of exchange in the production of academic ideas primarily in the first world, which results in feminist theory that universalises whiteness by operating within the prevailing logic of sameness. The failure of Australian feminism to take account of its whiteness masks its partiality. Although white feminist theorising may have problematised the category woman, the subject position middle-class white woman remains centred as the dominant subject position from which white feminists theorise, write and speak. Theories that fracture white womanhood "have been enormously productive, but at the same time that they challenge white womanhood, they depend on it and once again circumscribe and consign to erasure those bodies that white womanhood nullifies historically and continues to negate" (Davy 1997:214).

Theorising about white women's issues remains the dominant paradigm within Australian feminism. Indigenous women's issues have been of little theoretical interest to white feminists. The majority of articles published by three of the oldest Australian feminist journals, *Refractory Girl, Australian Feminist Studies* and *Hecate,* are written by white women.[5] As of March 1998, the published articles on Indigenous women are predominantly by non-Indigenous women. *Refractory Girl* has published approximately 16 articles; since its inception in 1985 *Australian Feminist Studies* has published 12; and since 1975 *Hecate* has published approximately 33. The majority of these articles are written about the relations between white women and Indigenous women and either rely on the historical journals of white women for their information or they use anthropological representations of Indigenous women in their accounts.[6] The majority of articles written by Indigenous women are autobiographical, although some engage with feminism and these will be discussed in Chapter 6.

Since the 1970s a few white feminists have discussed the relationship between Australian feminism and Indigenous women to varying degrees, often theorising about the intersections of race, class and gender. Anne Summers (1975), Patricia Grimshaw (1980), Jan Larbaliester (1977, 1980, 1990, 1991), Meredith Burgmann (1984), Sue Sheridan (1988b), Kay Saunders (1991, Saunders and Bolton 1992, Huggins and Saunders 1993), Anna Yeatman (1993) and Jan Pettman (1988, 1991, 1992) are perhaps the most well-known feminists. Anne Summers incorporates Indigenous women in her theory of the construction of Australian womanhood embedded within the "God's police versus dammed whores" binary by locating Indigenous women in the latter category. Some feminists explicitly connect us to feminism through racial oppression and argue that feminism is a white women's movement which has yet to theorise its complicity in colonisation (Sheridan 1988, Saunders 1991, Saunders and Bolton 1992, Huggins and Saunders 1993). Others such as Burgmann (1984) and Larbaliester (1977, 1980) argue that class differences between feminists and Indigenous women account for their non-participation in feminism, and Pettman (1992) theorises an intersection of class, race and gender relations in understanding the position of Indigenous women in society. Yeatman (1993, 1994) offers a theory of interlocking oppressions to analyse the position of Indigenous women in Australian society. Her theoretical framework sees sexuality, race, class, ethnicity, nationhood and gender as interconnecting and combining in different ways to position women in a variety of contexts of social existence that are an outcome of historical and material processes.

Recent feminist literature about Indigenous women and feminism disrupts and historicises the universal category white woman, but it does so from the subject position middle-class white woman. Indigenous women's subjectivity and experiences are often missing or subsumed within the literature, which tends to speak *for* Indigenous women. The specifics of Indigenous women's accounts of white race privilege and domination, which can offer insights into incommensurabilities and limits to knowing "Other", are invisible. As important as this literature is to feminist theorising and pedagogy it is limited because it does not make problematic how the social construction of the subject position white woman is represented, "taught, learned, experienced, and identified in certain forms of knowledge, values and privileges" (Giroux 1997:296). Whiteness is so pervasive as an invisible norm that race, as difference, still belongs only to women who are not white in Australian feminism.

Since the 1990s Australian feminism has moved from a politics that advocated unity in diversity to a politics of difference influenced by postmodern, deconstruction and poststructural theories and challenges from Indigenous women, women of colour, immigrant women and lesbian women (Magarey et al 1994; Gunew and Yeatman 1993; Yeatman 1994). Challenges to feminist practice and the development of new theories inform feminists of the multiplicity of differences, but whiteness is not positioned within the new theories as a "difference". Australian feminists live racialised lives in a racialised society, yet whiteness remains uninterrogated in feminist theory and practice. This discrepancy remains invisible, unmarked and unnamed, yet it is enmeshed in a feminist politics of difference.

A feminist politics of difference: when the object speaks

Some Australian feminists engaged with the politics of difference in their work such as Bottomley et al (1991), Pettman (1993) and Gunew and Yeatman (1993), and a few entered into the Bell–Huggins debate mentioned in Chapter 3. To reiterate, the debate arose in 1989 over an article written by Diane Bell and Topsy Napurrula Nelson in which it was argued that rape in Indigenous communities is everybody's business. Indigenous women contested the article. During the debate Bell stated that she and Topsy were compelled to speak out about intra-racial rape because it was an issue that had to be placed on the public agenda. Bell advised her audience that she could write about this issue because she was "authorised" by her friend, Topsy Napurrula Nelson, to speak. Topsy was born south of Tennant Creek and Bell says she "grew up with her extended family, wise in the ways of the land. Responsibilities for the maintenance of the mythology, songs, paintings, dances and ceremonies which commemorate these places is one [sic] Topsy has taken seriously" (Bell 1989:405). Bell's definition of Topsy positions her as a "traditional" woman.

According to Bell, rape and intra-racial rape have been interrogated and outed by feminists elsewhere because:

> no matter how unpleasant, feminist social scientists do have a responsibility to identify and analyse those factors which render women vulnerable to violence. The fact that this is happening to women of

another ethnic or racial group can not be a reason for ignoring the abuse (1989:404).

Bell then provides her audience with a brief overview of colonisation and its impact on gender relations in Indigenous society, followed by an outline of Indigenous women's perspectives on rape, which she argues, are confined to perspectives on inter-racial rape. Bell asserts that, unlike African American women, Indigenous women have not engaged in theoretical debates about rape because we have not recognised some of the feminisms that are relevant to us, and we have been unduly influenced by the socialist left in our political activity. She also asserts that "the underlying dilemma in the theoretical positioning of the topic of rape which polarised feminists in the seventies is now entering the writing of Aboriginal women" (1989:411). Bell deploys the subject position middle-class white woman to speak for us as the authoritative voice of the all-knowing subject.

Bell's narrative displays a striking contradiction. Indigenous women are not able to discern which feminisms are relevant to us and yet we now seem to have been able to distil the underlying dilemma in the theoretical positioning on the topic of rape in feminism. Indigenous women are positioned as uninformed girls who cannot discern theory and develop political strategies, but are positioned as "women" when we write about the same things as white feminists. This positioning is not arbitrary; it is grounded in the historically constructed premise of inferiorisation within the hegemony of white ideology which positions Indigenous women on the racial continuum as the most encumbered by nature and, therefore, the least civilised or most degenerate. This same ideology allows white women to be positioned closer to the other end of the continuum, where the dominant subject position "white male" represents culture and civilisation (Davy 1997:212). Bell is thus able to exercise her white race privilege to include or exclude Indigenous women from the category "woman" according to her current purpose.

The remainder of Bell's article is devoted to an analysis of the relationship between the judiciary, bureaucracies, Indigenous Legal Services and Indigenous women on intra-racial rape. Bell concludes by identifying common problems faced by Indigenous and non-Indigenous rape victims. She states that "it is the radical feminist strategies which emphasise the universality of key experiences of women and the need for separate institutions and it is this which offers Indigenous women the most likely strategy for success" (1989:415). Bell then identifies areas for reform in the area of intra-racial rape. She again provides us with an interesting contradiction. Bell, the white feminist anthropologist, sees no differences between the key experiences of white and Indigenous women, yet her academic career is based on constructing and representing the cultural differences of "Other".[7] How do we reconcile Bell's acceptance of radical feminism's subscription to the universality of women's experience and the strategies it offers Indigenous women as being correct and proper, and her career based on constructing cultural difference? Bell, speaking from the subject position middle-class white woman, centres the experiences of white women in two ways. White womanhood is the universal and the norm from which to judge and include the experiences of Indigenous women and it is white radical feminists who have the solutions to Indigenous intra-racial rape. Bell deploys the subject position middle-class white woman to exercise her white race privilege to include Indigenous women in the category "woman" although simultaneously denying our subjectivity so that in effect we remain objects. She then positions Indigenous women as children who do not know what the correct strategies are, and by implication are unable to develop them. In both positionings the subject position middle-class white woman represents the standards by which Indigenous women are measured and from which we are distanced.

In the article, Bell positions Nelson as the authentic voice that speaks for the women who have been raped and the families who have experienced this violence; she is the only informant. We do not hear from the victims themselves. Bell acknowledges in this article that she is walking on controversial ground. She recalls that at a conference when she and Nelson spoke about white women writing about Black women there was hostility.[8] The hostile audience consisted of urban Indigenous and Black American women. However, she defines her position on writing about Indigenous women in the following way: "I did not speak for, nor did I merely report, but rather my task was to locate issues of gender and race within a wider perspective ..." (1989:405). Bell tells the reader that Nelson also faced "hostile urban Indigenous and black American women" in relation to this issue. Nelson defined her position on the issue by stating that it was the quality of the relationship between the two women involved that was important when white women write about black women. Nelson could trust Bell to write about her ideas.

Despite the problems of representation raised at this conference Bell submitted the article for publication. It is not surprising that it generated debate and a written response by Indigenous women. In 1990 Jackie Huggins, on behalf of a number of Indigenous women, wrote a letter of protest to the editors of the *Women's Studies International Forum* objecting to the publication of the article on the grounds that Bell did not have the right to speak for all Indigenous women on the issue of rape. The Indigenous women also took issue with Nelson being positioned as the co-author in the article on the grounds that her voice had been appropriated by Bell and relegated to that of authoritative informant. The editors of the journal did not publish the letter. In the words of Renate Klein, one of the editors:

> ... we never refused to publish the letter by the Aboriginal women. But we felt that the debate deserved more than an unsigned letter with typed names, and no return address(es) — our managing Editor wrote twice to Jackie Huggins asking her to sign and fill out a copyright form with all the signatures as is standard practice. Neither response nor signatures were forthcoming. Consequently, we had to ask our publisher to seek legal advice in order to protect the 12 writers as well as the journal in case of legal action (Klein 1991: 505).

Jackie Huggins' recollection of events is that she was told that the letter lacked "academic rigour" and was seen to constitute "a personal attack on Bell" (pers. com.). Implicit within the editors' explanation for not publishing is the positioning of Huggins as the uncooperative black woman who lacks professionalism because she does not seem to understand white procedures. Effectively these seemingly neutral white procedures worked in the interests of the white feminist editors. They were able to control the debate by blaming Huggins for their inability to publish her response. In her letter of explanation to readers of *Women Studies*

International Forum Renate Klein exposes the political position of the white feminist editors:

> We find it deplorable that speaking out about rape still means paying a price — even in feminist circles. We are deeply distressed about these happenings but more than ever determined to continue publishing radical analyses of the grim realities women continue to face globally. We urge our readers to send us papers on violence against women: we must continue to speak out in order to devise strategies to stop the abuse of women (Klein 1991:505–6).

If Huggins et al.'s position is defined as "an unsigned letter", it is logical to assume that it is Bell's paper that is located within the category "radical analyses". The white editors here positioned Bell's paper as academic and Huggins et al.'s response as a letter, despite the fact that the letter contained an analysis of Bell's misrepresentation. The distinction made between the texts is consistent with Huggins' recollection. The editors exercised their race privilege to further their political agenda from a position of dominance. The subject position middle-class white woman was deployed by them as the universal woman who has the right to speak on behalf of all women. White feminist values and interests are centred and represented as being right and proper and the values and claims of the Indigenous women are positioned as being improper, unjustifiable and ignominious.

The article became the subject of further debate. In April 1990 Jackie Huggins, Jo Wilmot and I participated in a discussion about the article at the "When the voice of the turtle shall be heard in the land" — Women and Australian Anthropology 1788–1990 Conference in Adelaide.[9] The issue of control and ownership of knowledge did not arise and although I attempted to raise problems with Bell's methodology, questions from the audience personalised the discussion. White women in the audience tended to position Huggins as the ungrateful and angry black woman who did not believe in the spirit of equal treatment for all rape victims irrespective of race and culture. The white audience members adopted the line that Indigenous women did not seem to understand that Bell was in fact doing us a favour by exposing intra-racial rape. By positioning Huggins, Wilmot and me in this way, white women in the audience used their race privilege to dismiss the issues and questions being raised by us.

Such a positioning allowed them to feel good about themselves although simultaneously reinscribing white superiority. What remained invisible to the white women in the audience was the way they were exercising their white race privilege to represent Bell's work as morally correct and the concerns of the Indigenous women as less morally sound. In the discussion Huggins, Wilmot and I were both objects and subjects of the audience's gaze. We were objectified to the degree that what we were — Indigenous women — was crucial to the discussion, and our subjectivity was acknowledged in that we were allowed to speak, but the unpalatability of what we said relegated us to being silenced as objects.

Indigenous women continued to comment and participate in the debate in public forums. Jackie Huggins and a few other Indigenous women in Adelaide discussed the article on "The Coming Out Show" on ABC National Radio in May 1990, which was the last public engagement about the issue. In September 1990 Professor Anna Yeatman intervened in the debate. She states that her intentions were "to accord more public representation of the objections to the Bell piece from Huggins et al. on the assumption that they were opening up an important politics of voice and representation in respect of Indigenous women and white Australian feminists" (1993:240). Yeatman argues that, when the hegemonic white feminist intellectual representations of "Other" are contested by those positioned as "Other", what tends to occur is that the Indigenous intellectual becomes scrutinised according to a binary of same/difference which seeks to disrupt and dislocate their representation. Yeatman states that "the Bell debate is more of a debate between the custodians as to which of them is the better advocate of Aboriginal women than it is yet an elaborated politics of difference within Australia" (Yeatman 1993:239). For Yeatman such a politics would require the current custodians to relinquish some control over the agenda so that women positioned as "Other" could have a voice and differences within the movement would not be accounted for by any one binary (1993:239). Yeatman acknowledges the existence of multiple differences, but her politics of difference does not make visible *why* white feminist values, privileges and knowledges remain dominant in Australian feminism. It is taken for granted that they do.

Jan Larbalestier, a white feminist anthropologist, responded to the Bell debate in her article "The Politics of Representation: Australian Aboriginal Women and Feminism" (1990). Larbalestier states that within the discipline of anthropology there is an emerging debate concerning the political nature of its endeavour. This debate seeks to unpack the way in which knowledge is produced, how it is understood and how it is represented within power relations. Larbalestier (1990:146) asserts that, for feminists of whatever variety, the concern with the Bell–Huggins debate was the "shaping of the speech, rather than what was spoken". Larbalestier argues, however, that the focus of Bell's article was the appropriateness of radical feminism in theory and practice for understanding and acting on male violence against women rather than providing an analysis of intra-racial rape. Bell does not provide an analysis of the culturally specific contexts of intra-racial rape; instead, the article is concerned with identifying the way in which the judicial system and Indigenous legal services fail to deliver for Indigenous women.

Bell's utilisation of the radical feminist framework is also problematical because it is predicated on universalising women's experiences. As Larbalestier states, "Bell seems to gloss over her own position as a white academic in settings that are inscribed with the politics, the considerations and the positions and the strategies of power." She fails to understand why "urban" (meaning contemporary) Indigenous women are challenging her right to speak. It is the basis on which this right is established that is at issue. Larbalestier asserts that Indigenous women are developing their own theories of the conditions of their existence and experiences. She states that this is a necessary starting point for "specific Indigenous perspectives"(1990:154). For Larbalestier the Bell–Huggins debate highlights conceptual flaws in feminist anthropology. What is required is the development of "theoretical and empirical grounds for a feminist anthropology based on difference — most importantly it is necessary to look at ways in which racial difference is constructed through gender and to deconstruct the category women"(1990:154). This would require changing the conceptual and analytical frameworks because

> difference is both a conceptual, cultural and material problem. It is embedded in politics of identity, which are in turn embedded in relations of power. Dealing with patterns of inequality along with its accompanying positions and strategies of power may well prove to be the greatest challenge for all of us (1990:155).

Bell responded to Larbalestier's critique by reasserting her claim that she has the right to speak because she is a feminist anthropologist and Nelson said she could. She dismisses Larbalestier's positioning her as creating a false binary between Huggins et al. and Nelson because "to note differences is not to fall into a racist division of authentic/unauthentic" (1990:62). Bell draws on the white authority of science and the authority of Nelson as a "traditional" Indigenous woman to speak, which is doing more than just noting differences. She strategically deploys cultural differences manufactured by anthropology to legitimate her position within the text and the debate. Bell provides another contradiction by positioning her radical feminist emphasis on the universality of key experiences of all women, but noting that there are differences in experiences between Indigenous women. This contradiction can only be reconciled by recognising that its function is to support Bell's political agenda. Bell states that she is not concerned with the way she shaped the speech in her article, as she wanted to get the debate focused on the substantive issue of intra-racial rape:

> My interest in the relationship was in as far as it illuminated the issue of intra-racial rape. In returning to the issues ... I argue that forging a sustainable vision of a meaningful future in the current crisis requires that the needs of women are addressed; that in pursuit of the politics of difference we not lose sight of questions of power; that the politics of law, the nation state, the academy, and Indigenous liberation struggles which shape the "master narratives", are interrogated from within and from "elsewhere" (de Lauretis 1987:25) (Bell 1990:164).

Bell's statement represents a privileged position where power is deemed to be external thereby denying the power she is able to exercise as a professional white middle-class woman. Although Bell acknowledges questions of power she appears to lack an understanding that she is immersed in racialised power relations that are both asymmetrical and reciprocal, involving power and resistance which can be unintentional, intentional, direct and indirect. Bell did not own her whiteness and her social authority as an academic, so she did not recognise that they provided her with more power than Indigenous women within the debate.

In 1991, in *Women's Studies International Forum*, Vol. 14, No. 5, the editors published their editorial on the debate, the letter from Huggins et al., a letter from Nelson and a response from Bell, as well as another article. The letter from Huggins et al. is clear in its intent and advocacy. Indigenous people have been and continue to be subject to the forces of imperialism. Rape in Indigenous communities is not everybody's business; it is the business of Indigenous people. Huggins et al. fundamentally challenge Bell's right to speak on this issue and the basis from which she derives her cultural authority. They position the article written by Bell as an example of racist imperialism at work in the 20th century. They also take issue with Bell's positioning of Nelson as co-author to legitimate the article; in their opinion Nelson's role was one of informant not one of co-author. Since Nelson is not a qualified anthropologist and has no other academic qualifications, her ability to co-author the article with Bell is therefore circumscribed. In effect, the article is informed by the different knowledges of both Bell and Nelson, but it is written in an academic genre.

Huggins et al. responded to Bell's assertion that Indigenous women have not recognised feminisms that are relevant to them. They state that they share common interests with social feminists rather than radical feminists because "our fight is with the state,. the system, social injustices, and primarily racism far in excess of patriarchy" (Huggins et al. 1991:506). They note that they are conscious of the way in which white women create divisions among Indigenous women and state that the article contributes to widening the gap. They point out that colonisation has impacted differently in different contexts and that white women have contributed to its application. They conclude by asserting that sexism does not overshadow racial domination in Australia. For Huggins et al., talking about rape as everyone's business

breaks Indigenous law and the racial damage it does far out-
weighs the importance of gender.

In her letter Nelson states that Bell has worked with her since
1975, and, despite the fact that she had asked Indigenous women
to write down her stories, they did not respond to her requests.
Bell is the person who listened and wrote down her stories.
Although Nelson positions the Indigenous women as not interested, it has to be acknowledged that Bell is in the privileged
position of having the resources, time, skills and knowledge to be
able to undertake the task. There could be a number of reasons
why Indigenous women in Nelson's community did not respond
to her request. Poverty often means Indigenous women's priorities are caught up in the daily struggle to survive with limited
resources. They do not have white race privilege or the luxury to
participate in what could be perceived as a difficult exercise. In
her letter Nelson does not present herself as the "traditional"
Indigenous woman of authority in her community as she is
represented by Bell; in fact, Nelson's self-presentation raises
concerns about Bell's use of Nelson's "traditional" authority to
legitimate her claims to speak on the issue of intra-racial rape.
Bell is able to make these claims because her white race privilege
allows her to take the morally superior position in the debate.

Bell reinscribes her morally superior position by reiterating in
response that speaking about rape is everybody's business. She is
concerned that the issue of women being hurt is being neglected
in the controversy and wishes to remind her audience that she is
driven by this pain to speak out despite being "white listed".
Apparently those who speak out against subjects that are taboo
to Indigenous people become "white listed". It is also unclear
what Bell means exactly by the term "white listed" other than as
an inversion of the racially pejorative term "black listed". It is also
clear who develops this list: one can only assume she means
Indigenous people, who have no power within universities over
research grants and academic positions. She further points out
that other researchers working in the field have had to temper
or withhold their findings "for fear of an attack on their personal
and professional integrity" (1990:508). She also fears for her
future work and that of her colleagues because they will be

reluctant to co-author with Indigenous people because of the attack on her collaboration with Nelson whose "imprint is firmly on the ideas and structure of the piece" (1990:509). Bell inadvertently shifts Nelson's position from being one of co-author to informant in this statement, which concurs with the Indigenous women's analysis of Nelson's role. Statistically and corporeally Indigenous women as a group constitute a powerless and underprivileged minority in Australian society, but Bell positions us as threatening, powerful, uncontrollable and ubiquitous when the authority of her work is challenged. Bell utilises her white race privilege by defining the boundaries between her and Indigenous women as being irrational and unreasonable.

Bell takes issue with Huggins' statement that rape is not everybody's business by rationalising how knowledge is situated and located in central Australian idiomatic formulation. She states that knowledge in Indigenous society is owned and highly valued: those who appropriate knowledge without consent are seen to commit theft. What Bell omits from this idiomatic formulation is that what constitutes public and private knowledge within Indigenous communities is contextualised by elders and the kinship relations of the participants involved in the event or circumstances that govern these deliberations. Bell states that she has abided by this law, which is not just restricted to central Australia, yet her statement that rape is everybody's business contravenes it, because she and Nelson are making public certain knowledge without the appropriate deliberations of the communities concerned. Bell refuses to acknowledge and accept that it is precisely this cultural premise which motivates Huggins et al. to take issue with her statement that rape is everybody's business. Bell does not have the authority of Indigenous women to speak on behalf of the communities represented by Huggins et al., but she does have the white cultural authority of "science" which is part of the white race privilege she exercises in asserting her "right" to speak. As Ma Rhea (1998) argues, universities were and are part of the colonising process:

> [It is] important to an understanding of the historical production and reproduction of ideas within the system of Commonwealth universities to recognise that the primary outcome of such a process was, and is, the globalisation of a scientific world view which is

ontologically and epistemologically committed to the idea of "white" superiority (1998:3).

Bell concludes by speaking out about the racial cringe displayed by white researchers who do not speak out on issues of concern to them because of the fear of backlash and the possibility of job discrimination. However, there has never been a case where an anthropologist has lost his or her job in a university as a result of criticism by Indigenous women. There is also a hidden assumption here which is consistent with a position of white superiority: Indigenous people have a duty to participate in research and researchers have an inherent right to jobs because the rationalist metaphysics of western science require it. The question that needs to be asked is: who benefits the most from the research? Bell believes that researchers have a right to do research among Indigenous people, and that, as long as they abide by the rules of white western disciplinary methodologies, it is not a problem. As argued in Chapter 3, anthropological methodology is problematical because it creates a racialised binary that centres the subject position middle-class white woman and produces distorted representations of Indigenous women. Bell positions herself as a feminist but fails to adhere to a premise of white feminist methodology: that all research is circumscribed, and that when researchers embark on research they must do so with some knowledge of the political context and the potential consequences to themselves.

Bell notes that some white women have pursued and encouraged the debate, but in all the responses there are no practical suggestions about how to change the situation of women being raped in Indigenous communities, through empowering them or forming national alliances. Bell appears to target Yeatman and Larbalestier by stating that instead "Aboriginal women's experiences are providing fodder for the deconstructionists' mill" (1990:512). Bell believes that the substantive issues have not been dealt with in this debate. She concludes that "in our article we asked: who speaks of the anguish, shame and risk for Indigenous women? The question is still floating out there" (1990:513).

The Bell–Huggins debate is more than an isolated case of contested advocacy. It speaks to central issues within feminism on irreducible differences, incommensurabilities and whiteness. The Huggins et al. critique challenged the authority of Bell's white race privilege and the white institutional basis from which she derives her knowledges and power. White Australian feminists have been, and continue to be, complicit in the exercising of power in their relations with Indigenous women. As beneficiaries of colonisation, white feminists have been able to challenge and remake themselves as white women through the state and other institutions. The complicity of feminism in the colonial project has not been erased by all white feminists, but the middle-class subject position white woman remains invisible, unmarked and unnamed in the work of such feminists. The exercising of white race privilege is not interrogated as being problematic, nor is it understood as part of the power that whiteness confers; instead it is normalised within feminist texts and practice.

The history of white feminist relations with Indigenous women reveals that both first-wave and second-wave feminists have sought to remake Indigenous women according to the subject position middle-class "white woman", but for slightly different reasons. During the first wave, white feminists, deploying the respectability and sexual propriety embodied in the subject position middle-class white woman, sought to civilise Indigenous women, in particular our sexuality, to minimise racial impurity. The second wave of feminism seeks our ideological reconstruction as white feminists despite its theoretical positioning on difference, which in practice amounts to little more than rhetoric. As Behrendt (1993) argues, white feminism tells Indigenous women "that their position in society is defined by their gender rather than their race, that the push for rights by white women will empower black women, that we are aligned with white women in the battle against oppression and that white women are as oppressed as we are" (1993:41).

The Bell–Huggins debate is an example of incommensurabilities that exist and unfold in inter-subjective relations in feminism in Australia. The white feminist anthropologist authorised herself to speak on behalf of Indigenous women and this authority was contested by the self-presentation of Indigenous women. Bell and the white editors' response to the Indigenous women was to represent them as inadequate academics and unauthentic Indigenous women, mediated through the dialectical triangulation of the middle-class subject position white woman, feminist academic and traditional Indigenous woman. They drew on the authority of white masculine modern foundationalist science and its discourse on racialising "Other", as a way of reinscribing the dominance of their subject position middle-class white woman in the debate.

What is evident from the interconnected relationships of white domination and Indigenous contestation is that as knowing subjects white feminists and Indigenous women speak out of different cultures, epistemologies, experiences, histories and material conditions which separate our politics and our analyses. What has been deployed and constituted historically is the subject position middle-class white woman as the bearer of true womanhood, which positions Indigenous women in particular ways. This subject position is socially empowered because it has a structural location as part of white hegemonic ideology and is embodied in various forms of white feminist agency. As Huggins (1994) argues, white feminists representations of Indigenous women are

> based on a menial or sexual image: as more sensual but less cerebral, more interesting perhaps but less intellectual, more passive but less critical, more emotional but less analytical, more exotic but less articulate, more withdrawn but less direct, more cultured but less stimulating, more oppressed but less political than they are (1994:77).

Indigenous women's communicative exchanges with white women have been imbalanced; we have been positioned as "little bit woman". White women have been the helpers and Indigenous women the helped (Sykes 1984:64–5). This inter-subjective relationship reflects the historicity of the interconnected structural relationship of domination and resistance between white Australia and Indigenous people. For Indigenous women, all white feminists "benefit from the continued dominance of their culture and the exploitative effects of their freely exercised power over our people, our lands and our place in our own country" (Trask 1996:914). All women live with the history of their subjectivity, but not necessarily with a consciousness of or consciousness about it. White women come to feminism with already formed subjectivities that are linked to different histories, discourses, privileges, power and oppression. They are socially situated subjects who are implicated and enmeshed in power relations where whiteness remains invisible, natural, normal and unmarked.

CHAPTER FIVE

White Women's Way:
Self-Presentation within White
Feminist Academics' Talk[1]

> Progressive white feminists, with anti-racist politics, seeking to edu-
> cate and explain the experience of sexism, often compare sexism to
> racism. The use of this analogy suggests that the "analogizer" believes
> her situation is the same as that of a person of color. Nothing in the
> comparison process challenges this belief, and the analogizer may
> think that she understands the other's situation in its fullness. The
> analogy makes the analogizer forget any difference and allows her to
> stay focused on her own situation without grappling with the person
> of color's reality (Grillo & Wildman 1995:171).

White women are represented everywhere in Australian feminism, but are not racialised as whites. Instead they are presented
as variously classed, sexualised, aged and abled even though the
social construction of their racialised subject position is tied to
the way in which whiteness "is taught, learned, experienced and
identified in certain forms of knowledges, values and privileges"
(Giroux 1997:296). What is evident from the previous chapters
is that middle-class white feminists and Indigenous women speak
out of different subject positions. The different knowledges that
inform both Indigenous and middle-class white feminists' speaking positions disclose that there are limits to knowing the
"Other". These limitations exist in any inter-subjective relationship. The degree to which they influence relations depends on
the power and privilege derived from the structural location of
the subject position deployed.

In this chapter it is argued that middle-class white feminist academics, who advocate an anti-racist practice, unconsciously and consciously exercise their race privilege. The analysis of the interviews of feminist academics discloses a deployment of the subject position middle-class white woman in professional and personal practice. The chapter begins by providing a description of the methodology, followed by an analysis of the interviews showing how feminist academics engage with race and how the subject position middle-class white woman is implicated in this engagement.

Indigenous on white: the interviewees and the method

Ruth Frankenberg argues that "race shapes meaning and experiences for social, political, historical and cultural reasons rather than as a result of essential race difference" (1993:148). In the earlier analysis of multiple texts, the subject position middle-class white woman was revealed in different historically constituted discourses. In these discourses, race as construct and category has been reserved for those designated "Other" and this subject position is invisible for those who occupy and deploy it. However, what is missing from the analysis is how whiteness, as a racial identity, was performed by feminist academics in their personal and professional practice in Australia in the late 1990s. The degree to which "race" continues to be externalised and yet shapes feminist thinking and practice requires further examination in the contemporary Australian context.

In order to explore the way in which race shapes the thought and experiences of white feminist academics, twenty women were selected for interview from three universities between November 1996 and February 1997. However, eight women did not consent to be interviewed as they were too busy or said they did not teach anything on Indigenous women. Feminist academics were chosen because since the second wave of feminism in Australia the feminist movement's presence is strongest in academia and the bureaucracy.[2] The ages of the women ranged from the early 30s to the mid 50s; all were middle-class but some had working-class origins.[3] They were predominantly single and the majority were positioned to be heterosexual.[4] Three women had migrated from England, one from South Africa, one from the United States of

America and another had been born in Canada but raised in South Australia. The remaining six women were born and raised in Australia. The interviews ranged in duration from twenty minutes to three hours. Copies of the transcripts were sent to each of the women for their perusal and amendment.[5] Some women provided additional information, some did not respond and some deleted sentences within the text. Only one of the women refused to allow me to use a number of pages of her transcript, because, she said, she was not aware that the tape was still on when we engaged with each other's comments. The women's status in academia varied. Three women were professors, two women were associate professors, and the rest were either at senior lecturer, lecturer or associate lecturer level. Although the group is not representative of the white female population as a whole, it is representative of the small number of white feminists in Australia who write on race, endorse an anti-racist politics and are members of the educated middle-class.

Framing and conducting the research: researcher and power

In order to elicit in-depth and diverse responses the questions were made as general as possible. The purpose of the questions was to gain an insight into the relationship between the interviewees' professional (public) life and their personal (private) life in relation to race and cultural difference. The questions were structured to move interviewees from their pedagogical practice and theory to life experiences as white feminists. Five questions were developed, influenced by the work of Ruth Frankenberg on the social construction of whiteness and my textual analysis of the relations between Indigenous women and white feminists in Australia.

The first and second questions were concerned with the ways in which these women gendered their curriculum and how they included cultural difference. The third question asked women to identify themselves as belonging to a racial or cultural group and whether they knew people from racial and cultural groups other than their own. The fourth question was concerned with asking when or how they knew that cultural difference was manifesting itself before them, and the final question asked them to discuss their relationship to racism. My research approach to the interviews was what Frankenberg names as "dialogical" (Frankenberg 1993:30). As the interviewer, I shared some information about my life and experiences in relation to cultural difference, race and racism with interviewees throughout the research process. I was aware of the discomfort my questions could bring to white feminists who, for the first time, were subject to an Indigenous gaze on social phenomena in which both researcher and interviewees were historically implicated. Feminists have long acknowledged the subjectivity of both researcher and interviewees and the imbalance in power relations between them (Harding 1987, Alcoff & Potter 1993, Behar & Gordon 1995). They have sought to minimise their power in the research process through various strategies, such as information exchange and interviewee interrogation of their analyses (Harding 1987:181–2, Frankenberg 1993:29–32). However, most empirical research undertaken by feminists involves researching women of their own race or white women researching non-white women. The capacity to share information or offer interrogation of one's analysis can easily be made from the location of privilege and power. I have not found any empirically based research conducted by a woman of colour on white women about their "Othering" and their experiences of the research process. Therefore, based on my experiences and knowledge about whiteness and the responses received from women who did not want to participate in the study, I would be positioned as both object and subject in the research process. "Race" would predominantly be perceived as belonging to me, the Indigenous "Other".

Unlike other informants or interviewees, who usually do not have knowledge of and experience in western research processes, the women I interviewed had both the knowledge and the skills to give measured and intellectualised responses. In order to minimise measured responses, I asked direct questions that specifically identified the subject matter but were generalised in format. The generalised nature of the questions yielded diverse and varied responses and allowed me some degree of intervention, despite the interviewees' familiarity with research processes.

This method was successful but it was limited by race. For example, when I compare the type of responses given by white women in Ruth Frankenberg's work on "race" with those in my study, it is obvious that Frankenberg's racial identity was invisible and familiar; not a reference point for racial difference. This indicates to me that had I been white I would probably have elicited a different range of responses from the feminist academics I interviewed. The interviews were both coherent and contradictory, and they provide insights about the deployment of the subject position middle-class white woman and her racialised invisibility.

Pedagogical practice

Feminists argue that universities are knowledge production sites where knowledges are contested, accommodated, created, reconstructed and deconstructed. They are sites for producing oppositional, revisionist and authorised knowledges which enter public discourses "in ways that may reinforce or unsettle our understandings of social problems, provide language for explaining or obscuring connections, and widen or foreclose conceivable political options" (Pettman 1992:131). In asking feminists the general question about how they gendered their curriculum, I wanted to ascertain to what degree the subject position middle-class white woman was centred in their pedagogical practice. All of the women interviewed stated that they gendered their curriculum, but in different ways.

Five of the women structured their courses specifically on the social construction of white masculinity and femininity. For these feminists, white women's gender is the primary difference acknowledged and engaged with; the universal subjects are white woman and white man. Whiteness is culturally central and normalised in their pedagogical practice. An unintended consequence is that the subject position middle-class white woman is essentialised as the embodiment of true womanhood. That is, through the exclusion of other women, the white woman becomes the universal standard for all women (Spelman 1990). The other seven women organised their courses around race, cultural difference, class and gender. They teach about structural inequality and the intersection of race, class and gender differences; they

are concerned with social structures that determine the characteristics and actions of individuals. However, in the interviews
they did not discuss the relationship between knowledges, social
responsibility and collective struggle which one would expect to
find in an anti-racist pedagogy (Mohanty 1990:192). Instead they
teach about the structural location of race as racial oppression
and do not engage with their whiteness or the subjugated knowledges of those who experience such oppression. Their pedagogy
is inclusive of the race of the "Other" but masks the subject
position middle-class white woman from which they teach. Their
pedagogy works to supports white people's externalisation of race
by restricting it to structure and "Other". In denying whiteness as
a racial identity, "race" is removed from white agency in their
analyses and this can diminish their students' scope for self-
reflection as an anti-racist practice.

A decolonising pedagogical practice places importance on the
relations between different knowledges, learning and experiences to understand differences (Mohanty 1990:192). Some of
the women interviewed sought to engage in a decolonising pedagogical practice. One feminist incorporated race and colonisation in her teaching on gender in Australian history. She sees her
role as

> to understand what happened and to use my education and training
> to bring it to other people's knowledge so that they can come to terms
> with what is our collective past. Because we have a collective past. We
> have a separate history, but we have a collective past as well and where
> it comes together is of course the total discrepancy of power.

The pedagogical aim is to develop critical thinking among
students so they can inform themselves and transform their world
view. The idea is to convey to their predominantly white students
that their respective positionings influence the way they interpret
the world. What is not taught as being problematic is "how
whiteness as a racial identity and social construction is taught,
learned, experienced and identified in certain forms of knowledge, values and privileges" (Giroux 1997:296). The determinate
connection between white feminist academic and white student
lives in the centre, and the lives of Indigenous women and
students on the margins remain invisible. Perspectives that ac-

knowledge the "Other" on the margins inadvertently privilege the subject position middle-class white woman because she remains uninterrogated and unnamed (Apple 1997:127).

In my questions, I sought to ascertain if cultural difference was included in their curriculum and how it was represented and interrogated. As stated previously, some of the feminists interviewed did not deal with cultural difference in their subjects. Three women gave priority to imparting knowledge that centres whiteness within the boundaries of white-male-dominated institutions. The subject position middle-class white woman — naturalised, unmarked and unnamed — is the centre of their gendered curriculum. The omission of the cultural difference of other women reinscribes a hierarchy of white cultural values that are enforced and built into the power structure of their respective universities. Other feminists sought to transform their curriculum and decentre the subject position middle-class white woman by including cultural difference through the use of texts by Toni Morrison, bell hooks and Gayatri Spivak. As one feminist stated:

> Racial/cultural difference questions are taken up to some degree in all these subjects but more so (sometimes much more so) in some rather than others — although cultural difference in one way or another is always an issue.

Cultural difference is incorporated within the curriculum through an "Other" literature that does little to disrupt the experiential knowledge of students in the Australian context. The racialised "Other" belongs to another country and is therefore culturally safe for interrogation. An assumption that underpins such a teaching strategy is: racialisation is the same everywhere. Other feminists taught cultural difference in terms of the problems faced by Indigenous and migrant women in the health care system in Australia. This suggests that students are not taught to recognise whiteness as shaping, for political, cultural and historical reasons, the normative practices and diverse relationships within the health system. Instead, the health system, like other institutions, is often presented as having shortcomings but it is racially neutral; whiteness remains invisible and unnamed. Similarly, another feminist taught cultural difference in terms of its impact on the legal personality:

One of the things I tend to do certainly in a first year subject, also I do it where the issue comes up in other subjects, there is this whole idea of legal personality which is one of those basics about who is entitled to claim legal redress and working with the idea that it isn't a natural concept. Law structures who is entitled to speak to it and in what contexts. In the last century, for example, companies enjoyed a far greater degree of legal personality than women, and women's legal personality tended to be structured according to marital status and according to race.

The primary referent here is the female gender (read "white"), although race (read "black") is identified as a marker that also changes the relationship of the female to the Law. Cultural difference is reduced to the way the law treats women. Although it is acknowledged that "race" is a factor that shaped a woman's legal personality, "race" is synonymous with the non-white "Other". "[S]ociety operates in such a way as to put whiteness at the centre of everything, including individual consciousness — so much so that we seldom question the centrality of whiteness, and most people, on hearing 'race', hear 'black'. That is, whiteness is treated as the norm, against which all differences are measured" (Reddy 1994:12). The legal personality of white women was tied to their marital status in the 19th century whereas the legal personality of black women was connected first and foremost to their "race" (Williams 1991; McGrath 1993).

The absence of an interrogation of whiteness as cultural difference is evident in the response of another feminist who utilises critical race theory to unmask the way race and gender position people differently within the Law. However, she claims that it leaves white students with a dilemma. Critical race theory accepts that all speaking positions are valid even though it forces students to recognise that the Law is grounded in a white value system that privileges white people over others. All speaking positions are valid but are not of equal worth. Who is listened to or heard depends on their ability and capacity to exercise power as part of the dominant group. White feminists and their white students practice cultural relativism every day, but do not perceive this as a dilemma for those positioned as "Other". In this way whiteness remains centred and is masked in pedagogy. It was clear from the interviews that where a feminist had a consciousness of her subject position as a middle-class white woman, and drew on her experiences and cultural locatedness to inform her pedagogy, whiteness was unnamed as the dominant cultural form. Her students are taught about how cultural differences are manifest in values, behaviour and ideas; different knowledges inform different behaviour. Although students can be taught to recognise that meanings have a culture specific context, only certain meanings are legitimate and accepted as official knowledge within Australian society. "These meanings, of course, will be contested, will be resisted and sometimes transformed but this does not lessen the fact that hegemonic cultures have greater power to make themselves known and acceptable" (Apple 1997:124).

The hegemony of whiteness manifests itself in pedagogical practice when feminists seek to recentre themselves by making "oppressions" the common denominator between themselves and Indigenous women. White women's oppression was mentioned repeatedly in the interviews, specifically in relation to the issue of cultural difference. So while cultural difference was equated with Indigenous women, the white race privilege, which confers dominance on its female members, remained unnamed and invisible. Race, class and sex oppressions were the key representations of the "Other's" cultural difference given by feminists. This reveals a limited capacity to identify the specificities of cultural differences grounded in different knowledges and realities from their own. The interviews also provide insights about how the invisibility of whiteness works in feminist pedagogy to normalise, naturalise and maintain its privilege while appearing to be culturally and racially neutral, progressive and inclusive. The way in which cultural difference is taught centres the concerns of the subject position middle-class white woman. As Carlson argues, "In the twentieth century, white hegemony has been maintained less through the legal denial of rights and military force and more through control of popular culture and education" (Carlson 1997:137).

Self-presentation, identity and sociality

Sociality plays an important part in affirming or disrupting subject positions in cultural contexts. As such, inter-cultural inter-subjectivity provides opportunities for encountering differences and similarities that may lead to the disruption of assumptions about the "Other". Ruth Frankenberg (1993) found that white women who socialise and work with the "Other" tend to advocate an anti-racist practice more than white women who remained socially distant. As the feminists I interviewed subscribed to an anti-racist politics, I was interested in ascertaining whether or not they socialised outside their racial group. I asked the questions: "Do you have contact with people of different racial or cultural groups from that of your own?" and "Do you see yourself as belonging to an ethnic or cultural group?"

All the women had contact with people from different cultural or racial groups. Four of the women had contact in their child-hood. Two socialised with migrant children from their schools. One lived next door to a Chinese family and spent time with them; her mother suffered from mental illness and she found refuge in their company. Another went to boarding school with Asian students. These women now have limited contact with students or colleagues from different cultural and racial groups; most contact occurs through their work as academics. This lim-ited contact with the "Other" was the case for most of the other feminists, with the exception of three women who had socialised or worked with people from different cultural or racial groups. One feminist had been involved politically with Indigenous women and another shared a house with Chinese and Indigenous women. Another feminist had been active in the civil rights movement in the United States and had a continuing friendship with an Australian Indigenous couple. However, outside the academic environment they socialised predominantly with white people. Their interaction with difference is a matter of *choice* — not an imperative.

Inter-subjective relations with the "Other" in academia occur through research or teaching. Here the power relations between student and lecturer, or researcher and researched, centre white dominance through the social organisation of the academic structure and the learning and exercising of western knowledges. These feminists have no imperative to step outside the beliefs, values and behaviours embodied in the subject position middle-class white woman. They live in a country where cities have been developed around invisible conveniences that give social preferences to whiteness in the location of municipal and other services. The design of suburbs and the naming of streets have been planned to serve white neighbourhoods and preserve their whiteness.[6] As one feminist noted:

> I live in — which is middle-class, white, orthodox, affluent, comfortable ... So I meet absolutely nobody in my suburban community who is anything other than myself. The place where I meet the "Other" is in my research.

The engagement with the "Other" remains predominantly, for these women, a dimension of their work practice — their public world — where their academic knowledges engage with difference to varying degrees. This reduces the opportunity for their experiential knowledges about the "Other" to be interrogated and disrupted, although their academic knowledge allows an empathetic appreciation of difference. Although these feminists advocate an anti-racist politics in academic contexts this appears to have little impact on their construction of subjectivity outside of academia. Their anti-racist politics are restricted to ensuring that they teach about the "race" of the "Other" in some manner, do not condone racial hatred in their classrooms, and make class and sex oppression explicit as social justice issues. In most cases the subject position middle-class white woman is not deployed in any social or political activity with "Other" outside the confines of academia.

When asked the question "Do you see yourself as belonging to an ethnic or cultural group?", all the feminists were confident and certain that they were white and middle-class, but they were ambiguous about different ethnicities. The mixed ethnicities identified by the women were Anglo/Celtic/Saxon or Scottish or Irish or English; one stated that she was of Jewish heritage and another Prussian. Their self-presentation as white implies that they recognise their racial assignment. The ambiguity of their ethnicities suggests that they unconsciously acknowledge the power that they possess because their race privilege is connected to a white cultural system that exists as omnipresent and natural. However, such a consciousness did not lead these feminists to discuss or mention what being white meant in terms of their ethnicity, identity and their anti-racist politics. It was taken for granted that they had options: they could claim a specific ethnicity, or be just white, and they could choose which of their European ancestry to include in their description of their identities. They were able to exercise their race privilege to choose or not choose an ethnic identity because as white feminist academics they are part of the white majority centre in Australian society. As Waters argues, "The option of choosing among different ethnicities in their family backgrounds exists because the degree of discrimination and social distance attached to specific European backgrounds has diminished over time" (1998:404). Ethnicity is a choice because there is no social cost involved in what are predominantly symbolic ethnicities. That is, the ethnicities of these feminists do not influence their lives unless they want them to; in effect their ethnicities are individualistic in nature. The problem with such a positioning on ethnicity is that it is easy to assume that all ethnic identities are in some sense interchangeable. Most of these white feminists, when consciously deploying the subject position middle-class white woman, did not recognise that their race privilege meant they were accorded choices about their ethnicities.

For some feminists, whiteness as a racial identity that confers dominance and privilege remains unmarked and unnamed in a different way. One feminist who comes from South Africa sees herself as white but not belonging to an ethnic or cultural group; rather she positions herself as an outsider. Another said she just did not see any ethnic differences. These feminists want to deny their racially assigned power. Both feminists want to remove themselves from white race privilege, one by individualising difference, and the other by invoking the notion of sameness. As one feminist said:

> I tend to bounce off my feelings of otherness as a woman and a particular sort of outsider woman because of breaking the rules of being a mother but not married, bright but not ugly, heterosexual but single [inaudible], so racism in its crude sense is of the greatest debate; it helps fuel my desire to press for more to be a transformative instrument and it also really does tend to isolate [inaudible] what we define as my feminist ethics.

Another feminist also denied her racially conferred privilege and dominance but in a different way. She identified as being white and stated that she could claim she had "Welsh blood" and "Irish blood" but they were not significant parts of her identity; she was "straight down the line, boring Anglo". It was interesting that this woman was the only feminist interviewed who used the metaphor of blood in terms of culture and ethnicity. Frankenberg (1993:144) argues: "The blood metaphor ... used is crucial, for it located sameness in the body — precisely the location of *difference* in genetic or biological theories of white superiority. Further, of course, blood is under the skin, and skin has been and remains the foremost signifier of racial difference". Sameness is a way of rejecting the idea of white racial superiority and distancing "race" and "racism" from the subject position middle-class white woman.

Identifying cultural difference in practice

In answering the questions "What does cultural difference mean for you in practice?" and "How are you conscious of it?", a variety of responses were given which indicated that cultural difference meant different things to different feminists. I expected to find that feminists who think that cultural difference means a different way of thinking, acting and behaving would be conscious of how these differences impact on their own behaviour in practice. I anticipated that they were conscious of how subjectivity is shaped by white culture, because they had knowledge about, and challenged, patriarchy — which would require deploying different subject positions.

The feminists who were most conscious of cultural differences had experienced the disruption of their subjectivity when socialising with the "Other" or they were raised in a household in which their mother's mental illness dominated daily life. They understood that living with such differences in practice meant living with uncertainty and sometimes denial in uncomfortable and liminal spaces. For example, the feminist who spent a good deal of time as a child with the Chinese family next door, because of her mother's mental illness, learnt an appreciation of cultural difference from the Chinese family, which she viewed as the antithesis, in many respects, of her own family. She learnt that there was a different way of dealing with conflict which contrasted with her white middle-class family's pretension and denial. The scope for deploying a different subject position was broadened. Another feminist was also raised in a household with a mother who suffered from mental illness:

> Her madness couldn't be fixed or ignored so you learn a new sense of tolerance and diversity where you are not in control as a kid [inaudible]. Because of this experience of being utterly powerless at the hands of a woman I find some of the feminist stuff a bit "twee" about all women being good. My feelings about difference and diversity are more complex and cynical and more aware of the real limits and frustrations. It left me with a different view of the world that you cannot change and managing living with that kind of uncomfortableness and madness. Life is about learning tolerance that's basically intolerably different, discomforted and there is a level at which you have to learn to live with incommensurate difference and discomfort and my mother taught me that. Although I grew up a white in many ways and privileged in many ways I think that [it] was the difference that made me think about oppression and power.

A disrupted childhood provided an awareness of cultural differences and tolerance, and this early training gave insights about living with difference that were drawn on when sharing houses with women from different cultures. However, her experience of living with the "Other" in different relations of power was that "in reality real tolerance of incommensurable difference is very hard to achieve ... who dominates matters a lot". Living with cultural difference means one has to deploy and negotiate different subject positions in order to function within an environment where a variety of power relations exist. In these contexts it matters who has the power to dominate; if one wants to work at minimising the oppression of others from a subject position of white privilege, one has to alter one's behaviour and attitude. Another feminist also lived with cultural difference through a childhood of family discord between a Dutch mother and an Australian father, but as soon as she left home "difference" became outside and beyond her experiences. Her ability to experience otherness disappearing off her horizon meant that cultural difference only mattered in her life when it was unavoidable. She was able to feel culturally safe in her new context at university because her white race privilege gave her the power to be able to choose whether or not she interacted with the cultural difference of the "Other". Despite the fact that all three feminists have an awareness of changing their subject positions in relation to cultural difference, they speak from a dominant subject position located within the centre of white Australian society. Cultural difference made an impact on their formative years, but its impact on their subjectivity was reduced when they left home and were able to exercise choice about their sociality in Australian society.

Another feminist's experience of living in France and China meant that she deployed different subject positions but retained her white race privilege in these contexts:

> I spent a lot of time in France and I feel very comfortable there, but I'm also very conscious of the way in which when you become part of a different cultural context different things become possible. There are different things you can say and different things you can do [inaudible]. In China it was a very different culture — we were honoured guests — [inaudible]. I had a badge that said I was [a] foreign expert so I was treated with great deference and people made a fuss of me, which was wonderful. [inaudible]. I am very much aware of the sort of things that what cultural differences consist of, but I think it's important to say that I have always been able to participate from a position of privilege which I think really does make a difference.

Her experiences reveal that she not only has a consciousness of her structural location in a different cultural context, but that she is also conscious of the need to deploy different subject positions to accommodate and enable cultural difference. She tries to resist the power of her structural location as a middle-class white woman at the inter-subjective level by having a consciousness of its privileges.

Other feminists interviewed had an awareness of structural inequality. However, this consciousness did not inform changes to their subject positioning on cultural difference. For some feminists cultural differences meant class and race differences:

> Now with Aboriginal cultural difference — at that stage there was more of a tension around that because this Purfleet township was poor. We used to drive through it on the way to Sydney or if we were going to the beach and I used to feel a little bit frightened because

the houses were run down compared to most of them in the town. And I do not know, but we might have stopped and bought something from the shop a couple of times, but mostly we just drove through it and I was sort of aware of a kind of tension. That might not be the right word, a sort of a stress or something with my mother and father that this was something that they were not neutral about, you know, and the children were wandering around a bit.

Poverty here is equated with cultural difference and is perceived negatively because of the value held for material things in the white system. The fear of the "Other" is derived from associating poverty with badness. What is missing from this gaze is that Indigenous people might not have the same values about these conditions because they share a different system of values. Within this narrative there is an awareness that cultural differences can manifest through behaviour and language, but the Indigenous social world imbued with meaning grounded in knowledges of different realities remains unknown. Several of the remaining feminists acknowledged that cultural differences exist within the landscape of the university, but they do not alter their subjectivity to accommodate it in their engagement with students and colleagues. That is, they do not position themselves through the eyes of the "Other" to change their behaviour and attitude, nor are any strategies in place for a reflexive anti-racist practice within their classrooms and the university landscape. In the words of Frye (1983: 115), "The concept of whiteness is not just used, in these cases, it is *wielded*". In deployment of the subject position middle-class white woman these feminists are able to exercise their race privilege to make choices about how and when they engage with, have an awareness of, or ignore the cultural difference of "Others".

Racism as a relationship

Racism is often represented and taught in universities throughout Australia as a problem associated with people of colour, and the study of Indigenous Australians has been informed by anthropological knowledge (Cowlishaw 1986a). Five of the feminists interviewed teach from the position that racism is not a white problem; they are not personally implicated in it and the gaze is fixed firmly on the "Other". As one feminist said:

I do not like it but obviously I am someone who is not directly affected by it. I might get offended by it but it is not as though I am an Asian or a black person except for this Jewish thing ... So my relationship to racism then in terms of being a political person of one kind or another and my academic work, my intellectual work, is to try and work against that.

The positioning here is contradictory in that she denies a personal relationship to racism because white women are not affected by racism, but she forms one in her pedagogical practice because this is the politically correct thing to do as a white feminist. She does not perceive herself as a racialised being who operates in racialised contexts; instead, her deployment of the subject position middle-class white woman allows her to exercise the privilege of racial invisibility. She is able to have an intellectual relationship to racism that is not personal and does not inform any altering of her subjectivity. "Racism" is thus relegated to something that operates in the public sphere but not the private.

Another feminist located her relationship to racism through her academic engagement. She says that her relationship to racism revolves around the word "racism" and what is associated with that label:

> I am very interested in the way in which our understanding of the language reflects a large part of our mental construct of who and what we are. My interest in psychoanalysis comes about through understanding our psychic relationship to language that I think gives us a transformative potential. Racism and racism in its crude sense of delivering the [inaudible] of cultural otherness as an [inaudible] for criticism is a place of great academic inspiration to work.

Here the person's relationship to racism is one through which she enhances her transformative potential as a feminist. Her intellectual engagement with racism inspires her and enhances her personal development. However, racism here too is treated as something public and external to the subject position middle-class white woman; it is something that one gets involved in by *choice*. Other feminists also implied that they had a choice about being involved in racism for moral as well as intellectual reasons:

> I suppose, in a sense to talk about it in terms of a relationship, it is something that on one level I suspect I see, this goes into a whole set of tensions about ideology and about where I position myself ideologically. I see racism in part, on an intellectual level at least, as a sign

that we have not yet buried what I refer to in some of the things I have written as the old loyalties of hearth and clan in the universal subject which liberalism was supposed to herald, because racism is a way of harping back to ways of defining citizenship [inaudible]. On another level there is another set of things going on which I suspect, on a much more contemporary level, this is true. I believe in Australia [inaudible] racism is one way of enabling members of the dominant group, who perhaps are unemployed or not making it or unsuccessful in a range of ways, to deflect away from themselves any possibility of accepting any responsibility for the fact that they have stuffed up. By laying that responsibility on a group, and it is easy to do it with a racial or ethnic group because there is the definition by visibility. Now so in those two, my understandings of what is going on with responses that are racist, which makes them somewhat less simple than they might otherwise be. The other element I suppose on a moral level is an understanding of it as evil and I have no trouble using the vocabulary of evil myself. I am certainly not a religious person but there is evil and there is good and they are thoroughly clear and distinct. The other thing, of course, it is a learned response.

At an ideological level this feminist understands that the practice of racism is connected to loyalty to the dominant group and allows for the scapegoating of "Others". Morally it is something evil and it is learned. However, white people as the dominant racial group remain invisible. Only the "Other" is visible; white race privilege is not perceived as being inscribed on white bodies. Here one's personal relationship with racism is through a moral position that allows one to put distance between oneself and other members of the dominant group who are evil and racist. By implication one is not an evil person, therefore one is not racist. One can deploy the subject position middle-class white woman to signify virtue and purity, because racism is perceived as racial hatred, not as racial supremacy in which all members of the dominant group are systemically implicated. As another feminist acknowledged:

I spend a lot of my career thinking about it and writing about it and trying to understand. I probably feel that racism is so pervasive in our culture that we never really escape it. It's there. You can consciously overcome a lot of it, you can academically understand it, but I think at some subterranean level it is always there in your psyche and what I am doing as a person who wants to promote social change and to have an Australia where we can have had separate histories but we [inaudible] what we did together and try and take it on from there.

I've overcome it more perhaps than a lot of people. But I think if you are honest there are bits and pieces [inaudible] but you are brought up to think that European culture is superior and that other cultures are exotic and that for various reasons Westerners should have been dominant. It's unfortunate, but what the subterranean things are we don't know, because we want to academicise to a certain degree and in that sense maybe you are not as honest. Maybe the person who just comes out with the abuse is more honest than the highly educated self-aware academic.

This feminist recognises that she has a personal and political relationship with racism that occurs on several levels. She registers discomfort at being in the subject position middle-class white woman because she perceives racism as integral to white culture and recognises the difficulties in struggling to forge out an anti-racist practice. She implies that an intellectual engagement with racism allows one to distance oneself from being personally located within racist practice while she acknowledges that she cannot escape it. Her relationship to racism reveals that, despite her consciousness of the pervasiveness of racism, she chooses to locate her anti-racist practice in an environment where her subject position will be safe, secure and invisible to her students. Her ability to make such a choice is part of her privilege as a middle-class white woman.

Most of these feminists positioned themselves as having an intellectual relationship with racism. It is positioned as an ideological and academic engagement by the subject position middle-class white woman academic and remains something that shapes the lives of "Others" rather than white experiences and choices. The reason one does not have to connect with racism in all aspects of one's life is the inability to see race as shaping one's life, and, as Frye (1983) argues this is part of the privilege of being white. Teaching racism as a people of colour issue fails to interrogate and locate white complicity. Intellectualising about racism allows the subject position middle-class white woman academic to be professionally, but not personally, engaged and is predicated on a mind/body split that works to allow the white female body to be separated from the mind. In other words, the mind creates a virtual non-racialised disembodied subject that knows and practises racism but does not experience it.

Some feminists were more overt than others in distancing

themselves from their white race privilege when describing their relationship to racism; inadvertently whiteness was recentred in their discussions. As one feminist stated:

It's clear to me from the engagements I've had — I've gone out to having engagements about being a white woman — let me just say this straight — you get beaten up a lot — because you get it wrong all the time — you get beaten up for being racist — not in the physical sense — but verbally beaten up and of course you get pissed off because, you know, I am really trying — why won't they accept that I am really trying! Of course, it [is] just like when men were trying to be pro-feminist and they suffered all the time and the women would slap them around and they would think well bugger this for a joke [inaudible] and I won't be a pro-feminist any more. I thought for a long time that I would try harder and get better and better and stop making these mistakes and I'm really learning something in this book about [inaudible] called *Racism and the Lives of Women.* It was written by mainly women working in the counselling type area. This woman described this racial incident where there were two [black] women in the office and one of the white women came in and called her Della for example; in fact the other woman was Della and said it's just an example of racism, we all look the same to them. I was thinking — I've done that — maybe it is! Maybe it is an example of racism and they all look the same, but you sometimes mix all sorts of people up with all sorts — oh God, we will never get it right; it doesn't matter what we do. You know what I mean?

The relationship to racism here is not perceived as being informed by the legacy of white colonisation in Australia, and one is able to distance oneself from white domination by adhering to a liberal position of universal sameness that evades power and erases race. She perceives herself to be a victim of the power relations involved in engaging with the "Other", and by implication the "Other" is not appreciative or grateful for her efforts. Her engagement with the "Other" is something she is doing for them, not for herself; the "Other" is the problem, not white domination. There is a denial of having white race privilege as a middle-class white woman, while being able to exercise it. Despite her intentions to be anti-racist, she preserves the power structure by recentring whiteness, as did others, who said:

I suppose sometimes I wonder whether I am racist — I wonder sometimes whether I don't find myself making allowances for someone because they are from a different race and I must be nice to them and I think that is racist. I think a funny thing about racism — in that basically I am colour blind, I don't actually notice people's race very much, and yet that's not true as I'm aware that this person is Asian and you're Aboriginal and I'm European, but it doesn't impinge on me somehow; they are just people.

I don't think I have to try — I just won't have any feeling about it at all. I don't notice. Well, for example, one of the things that my relatives commented on, when they came out from the country, that there is a lot more Asians around than there were the last time they were here. I don't know, there are just more people around, but I'm not conscious of their background. Is that strange?

The idea that one does not notice colour is an explanation that allows these feminists to distance themselves from racism by rejecting white racial superiority. Both feminists have a relationship to racism that is power evasive in the sense that, if treating or noticing people of colour as different is racist, by implication treating them the same as members of the dominant group is not racist. As Frankenberg points out, if noticing a person's race is not a good thing to do, then by implication colour, meaning non-white, is seen as being bad in and of itself (1993:145). Whiteness is recentred by rendering it invisible, unnamed and unmarked in their relationship to racism. Another feminist said:

I think racism is the thing inside me I must fear and I think that I've had a lot of resistance to wanting to open it. I shudder to think what's there. I also know that [wallowing] in guilt is not the way to deal with that either. We have to figure out what a non-oppressive whiteness can be like, and I think there is a big fear, in that men must fear [in] relation to women. [inaudible] I think there is a difference to sort of throwing that back in a defensive way — oh, you know you are not the only ones — to sort of being aware that it is [inaudible]. We'll ultimately find ways about being assertive without being oppressive [inaudible]. I think the next millennium will be Asian. Obviously the Pauline Hanson stuff taps into the kinds of fears that we have about that, but people dare not talk about it. Bring back the white Australia or something, that is the context in which whiteness has to be renegotiated. [inaudible] I mean, it does mean that in terms of reconciliation and indeed reading out multiculturally, I mean we do that in a sense of not necessarily drawing boundaries about who we are, but enlarging who we are and creating new identities rather than seeing identity as something that is fixed.

There is an implicit acknowledgment about who has power in this statement: white people have to learn to be assertive without being oppressive. What underpins her idea of some form of resolution of racism is to create new identities, which implies that ethnicity is individualistic, voluntary and therefore changeable. Symbolic ethnicities are confined to white Australians, who, as Waters points out, "have a lot more choice and room for manoeuvre than they themselves think they do" (1998:405). Having a place in the centre of white culture confers privilege and the capacity to be able to make choices about one's identity that is not accorded those positioned in the margins.

Race does matter in shaping the meaning and experiences of white feminist academics, for political, historical, economic and cultural reasons. White feminist academics who participated in this study utilise "race" as a marker of difference that is deployed in modes of thinking on race, gender and cultural difference. This illuminates the contradictory and inconsistent, complex deployment of the subject position middle-class white woman. In discursive practices the subject position middle-class white woman remains centred, but is unmarked, unnamed and structurally invisible. White feminist academics perceive themselves as autonomous independent individuals, whose anti-racist practice is orchestrated through an intellectual engagement based on objective rational thinking and behaviour. They speak with certainty and confidence from a subject position structurally located in a white cultural system that exists as omnipresent and natural yet invisible — a cultural system that confers on white people certain privileges and dominance.

The complex and contradictory positioning of white feminist academics on "race" demonstrates that their consciousness of structural inequality, without an interrogation of, and change in, the subject position middle-class white woman, results in intersubjective practice that centres whiteness and reproduces inequality. Teaching "race" in terms of structural inequality more often than not results in reducing it to a biological category that has social consequences only for the "Other". By not naming and interrogating white race privilege in such analyses "race" remains extrinsic to white subjects whose complicity in racial oppression is intentional and unintentional. "Race" remains extraneous to whites and its relevance and meaning is depoliticised for those positioned as "Other".

In their social lives, sociality is restricted to mixing predominantly with one's own race, thereby reducing the chances of evaluating one's anti-racist practice. The lack of sociality with "Others" reinforces the disparity in experience and meaning between women who are "Other" and white feminists in relation to systems of domination and the depth of cultural differences. The knowledge these feminists have about "race" in relation to women who are "Other" is predominantly derived from texts; they have academic knowledge. If there is limited or no inter-subjectivity between women who are "Other" and white feminists, then knowledge of the "Other" is restricted to imagination and theory.

In imagining someone there is never resistance from the image:

> ... for you never find anything in an image except what you put there. You don't investigate or interrogate an image to find out about it; there is nothing to learn from it because it only contains what you posit as being in it. Objects of the imagination only exist insofar as they are thought of, and they can be destroyed by the simple act of turning away from them in consciousness (Spelman 1990:180).

Social distance between white feminist academics and women who are "Other" reduces the risk of disruption to and interrogation of the subject position middle-class white woman. Their white race privilege means that there is no imperative for these feminists to change their sociality. For most of the white feminists, teaching race difference within academic institutions means including the literature of women who are "Other" in the curriculum without challenging the subject position middle-class white woman in either theory or practice. Any inter-subjectivity in the cultural borderland of the university between white feminist academics and the "Other" is always circumscribed by the way in which white normality and otherness is invisibly retained. In effect, the cultural values, norms and beliefs of "Others" are subordinated to those of the institution.

In academic institutions, race privilege accords white feminist academics choices about altering their subject positions to accommodate the "Other's" cultural difference. There is no imperative for them to acknowledge, own and change their complicity in racial domination, because the mind/body split allows them to position "race" as extrinsic. Their anti-racist practice, as an intellectual engagement, is evidence of their compassion, but racism is not experienced as part of their interiority. Their extrinsic and almost extraneous relationship to "race" is evidence of why the subject position middle-class white woman, as a site of dominance, needs to be interrogated.

Making the subject position middle-class white woman visible in white feminist academic discourse can only displace it from the unmarked and unnamed status that is itself an effect of its domination. The dominance of this subject position diminishes the inclusiveness of a politics of difference in Australian feminism. White feminists who teach about "race" leave whiteness uninterrogated and centred but invisible. "Race" and "racism" in relation to the "Other" are important intellectually to the politics of the subject position middle-class white woman academic. However, her anti-racist practice is reduced to teaching within a limited paradigm that has little impact on her subject position both outside and within the university context. Finding ways to put a politics of difference into practice will require more than including Indigenous women in Australian feminism and allowing us to speak. It requires white race privilege to be owned and challenged by feminists engaged in anti-racist pedagogy and politics.

CHAPTER SIX

Tiddas Speakin' Strong: Indigenous Women's Self-Presentation within White Australian Feminism[1]

Feminism was presented initially to me as a political tool that addressed the oppression of Women. When I say I am a Black Feminist I mean I recognise that my primary oppression came as a result of my blackness, my Aboriginality, as well as my womanness and therefore my struggles on all these fronts are inseparable. A willingness and preparedness by white women to listen to Aboriginal women's experiences is not enough. Cultural and racial components of white femininity and histories have to be interrogated and dissected in a relational way, including the limitations of White Feminism, as we know it now (Johnson 1994:256).

As beneficiaries of colonisation, white feminists have challenged, gained concessions and remade themselves as middle-class white women through the state and other institutions in Australia. Although white feminists have theorised for, and about, the social location of Indigenous women and their experiences, they have not written from what hooks calls the "location of experience". She states that "when initiating theory from the location of experience, one can be less concerned with whether or not you will fall into the trap of separating feminist theory from concrete reality and practice" (hooks 1996:18). Due to the legacy of colonisation it has only been since the second wave of feminism in Australia that Indigenous women have engaged with feminist theory and practice, but many remain sceptical of the offer of accommodating difference by allowing us voice and space within feminism. In Australia, white feminists' theory of accommodating difference has often required, in practice, the commitment of Indigenous women to the dominant framework of a democratic white feminism which affords us voice and space while imposing a duty of tolerance for and adherence to its own fundamental values and goals.

This chapter argues that critiques of white feminism by black and Indigenous women challenge the universality of the subject position middle-class white woman in different but interconnected ways. These critiques are grounded in different experiences from those of white feminists, and they expose the reproduction of power relations between the white community and the Indigenous community within feminism. The priorities of Indigenous women are often in opposition to and are different from those of the white feminist movement and the nation state. Indigenous women's political activity and engagement with white feminists in text and practice reveal that, from the standpoint of the subject position "Indigenous woman", incommensurabilities and irreducible differences exist between us and white feminists — differences that are inextricably linked in different ways to the centring of the subject position middle-class white woman.

As knowing subjects, middle-class white feminists and Indigenous women speak from different cultural standpoints, histories and material conditions. These differences separate our politics and our analyses. Indigenous women do not want to be white women; we want to be Indigenous women who exercise and maintain our cultural integrity in our struggle for self-determination as Indigenous people. The chapter begins with an overview of the history of Indigenous women's public political activity since the 1970s. This is followed by an analysis of Indigenous women's self-determination and cultural integrity as incommensurable experiences and irreducible differences. The sexual oppression of Indigenous women is then explored to illuminate the experience of not being located in a white female body. The centring of whiteness in feminism is then unmasked through an analysis of the textual engagement with white feminists by individual Indigenous women.

The public politics of Indigenous women: an overview

Through our oral tradition, Indigenous women learn of other Indigenous women who have been, and are, involved in the political struggle of Indigenous people, whether as grandmothers, aunties, mothers, sisters and lovers or as activists in their own right. And in the documentary records of white people there is evidence of Indigenous women's political activity in the 1800s (Ryan 1986a). It is recorded, for instance, that young Indigenous women were sent by their elders to keep constant surveillance of explorers such as G. A. Robinson in Western Tasmania. Unfortunately, a comprehensive herstory of resistance by Indigenous women has not been researched and documented, unlike the frontier political activism of Indigenous men, which has been recorded in the works of historian Henry Reynolds (1981; 1987; 1989). In the 20th century, particularly in the 1920s, the political activism of William Ferguson and the Aborigines Protection Society is documented and recognised within academic political discourse (Stokes 1997:159–64). However, little is recorded of the Indigenous women who participated in and organised food for political meetings addressed by Ferguson, which were held on reserves and missions in New South Wales. What we do know from the life writing of Indigenous woman Margaret Tucker is that she assisted regularly in setting up meetings in Sydney and relaying information to rural areas on Ferguson's activities. Other Indigenous women, such as Monica McGowan, became involved in Labor politics in the late 1940s, working for the then federal Labor politician Dan Curtin (Clare 1978: xii).

The 1960s and 1970s in Australia proved to be a time of change for Indigenous people. This was due to a number of factors, including white economic prosperity, the Declaration of Human Rights passed by the United Nations, the civil rights movement in the United States, organised Indigenous political action and a change in attitude by the Commonwealth government. Since the late 1950s, Indigenous women such as Oodgeroo Noonuccal (formerly Kath Walker) and Faith Bandler undertook political action to improve the living conditions and legal status of Indigenous people. These women and some Indigenous men were members of the white-majority Federal Council of Aborigines and Torres Strait Islanders (FCAATSI), the organisation that led the campaign to gain support for improving the impoverished conditions of Indigenous people. Roberta Sykes (1989) argues that a change in government attitude to the concerns of FCAATSI came after a meeting with the then prime minister, Sir Robert Menzies, who offered Kath Walker a drink. Sykes writes:

> And Kath Walker replied: "Mr. Prime Minister, if you were in Queensland and offered me a drink like that, you would be put in gaol." The Prime Minister was shocked. There is every likelihood that this small incident was a turning point in history — the highest "citizen" in the land caught out by his country's racist legislation. These laws denied Aboriginal people, including Kath Walker, a legitimate place in their own country, and made it a crime for any citizen to offer — or for an Aboriginal to accept — an alcoholic drink in any circumstances. So it was that, shortly after Menzies' retirement, the government of his successor, Harold Holt, succumbed to growing pressure to place a referendum before the public on the question of rights for Aboriginal people. In May 1967, votes approved the proposal, giving the Federal government power to legislate on behalf of Aborigines, and to include them in the national census. Despite the popularity of the issue at the time, the vote was by no means unanimous (Sykes 1989:2).

However, the referendum did not automatically change the position of the majority of Indigenous women, who lived on missions, reserves and worked for payment in kind on cattle and sheep stations. Hope Neill, an Indigenous woman from Queensland, states that "other rules and regulations which governed our lives were still enforced. We were still given rations of meat, flour, treacle etc. There were still restrictions on our movements on or off the mission, and the managers still had total control over our property and money" (Neill 1989:69). White women had formal citizenship, the right to drink (but not in public bars), and were free to travel.

Major changes in government policy, and political commitment to the improvement of the conditions under which Indigenous people lived, did not occur until after the establishment of the Aboriginal Tent Embassy in Canberra in 1972. The Tent Embassy was set up in the grounds opposite what is now the old Parliament House, in protest at the apartheid conditions under which Indigenous people laboured and to draw attention to our claims to land rights and sovereignty (Sykes 1989:93). Indigenous women, including Cheryl Buchanan and Cilla Prior, were at the forefront of the tent embassy protest and were in the firing line the day the police came to remove the Embassy, as one woman recollects:

> I remember the day so clearly. We were all just standing around the tent and singing. Suddenly the air was charged. The squads of police were coming around the corner. They were marching, and we could hear their bloody big boots coming down on the road. Like that sound you hear in Nazi war films. We kept on singing. Men were on the inside, near the tent, protecting it. Women stood all the way around them. When we saw the police pause for a few seconds, you could tell they were going to attack us so we sent the children out of the way. And then it was on. I couldn't believe it. TV cameras from all the channels blazing, but still them [sic] kept on coming. They beat down all the women, walked over the top of them after they knocked them down, kicked them out of the way, and began slogging into the blokes. Some of the coppers had things held tightly in their hands to give extra weight, ballast, to their punches. They also had other things they hit us with. Some of our people were given electric shocks. It all happened so fast. We think they had electric pig prodders. But the main thing was that they were doing it in public. I don't think for one minute that — for any of the Blacks there it was their first beating from the coppers. But before that, it was all dark lane stuff. In cells. Or in paddy-wagons. No witnesses. If we didn't achieve anything else by that protest, we at least flushed out the truth about police bashing Blacks. The whole world saw it (Sykes 1989:95–96).

Kaplan (1996:143) asserts that a profound difference between white women and Indigenous women is revealed here. She argues that had the protesters been white we would expect the women to be in the middle of the circle surrounded by the men. She is correct to assume that a difference in gender relations is being performed. In Indigenous communities it is usual for women to place themselves between men in their disputes as a way of resolving or diminishing the incident. The Indigenous women at the Tent Embassy maintained their cultural integrity by performing the same cultural practice despite the history of violence suffered at the hands of the police.

After this incident, Labor Members of Parliament in opposition, who were acquainted with Indigenous protesters, capitalised on the event to call for the nation's support. As the future

Labor prime minister Gough Whitlam, then stated, "Our treatment of the Aboriginal people of Australia is the litmus test of
our dedication to justice, peace and equality in the world. By our
conduct in this area, the world will judge us" (Sykes 1989:96).
When Labor came to power in 1972 they created Aboriginal
Affairs as a separate portfolio, and established the Department
of Aboriginal Affairs and an elected National Aboriginal Consultative Committee to provide advice on matters and issues it wished
to raise with government (Rowley 1986:30–42). When Labor lost
office in 1975, the Liberal-National party coalition government
changed the title of the NACC to the National Aboriginal Conference and restricted its role to advising only on matters referred
by government.

The Tent Embassy protests in Canberra highlighted the struggle and impoverished conditions of Indigenous people. Some
white feminists participated in protests and others wanted to hear
more about Indigenous women: Indigenous women were invited
to feminist conferences and rallies. The first recorded major
conference in which Indigenous women participated was the
Women and Politics conference in Canberra in 1975, at which
Pat Eatock, an Indigenous woman, was an official rapporteur
(Eatock 1987:28). At this conference Indigenous women called
for an end to forced sterilisation, instead of supporting the white
feminists' demand for the right to abortion (Burgmann 1993:41).
White women were also seeking the right to say "yes" to their
sexual freedom, whereas Indigenous women wanted the right to
say "no" to sexual harassment. Differences such as these meant
that Indigenous women had limited involvement in what were
fundamentally white women's conferences; we were often positioned as tokens, assimilated or angry, by white participants
(Eatock 1987:27; Huggins 1994:76). Such experiences reinforced
the pattern of white women not respecting our differences as
Indigenous women. It is a pattern repeated many times since the
1970s, for example in the Bell–Huggins debate. In practice, white
feminist organisers failed to change the power relations between
themselves and Indigenous participants, which in theory they
were seeking to overcome. At feminist conferences the agenda
of white women remained centred.

Indigenous women were feeling alienated by the white women's movement. Our concerns were not being supported either within the movement or by the white males who controlled the Indigenous bureaucracy. In the late 1970s Indigenous women publicly sought recognition and implementation of our demands. In 1979 in Sydney, at a Teach-In on Land Rights, Indigenous women passed a resolution requesting the establishment of a Task Force on Indigenous women to evaluate our role and status in the Land Rights movement (Daylight & Johnstone 1986:85). This resolution was forwarded to and supported by the National Aboriginal Conference in June 1979. Indigenous women's issues were gaining momentum. In May 1980 at the Australian and New Zealand Association for the Advancement of Science (ANZAAS) conference, Indigenous women from around the country attended sessions set aside for their participation. They voiced their concerns through resolutions on income maintenance, employment, education, land rights and treaties, community services, health, housing, cultural traditions, child care and social problems (Fay-Gale 1983).

In July 1981 Indigenous activist and lawyer Pat O'Shane was appointed to the Office of Women's Affairs (OWA), which in October 1982 was renamed the Office of the Status of Women. Her appointment, together with the political action taken by Indigenous women, led to the adoption of a more inclusive policy agenda by the OWA. On 27 July 1982 a working party of one member from the OWA, Mary Sexton, and a group of Indigenous women set out the aims for an Indigenous Women's Task Force. The women were Eleanor Bourke, Vera Budby, me (formerly Aileen Buckley), Pearl Duncan, Flo Grant, Marcia Langton and Patricia Williamson (Daylight & Johnstone 1986:86). Indigenous women were committed to the concept of a Task Force, but became frustrated by the lack of commitment by government. Indigenous women in Canberra secured funding to hold a national conference for Indigenous women, which was held in November 1982. This conference saw the establishment of the Federation of Aboriginal Women (FAW). The FAW voted on and established a national executive, of which I was a member, and produced 42 resolutions on political issues, some of which were forwarded to the National Aboriginal Conference (NAC) for action. These issues differed from those of the white women's movement. Indigenous women sought the protection and preservation of Indigenous cultural heritage and customary law; representation and advocacy at all levels of government and in our communities; national land rights legislation; Indigenous people's sovereignty and the adoption of self-determination as policy. Indigenous women also called for improvement in, and the development of, culturally appropriate service delivery in the areas of education and training, employment and income, alcohol and substance abuse, health, housing and legal aid. After its inaugural meeting, the FAW did not receive any further funding and was effectively erased from the political landscape. However, members did have input into the support group of the Task Force that was eventually established in the Office of the Status of Women in August 1983.

The Indigenous Women's Task Force consulted with Indigenous women nationally and provided a report to government in 1986. Since the tabling of the Report of the Task Force three Indigenous women's conferences have been held: the First International Indigenous Women's Conference in Adelaide, 7–18 July 1989; the Remote Area Aboriginal and Torres Strait Islander Women's Meeting in Laura, 1–4 July 1991; and the ATSIC National Women's Conference in Canberra, 6–10 April 1992. A major outcome of the Task Force's report was the establishment of the Aboriginal Women's Unit in the Department of Aboriginal Affairs. After a change of government which saw the Labor party return to power, the Department of Aboriginal Affairs was amalgamated with the Aboriginal Development Commission (ADC) in 1992 to become the Aboriginal and Torres Strait Islander Commission (ATSIC).[3] The Aboriginal Women's Unit became the Office of Indigenous Women, and is located in ATSIC's central office in Canberra. Although there has been a dialogue between the Office of Indigenous Women and the Office of the Status of Women, there has been virtually no policy development between the two offices, because their priorities and issues differ. As Huggins points out, "femocrats have not opened up areas where Indigenous demands are respected and the politics of difference is understood" (1994:75).

Statistically, on all social indicators, Indigenous women are socially separate from white feminists. Indigenous women's life expectancy is 20 years less than that for white women, and at any age we "are more than twice as likely to die as are non-Indigenous people. For those aged 25 to 44, the risk is five times greater than the national average" (Antonios 1997: 24–28). Diabetes affects 30 per cent of the Indigenous population and Indigenous infant mortality is three to five times higher than for white Australia. Infectious diseases in our communities are 12 times higher than in the general population, and Indigenous women's chances of being admitted to hospital are 57 per cent higher than for white women. Indigenous people have the second highest leprosy rate in the world, and Indigenous families are 20 times more likely to be homeless than white families. Nationally, 32 per cent of Indigenous people do not drink alcohol and out of the 68 per cent who do drink, 22 per cent drink at harmful levels compared with 10 per cent of the non-indigenous drinking population in Australia. Only 33 per cent of Indigenous children will complete Year 12 of secondary school compared with 77 per cent of the rest of the population. In 1994 the unemployment rate for Indigenous people was 38 per cent compared with 8.7 per cent of the rest of the population; of the 62 per cent who were employed, 26 per cent work for their social security benefits under community development employment schemes.[4] In 1994 the mean individual income for Indigenous people was 65 per cent of that of the general population. Compared with 29 per cent of white women only 17 per cent of Indigenous women are employed in administrative, professional or para-professional positions. Labour markets for Indigenous women are either in government departments established to fund programs for Indigenous people or government-funded community based service delivery organisations. Few Indigenous women are employed in the private sector (Runciman 1994:47).

Indigenous children are over-represented in corrective institutions. They are more likely to appear before the children's court or panel and be placed in non-Indigenous substitute care as wards of the state. Indigenous imprisonment rates are up to 14.7 times higher than for other Australians (Antonios 1997:24–28). Indigenous women and men represent 40 per cent of the incarcerated population while representing only 2.5 per cent of the Australian population. In the Northern Territory Indigenous women die from homicide 28 times more often than the rest of the population (O'Donoghue 1992:19). A National Police Custody Survey in 1990 revealed that Indigenous people are under-represented in the commission of major crimes such as homicide, theft and robbery, with the exception of assault, but are more likely to be incarcerated for offences such as disorderliness and drunkenness (Kaplan 1996:138).

These social indicators reveal that statistically and corporeally Indigenous women as a group constitute a resource-deprived and underprivileged minority in Australian society. White feminists have less power than white men, but they hold a higher socioeconomic position than Indigenous women (Kaplan 1996; Bulbeck 1997). Differences in socioeconomic positions mean that the life chances, opportunities and experiences of Indigenous women will differ from those of white middle-class feminists. Indigenous women are aware of the discrepancy in socioeconomic status and power between themselves and white feminists, which is why we expect white feminists, who advocate to improve the conditions of all women, to support our claims. The Indigenous custom of sharing, which sets up relations of reciprocity and obligation, also informs Indigenous women's perceptions of being asked to participate in the women's movement. Indigenous women will lend support to white feminists in exchange for their support. However, Indigenous women believe that when white feminists advocate equality for all women, this should mean that the needs of those women who are in the most unequal position in society will be the first to be attended to within the women's movement. Indigenous women assert that by working to improve the conditions of impoverished women in Australia, the status of all women will be enhanced. This differs from the position of white feminists, who aspire to live under the same conditions and have the same opportunities and rights as white men.

Indigenous women's self-determination and cultural integrity

The struggle for Indigenous rights, citizenship rights and justice means that the basis on which Indigenous women challenge the nation state is different from that used by white feminists. Feminists have not challenged the legitimacy of the nation state on the basis of the murder of Indigenous people or the theft of our lands under the legal fiction *terra nullius*. White feminists have challenged the nation state on the basis of, and about, their rights as white female citizens (Watson 1992; Grieve & Burns 1994). Indigenous women give priority to the collective rights of Indigenous people rather than the individual rights of citizenship. This does not mean that they are unconcerned with rights of citizenship or women's representation and advocacy in society. What Indigenous women embrace is a politics of Indigenous rights which encompasses the collective rights of Indigenous people and their individual rights as citizens, as the following resolutions reveal. In 1980 at the ANZAAS conference in Adelaide, Indigenous women resolved that:

> The Australian Aborigines are the land owners of the country. The government needs to recognise this and meet the needs of the Aboriginal people by ensuring land rights, better education, employment and housing (Gale 1983:175).

And in 1989, at the first International Indigenous women's conference, it was recommended "that the State and Federal Governments recognise the right of Aboriginal people to maintain and foster our way of life and our own system of law and self government" (Huggins et al. 1989:8). The demand for the collective rights of sovereignty and rights of citizenship were echoed again in 1992 at the ATSIC National Women's conference, where it was resolved:

1. That we the Australian Aboriginal and Torres Strait Islander Indigenous women demand a commitment of:
   a. the recognition of sovereignty rights of Aboriginal and Torres Strait Islander people;
   b. increased socio economical and political status of Aboriginal and Torres Strait Islander people;

c. the preservation of Aboriginal and Torres Strait Islander culture and customs;

d. introduction of immediate strategies to combat racism;

e. the immediate equitable delivery of quality federal social services to Aboriginal and Torres Strait Islander people (ATSIC 1992:7).

The collective rights of sovereignty are perceived by Indigenous women as being synonymous with the rights of self-determination, which in response to the effects of colonisation and decolonisation, particularly since the 1970s, has become locally and globally the objective of Indigenous peoples. The right to self-determination is embedded in a number of United Nation's conventions as part of the human rights discourse, and is accepted as a fundamental right of all peoples by the international community. Marcia Langton, who worked on developing the United Nations draft universal declaration on the rights of Indigenous peoples, outlines the goals of Indigenous Australian self-determination, which include:

- the right to sovereignty and to self-determination as stated in the draft declaration of indigenous rights prepared in the United Nations;

- the right to self government currently being elaborated by the National Coalition of Aboriginal Organisations;

- land rights legislated at the federal level. The Federal Government should legislate for communal and inalienable landrights for Aboriginal people throughout Australia which recognises Aboriginal sovereign rights and prior ownership of Australia, and which gives Aboriginal people the right to claim all unalienated land including public purpose land;

- the right to control access to Aboriginal land;

- the right to control access to rivers and waterways on or adjacent to Aboriginal land;

- the right to all minerals and resources on Aboriginal land;

- the right to marine resources of the sea and sea bed up to a limit of ten kilometres where the sea is adjacent to Aboriginal land;

- the right to refuse permission for mining and other developments on Aboriginal land;

- the right to negotiate terms and conditions under which developments take place, and the right to statutory and mining royalty equivalents;

- the right to compensation for land lost and for social and cultural disruption;
- the right to convert Aboriginal properties to inalienable freehold title;
- the right, guaranteed by legislation, to living areas or to decisions on pastoral leases, these areas to be of sufficient size to allow for the development of economic activity and to be made available on the basis of need and/or on traditional or historical affiliations.
- All reserves currently occupied by Aboriginal people to be granted to Aboriginal people on the basis of occupation, needs and historical or traditional affiliation by way of direct executive action as for example has occurred in the reserves in the Northern Territory. In the case of the former Aboriginal reserves, which are currently vacant crown land, such land to be granted by way of direct executive action, to appropriate Aboriginal groups. Legislation for national compensation to be based on a formula as a percentage of the Gross National Product, to be agreed to by negotiations between Aboriginal people and the Australian government. These negotiations to be supervised by an internationally respected body acceptable to both parties (Langton 1988:4–5).

Langton's summary of the goals of Indigenous self-determination are clearly not based on the same historical experiences, priorities and practice or theory of the subject position middle-class white woman as are embedded in Australian feminism. The goals of Indigenous women's and men's self-determination are underpinned and informed by the inter-substantiation of relations between Indigenous land, spirit, place, ancestors and bodies. The connection between self-determination and these relations is evident in the words of Barbara Flick, who states:

I say that our struggle for independence is one that could be described as a marathon rather than a sprint — We hunger for the loss of our lands and we continue to struggle for repossession. We continue our demands for our birthrights. We struggle for the rights of our children to their own culture. They have the rights to learn about our religion and our struggle and they need to be instructed by us in the ways in which this world makes sense to us. We'll tell them the stories about our ancestor spirits, their travels and their adventures. And about morality and the attitudes that we have towards all living things in our world. We can make them strong (Flick 1990:65).

The irreducible difference exemplified here, between white feminists and Indigenous women, is the embodied experience of

Indigenous subjects, who have a connection to land that is not based on white conceptualisations of property. Indigenous self-determination thus encompasses our cultural sustenance and our political and economic empowerment; consequently, the nation state is positioned by Langton and other Indigenous women as a contractual partner in negotiations between a nation of Indigenous people and a nation of white people. Indigenous women are committed politically to achieving self-determination and maintaining their cultural integrity. Irene Watson, an Indigenous lawyer, asserts:

> It is vital for our survival as a people to assert the right to self-determination on all aspects of lives — our legal rights, health, housing, education, all functions of our existence must be determined by ourselves, from the perspective of positive Indigenous development and not welfare dependency (1992:180–81).

Indigenous people utilise the contradictory nature of power to position our politics on self-determination. We deploy a politics of embarrassment, which draws on the liberal democratic ideal of equal and human rights for all citizens in our struggle for self-determination, in order to expose the legacy of colonisation. In this struggle, Indigenous women are politically and culturally aligned with Indigenous men because, irrespective of gender, we are tied through obligations and reciprocity to our kin and country and we share a common history of colonisation (Behrendt 1993:32; Dudgeon et al. 1996:54). Individual accomplishment, ambition and rights are the essential values of the white feminist movement, whereas the family and kinship system in Indigenous communities means that Indigenous women's individual aims and objectives are often subordinated to those of family and community. Culturally and politically it is an irrelevant luxury for Indigenous women to prioritise white feminist issues over Indigenous issues for the sake of gender solidarity (Lucashenko 1994:22; Johnson 1994: 256; Behrendt 1993:41).

The goals of self-determination in practice warrant the recognition, acceptance and accommodation of Indigenous cultural differences within Australian society on equal terms with the dominant values, beliefs and practices of white culture. Indigenous women seek to transform cultural and educational institutions so that our ways of knowing will be taught and respected, whereas white middle-class feminists seek to gender institutions from within the epistemological framework of the dominant white culture. Indigenous women's relations to country mean we have specific concerns about the lack of protection of our sacred sites and our lack of formal ownership. Under Australian law it is the Crown who owns our sacred sites not the custodians, Indigenous women. Moreover, "the culture and spirituality [of Indigenous women] is being destroyed at a faster rate than that of Indigenous men", because the patriarchal discipline of anthropology has fundamentally designated Indigenous men as the land owners (Behrendt 1993:28). Indigenous women continue to demand and struggle for the return of our lands, the right to our intellectual property, cultural heritage, religion and spirituality, and the right to learn and pass on our morality, attitudes and world view (Flick 1990:65; Jarro 1991:16; Smallwood 1992:75; Felton & Flanagan 1993:59).

Self-determination for Indigenous people involves cultural practices derived from knowledges that are outside the experiences and knowledges of the white feminist movement. Cultural oppression in the form of the erasure and denial of Indigenous cultural knowledges by white people is a part of our everyday existence; we must participate in a society not of our making under conditions not of our choosing. Ideologically and in practice, white feminists' complicity in reproducing cultural oppression, which renders inferior such "differences", is part of the white patriarchal cultural hierarchy. Feminists exercise their white race privilege in the women's movement because "issues of importance to Indigenous women such as the preservation of culture are not part of the political agenda for white women" (Behrendt 1993:35). As argued in the previous chapter, even where white feminists have made Indigenous women's business a priority, as in the Hindmarsh Island issue, their capacity and ability to support Indigenous women is predicated on the use of their race and class privilege.

Unlike white middle-class feminists, when Indigenous women assert their rights of citizenship in relation to the provision of services from the state they do so on the basis that their cultural difference and integrity be maintained. In the resolutions from the six Indigenous women's conferences, service delivery was identified as inadequate in the areas of: child care; fostering and adoption; employment and income; education and training; family violence; alcohol, substance and sexual abuse; health; housing; law and legal aid; and sport and recreation. In these resolutions Indigenous women advocated that the development and provision of service delivery be culturally appropriate; that more Indigenous people be employed and trained in white departments providing services; that Indigenous people be consulted and provide advice on policy formulation and service delivery; that at the community level Indigenous people determine and have control over service provision; that culturally appropriate information be developed on service delivery for distribution to Indigenous communities; and that white service providers be taught about their racism and the cultures of Indigenous people (Fay-Gale 1983; Omand 1983; Daylight & Johnson 1986; Huggins et al. 1989; Renour 1991; ATSIC 1992). Indigenous women extend the politics of Indigenous rights to encompass self-determination and the rights of citizenship. However, rights of citizenship are not divorced from Indigenous rights. As Gracelyn Smallwood argues, improvements in Indigenous health will be brought about only by Indigenous women and men's ownership of their country and control of its resources, in addition to improved health care provision (1992:73). White middle-class f minists are not by experience and descent situated within a politics of Indigenous rights, as they do not have the same relation ship to the land as Indigenous women; it is outside their bodies, culture, memories and identity.

Representations of the "Indigenous woman" as sexual object

From the time white men invaded our shores Indigenous women's sexuality was, and still is in some discourses, represented as something to be exploited and mythologised (Reynolds 1981). White men misunderstood and ignored the social and political ramifications of participating in the Indigenous protocol of exchanging sex as a means of binding white men into relations of reciprocity and obligation. Conflict usually followed such encounters, when white men did not behave like classificatory male kin who would have reciprocated with goods. White men positioned Indigenous protocol within the 18th century discourse of the sexually deviant native, which was used to justify the rape and sexual abuse of Indigenous women for over a century (Gilman 1992). Pat O'Shane argues that part of the destruction of Indigenous society can be attributed to miscegenation; Indigenous men's dignity and identity has suffered because of the sexual exploitation of Indigenous women (1976:32). In the previous chapter it was argued that miscegenation impacted on both Indigenous men and Indigenous women. White middle-class feminists in the late 19th and early 20th centuries perceived miscegenation as being the result of Indigenous women's sexual promiscuity, lack of dignity and lack of self-respect.

Sexual relations between white men and Indigenous women were of concern to first-wave feminists up until World War II and were still of concern to governments in the 1960s:

> Of the five states and the Northern Territory, four authorities in 1961 exercised control of Aboriginal property; two required consent to marry; four exercised restrictions on freedom to move; two maintained special conditions of employment (and in two others there were *laissez-faire* conditions in the pastoral industry with the Aborigines excluded from the award); all but Victoria had laws against alcohol; four had laws to control cohabitation; three limited the franchise (Rowley 1972b: 401).

Despite prohibitions on cohabitation, the Indigenous population continued to increase. However, the effects of miscegenation have been a burden carried predominantly by Indigenous women and their extended families. Indigenous women who had sexual relations with white men produced children who the men, more often than not, did not support in any way, shape or form. Indigenous women were then positioned in public discourse as being promiscuous. In the 1980s, after Indigenous women were entitled to receive single-parent support, they were labelled as "welfare bludgers" because it was perceived that they were breeding so they could receive welfare payments. Indigenous mothers, judged by the standards of white motherhood and deemed to be unfit, had their children removed from them, usually by white middle-class women who worked for welfare agencies. Huggins argues that

> ... many Aboriginal children have suffered brutally at the hands of white women who have always known what is best for these children. White women were and still are a major force in the implementation of government policies of assimilation and cultural genocide. As welfare workers, institution staff, school teachers and adoptive and foster mothers, white women continue to play major oppressive roles in the lives of Aboriginal women and children. Racism in the welfare and education systems continues to be a major focus of Aboriginal women's political struggles today. These are the issues which Aboriginal women activists often see as priorities rather than those taken up by white feminists (Huggins 1994:75).

Unlike white feminists, Indigenous women are not concerned with child-minding centres for working women. Indigenous women want control of the fostering and welfare of Indigenous children to be placed in the hands of Indigenous people. From 1965 to 1980 approximately 2,000 Indigenous mothers had their children removed from them, some never to be returned (Gale 1983:170). The National Inquiry into the Separation of Aboriginal and Torres Strait Islander Children from Their Families found that from 1910 to 1970 "between one in three and one in ten Indigenous children were forcibly removed from their families and communities" (Wilson 1997:37). The Inquiry also found that Indigenous children who were removed have worse health and are incarcerated more often than the rest of the Indigenous population.

Indigenous women now have the legal right to take the fathers of their children to court for maintenance, but lack the financial support to take such action. Indigenous legal services are so overloaded with criminal work that family law cases do not take priority. Indigenous women called for an extension of Aboriginal Legal Service provision, as is evidenced in the resolution put forward in 1982 by the Federation of Aboriginal Women, which requested

> ... that the Department of Aboriginal Affairs take the necessary action to amend the existing Charter of Aboriginal Legal Services, by the end of 1986, so that the Aboriginal Legal Services broaden their function beyond defending criminal matters to include legal work (Omond 1983:17).

In 1992, after reports from Indigenous women in various communities around Australia about the continued lack of access to legal services, Indigenous women at the ATSIC national conference put forward the following resolution:

> That the Office of Indigenous Women prepare a report to all commissioners, regional councillors and regional women's advisers on the Aboriginal Legal Service, including:
>
> a) all expenditure that involve[s] representation of Aboriginal and Torres Strait Islander women by the legal service.
>
> b) to determine the level and nature of services highlighting any special project involving Aboriginal and Torres Strait Islander women.
>
> c) to ensure that the needs of Aboriginal and Torres Strait Islander women is further addressed with the new funds made available to Aboriginal Legal Service as a result of the Royal Commission into Aboriginal Deaths in Custody (ATSIC 1992:10–11)

Since this resolution ATSIC has implemented an Access and Equity plan designed to make its services, including legal services, more accessible to specific target groups within Indigenous communities (ATSIC 1993). In the past, Indigenous women had no legal avenue to take action against white men even though laws existed that made sexual intercourse between white men and Indigenous women illegal. Police who participated extensively in the same practices did not enforce these laws. Sexual intercourse was, and still is, an important social practice whereby heterosexual identities of masculinity and femininity are reinforced (Sullivan 1995:189). Sexual intercourse between Indigenous women and white men is a social practice which reinscribes white racial superiority into identities of white masculinity, because for over 200 years the Indigenous woman's body has been positioned within white society as being accessible, available, deviant and expendable.

The myth of the sexually promiscuous and deviant Indigenous woman meant that middle-class white women positioned her as competition (O'Shane 1976:33). First-wave feminists wanted Indigenous women removed from the approach of white men and remade in the image of their white sisters, who saw sexuality as inherently degrading (Saunders & Evans 1992; Lake 1996). The

fathering of mixed descent children, while not condoned publicly, was and still is supported by cultural constructions of white
masculinity which subscribe to the myth that male sexuality is an
irrepressible force and male needs must be provided with an
outlet. Indigenous women have been, and are, the object of white
male sexual desires. Although there still is a stigma attached to
such relationships, they are tolerated by white society on the basis
that sex for men is impersonal and biologically driven and Indigenous women are sexually promiscuous and deviant. Middle-class
white feminists have fought for sexual freedom outside marriage
and the right to say "yes" without being positioned as whores
(Summers 1975). Indigenous women, who have been positioned
as sexually deviant whores, want the right to say "no".

This has led Roberta Sykes (1975:301–2) to argue that feminism has not understood who is the true victim of sexual oppression in this country. The sexualisation of Indigenous women has
been and continues today to be one of the means by which white
males exercise their control and reinforce their white privileged
position in Australian society. The black female body has been
represented in the West as an icon of sexual deviance since the
18th century. White men sexualised Australian society by inscrib-
ing onto Indigenous women's bodies a narrative of sexualisation
separated from whiteness (hooks 1997:114). This distance is
evident in the following conversation reported by Sykes. The
white male owner of a cattle station was moving his Indigenous
workers off the property when his brother asked, how could you
do that when you sleep with the women? The white male owner
replied that while he may have sex with black women he never
gets intimate (Sykes 1975:302). Indigenous women were and are
"considered easy game for the racist rapist" (O'Shane 1976:33).
Daisy Corunna recalls her experiences of being a domestic servant in the early 1900s:

> We had no protection when we was in service. I know a lot of native
> servants had kids to white men because they were forced. Makes you
> want to cry to think how black women have been treated in this
> country (Morgan 1987:329).

The rape and sexual abuse of Indigenous women by white men
is tolerated in society because the imagined sexual promiscuity

of Indigenous women is perceived to be biologically driven. Indigenous women are positioned as being either primitive or exotic sexual subjects. As primitive sexual subjects they are seen to be closer to animals than white women and therefore naturally predisposed to sex in any form, which is one reason why Indigenous women find it difficult to report rape.

Two reports on the rape of Indigenous women show that they are more susceptible than white women to rape by white strangers but will more than likely know their Indigenous attacker. The Human Rights Commission's Inquiry into Racist Violence found that it was common for white police to rape Indigenous women after taking them into custody (1991:88–89). Indigenous women's presence in predominantly white social domains is often consciously or unconsciously interpreted by white men as signalling sexual availability. Although white women may be propositioned in the same space, their whiteness means that they will not be approached as often and a rebuff is likely to be interpreted as an insult to the male's ego rather than as a challenge to the white patriarchal supremacy. A rebuff from an Indigenous woman can lead to retribution in the form of verbal or physical abuse or gang rape. Indigenous women have a fear of white social spaces inhabited by white males and will usually not enter them unless accompanied by several Indigenous people. Indigenous women are conscious of their personal safety because their positioning in white society as sexual deviants means that they are represented as being sexually available and easily accessed.

Rape of Indigenous women by Indigenous men occurs in our communities. Payne argues that, unlike white women, Indigenous women are subject to three types of law: "white man's law, traditional law and bullshit law, the latter being used to describe a distortion of traditional law used as a justification for assault and rape of women" (Payne 1990:10). In court Indigenous women who have been raped are subject to white male lawyers who argue what they claim to be the "traditional law" line. They also argue that rape by Indigenous men is part of "murri love-making" and is not as hurtful or serious for Indigenous women as it is for white women (Atkinson 1990:6). Such a positioning supports white ideological constructions of Indigenous women's sexuality as deviant; it is disconnected and different from white women's sexuality. Indigenous women believe that we must empower ourselves to find solutions to problems such intra-racial rape and sexual abuse in order to be self determining as a people (Atkinson 1996:9). At the International Indigenous Women's conference held in Adelaide Indigenous women requested, to no avail, from government

> that funding be provided to train and employ more Aboriginal people, to deal as a priority with the issue of child abuse and emotional abuse, rape, incest, sexual abuse, physical abuse, verbal abuse and emotional abuse (Huggins et al. 1989:15).

Whereas feminists demand legal abortions, Indigenous women want stricter controls over abortions and sterilisations because they have been practised on our bodies without our consent. In the 1970s Indigenous medical services were using Depo Provera as a form of cheap contraception: it did not work and many Indigenous women became pregnant and suffered spontaneous abortions. Depo Provera was banned as a form of contraception in the United States in the 1960s and it was not approved as contraception in Australia, yet Indigenous women were talking of its use when interviewed about contraception by members of the Indigenous Women's Taskforce in 1985 (Daylight & Johnson 1986:64). The Department of Aboriginal Affairs knew of its use and by omission endorsed its application to the bodies of Indigenous women, who experienced the drug's impact, but lacked the power to challenge its widespread use. The Department's sanctioning of such practices indirectly reinforced the racialised systemic oppression and mistreatment of Indigenous women who were denied subjectivity. As in the United States, the use of Depo Provera in Australia can be linked to "the culmination of decades of eugenically informed birth control — promoting white women's fertility while constricting that of black women" (Amos & Parmar 1984:13). When white feminists of the second wave fought to take control of their fertility and demanded contraception, they were not coerced into taking Depo Provera by the state.

Indigenous women's representations of whiteness in feminism

Indigenous women such as Pat O'Shane (1976) and Jackie Huggins (1987) assert that Australia was colonised on a racially imperialistic basis, but such a statement does not assist us to understand the gendered nature of the racism. Both white women and white men benefited from and participated in the dispossession, massacre and incarceration of Indigenous men, women and children, but they did so to different degrees (Sykes 1984:68). White women civilised, while white men brutalised. Whiteness in its contemporary form in Australian society is culturally based. It controls institutions that are extensions of White Australian culture and is governed by the values, beliefs and assumptions of that culture. Whiteness confers both dominance and privilege; it is embedded in Australian institutions and in the social practices of everyday life. It is naturalised, unnamed and unmarked, and it is represented as the human condition that defines normality and inhabits it (Moreton-Robinson 1998:11). For Indigenous women whiteness represents dominance and privilege, which is why the concept "racism" features predominantly as the causal connection in analyses of power relations between Indigenous women and white feminists; the term "white" is used by Indigenous women as an adjective to identify feminism, racism and the beneficiaries of our oppression as well as Australian society (O'Shane 1976; Corbett 1994; Fesl 1984; Watson 1987; Huggins 1987, 1992, 1994; Huggins and Blake 1990; Huggins and Saunders 1993; Willets 1990; Andrews 1992; Liddy-Corpus 1992; Watson 1992; Johnson 1994; Behrendt 1993; Felton and Flanagan 1993; Lucashenko 1994; Wingfield 1994).

In their critiques of feminism, Indigenous and Black women have various positions on the extent and nature of white women's oppression. Some Indigenous women's critiques position whiteness as institutionalised racism in which the cultural pattern of the distribution of social goods and opportunities, including power, regularly and systematically privileges white women on the basis of their race. Roberta Sykes, a Black woman, argues that racism is institutionalised, and is a process that supports the dominant position of white women and white men. Both sexes have benefited from the dispossession and massacre of Indigenous people because they own land and stand to inherit it (Sykes 1984:68). White women have less economic, social and political power than white men but they have more than Indigenous women. Indigenous women such as Pat O'Shane argue that the social organisation of Australian society is based on white male supremacy and that white racism is embedded in the education, political, legal and economic institutions. White values, norms and beliefs permeate these institutions which confer dominance and privilege on both white women and white men. O'Shane identifies the women's movement as "white" because the norms, beliefs and values of the women's movement are those of white women. She states that white women want Indigenous women to be involved but only on the condition that they embrace feminist principles and support a white feminist agenda. O'Shane argues that racism, not sexism, is responsible for the dispossession and resulting disadvantaged position of Indigenous people in Australian society; therefore the women's movement should be fighting racism if white women want sisterhood with Indigenous women (O'Shane 1976:33). Eve Fesl concurs with O'Shane. She argues that Indigenous women do not want to join the women's movement because we have a sisterhood of our own, and it is racism which is the primary form of oppression Indigenous women experience at the hands of white women and white men (Fesl 1984:109). Elizabeth Williams (1987) asserts that racism not sexism is the overwhelming concern of Indigenous people because the priorities of white women are at the expense of Indigenous people's self-determination.

Indigenous women use the concept "racism" to encompass white dominance, privilege, discrimination and Indigenous subordination. Helen Boyle argues that racism and class inequality have placed Indigenous women in the role of the submissive sex in the wider society and the dominant sex within the Indigenous community (Boyle 1983:47). Lila Watson states that she has listened to the voices of women's liberation but they speak only of white women's liberation. Watson argues that white women have not understood Indigenous society and values, so myths and misconceptions have developed over time (1987:7). Jackie Hug-

gins argues that Australia was colonised on a white racially imperialistic basis which gave white women power over Indigenous
men and women. White women have not chosen to examine the
oppression of women by focusing on Indigenous women's experiences; instead they have been concerned with white middle-
class women's oppression. Huggins further argues that white
upper-class women are involved in the exploitation of other
women through their alliances with their husbands and their
economic, social and political commitment to private property,
profiteering, militarism and racism (1987:78). She states that for
these reasons Indigenous women have not joined the women's
movement, which is fundamentally an argument between white
women and white men. Huggins asserts that because of the white
power structure in Australian society Indigenous women's alliances are with the Indigenous liberation movement (1987:79).
She states that white feminists want to recruit into the women's
movement Indigenous women who are compliant and uncritical
of white experts who write and speak about them. She says there
is little evidence of white feminists interrogating their racism and
transforming their behaviour towards Indigenous women; instead, white feminists have sought to control and silence Indigenous women who speak for an anti-racist feminism (Huggins
1994:75–76).

Whiteness as a hegemonic ideology centred in feminism is
evident in the works of Behrendt (1993), Lucashenko (1994) and
Felton and Flanagan (1993). In Behrendt's work the centring of
whiteness in feminism is made visible through exposing the
complicity of white women in Indigenous women's oppression.
Behrendt (1993:29) argues that Indigenous women's herstory is
"one of invasion, dispossession, destruction of culture, abduc-
tion, rape, exploitation of labour and murder". In white people's
history white women are mythologised as the brave women who
fought against the harsh climate, but no mention is made about
how they lived and profited from the land stolen from Indigenous
women. White women have privileges accorded them by their
membership of the dominant group. They have access to more
resources, enjoy a better standard of living, earn more money and
are better educated than Indigenous women. Indigenous

women's priorities are not the priorities of white women; if the specific needs of Indigenous women can be contained within a feminist framework, then resources do not have to be allocated to them and ideologies remain intact. Beherndt argues that white feminism is

> telling Aboriginal women not to see what they see: that their position in society is defined by their gender rather than their race, that the push for rights by white women will empower black women, that we are aligned with white women in the battle against oppression and that white women are as oppressed as we are. We do not believe any of these white lies. The experiences of black women are trivialised when viewed as merely an extension of the experiences of white women — The failure of the feminist movement to meet the needs of minority women shows that just as men in our society will never know what it is like to be a woman, a white woman will never know the reality of living as a black woman (Behrendt 1993:37–43).

Melissa Lucashenko argues that white racism is the dominant form of oppression experienced by Indigenous women (1994:21). For Lucashenko, Indigenous women are not part of the feminist struggle because white hegemonic ideology is subscribed to by white women who rely on their race privilege to remain ignorant and avoid objecting to Indigenous women's oppression. Addressing white feminists, she states that Indigenous women are not a part of the white feminist struggle:

> ... because in 1993 you have little or no understanding of your colonial presence; because you believe the media images of Indigenous women and Indigenous society; because you fail to recognise that Black Australia is as diverse as your Australia; because you think that "part-Aboriginal" is a meaningful concept; because Black Australian history to you is a void or an irrelevance; because no major women's body in Australia has come out publicly in favour of the High Court's native title finding; because women's services have few if any Black workers; because you insist on burying your own racism under an avalanche of pseudo-solidarity; because you do not know whose traditional land you stand on; because you are baffled by the idea that Black women are justified in fearing you; because you want to "help" Black women; because you presume that having attempted our genocide you can attempt our ideological resurrection; because you think that Indigenous culture survived for millennia in this country *without* Black feminists, and because of your imperialist attitude that you alone hold a meaningful concept of female strength and solidarity, for these and for many other reasons, we Black

feminists are not a part of the Australian women's movement (Lucashenko 1994:24).

Felton and Flanagan argue that feminism is an ideology, which belongs to the dominant white culture. Feminism is perceived as a white middle-class movement where white feminist academics centre themselves as the norm (1993:53–54). Felton and Flanagan argue that "white feminists possess an inability to look outside their own cultural perspective. Yet they constantly speak with some apparent legitimised authority about our experiences". White feminists have either positioned Indigenous women as anti-feminist or they attempt to include us by requiring us to assimilate white feminist thought. Felton and Flanagan assert that because white feminists have not challenged racism or placed colonisation on their agenda, Indigenous women perceive feminism as another white politically controlled institution. They argue that a new feminism needs to be constructed through a critique of white women's racism and Indigenous women's experiences of it. Felton and Flanagan conclude by stating that Indigenous women's fight for equality is not about being equal with Indigenous men, but rather having the same human rights as white men and white women. Whiteness is not invisible but is normalised, centred and imbued with power for Felton and Flanagan. White women are positioned as having the power and the belief that they think, feel and act like and for all women.

The identification of white racism as the dominant causal connection in power relations between white feminists and Indigenous women shows that the organisation of social relations and public life on the basis of whiteness plays an important role in the cultural formation of experiences of both Indigenous and white women. A covert subjective experience of white racism is demonstrated in the example given by Pat O'Shane (1976:32–33). When O'Shane was admitted to the Bar, a number of members of the Women's Electoral Lobby in New South Wales would not support a resolution congratulating her on her admission because she did not look Indigenous enough. Through the actions of these white feminists Pat O'Shane was rendered invisible by the forced disappearance of her claim to be Indigenous. She was evaluated as being non-Indigenous on the basis of how whiteness represents Indigenousness. How Indigenousness is defined is also central to the construction of the middle-class subject position white woman because it signifies difference and distance. For the possessors of the middle-class subject position white woman it remains invisible, unmarked and unnamed but centred as the norm in the Women's Electoral Lobby. For Pat O'Shane this subject position was visible and had the power to deny her reality by erasing her Indigenousness on the basis of its white representation. This is a quintessentially Indigenous experience because anthropological representations of the authentic "Indigenous woman" are a part of middle-class white feminist discourse. Therefore, it is not exceptional for an Indigenous woman within Australian feminism to feel that she is defined as a non-entity solely on the basis of being Indigenous (Gould 1992:84).

Indigenous women have been able to occupy a space to challenge the epistemic authority of white feminism through a counter hegemonic discourse. Indigenous women do not want to be white as Joan Wingfield's narrative illustrates:

> When I get together with other Aboriginal and Indigenous women it feels really close. We call ourselves "sisters". Because their society is much the same, they can understand a lot better than most Whites. It's just so much easier getting on with them, because you don't have to explain anything: they understand and accept. We're not all the same, we have differences but they can accept the differences without trying to change us to being the same as them, which is done by White society. Many Whites don't accept differences — they think they're better and that we should change to be like them (Wingfield 1994:154).

Indigenous women's politics are about sustaining and maintaining our cultural integrity and achieving self-determination. Indigenous women's critiques of feminism reveal that second-wave middle-class white feminists have the power to define and normalise themselves within feminist discourse through their centring as the all-knowing subject who constructs the "Other". The middle-class subject position white woman has been historically the symbol of true womanhood in Australian society. This subject position has socially supported race and class privileges and it is deployed in the everyday practices of white feminists and the setting and prioritising of white middle-class feminist goals. It is present by its absence in the sexualisation and racialisation of Indigenous women.

Indigenous women perceive that white women are overwhelmingly and disproportionately dominant, have the key and elaborated roles, and constitute the norm, the ordinary and the standard in Australian society. White women are represented everywhere in Australian feminism, but are not represented to themselves as "white"; instead they position themselves as variously classed, sexualised and abled. In other words, white women are not of a particular race; they are members of the human race (Dyer 1997:3). Felton and Flanagan argue that "white feminists possess an inability to look outside their own cultural perspective. Yet they constantly speak with some apparent legitimised authority about our experiences" (1993:54). For Indigenous women, white feminists centre their own experiences, ideologies and practices as part of their invisible race privilege.

What is evident from the positionings of middle-class white feminists and Indigenous women is that our respective subject positions speak out of different cultures, epistemologies, experiences, histories and material conditions which separate our politics and our analyses. White Australian feminism is incapable of theorising from the lived experience of Indigenous cultural worlds because white culture and history can not link feminists with the land as an Indigenous familial extension. Our claims to land invoke different sets of relations between land, place, people, spirits and history which form the basis of irreducible differences and incommensurabilities between white feminists and Indigenous women. These sets of relations are grounded in a different epistemology that privileges body, place, spirit and land through descent, experience and oral tradition.

CHAPTER SEVEN

Conclusion:
Talkin' Up to the White Woman

... women of color who are feminist live on "the borderlands". We know more than one world and "travel" between different "worlds". In doing so, we develop new experiences, new territories and new languages not known by those who inhabit only one world or speak in only one language. We know possibilities unknown by others. We can develop those possibilities to the enrichment of everyone, but only if we are *subjects*, known and respected as equals in the task of building a new world for all women. If we continue to be treated as *objects* when acknowledged at all, we will never be known by others and perhaps not even fully by ourselves. The richness and knowledge we could offer the feminist movement in general ... will be forever lost. I believe that all of us ... can play a role in steering the feminist movement in this most enriching direction. We are all, together, the subjects and the owners of this movement (Espin 1995:135).

Indigenous women's experiences are grounded in a different history from that which is celebrated and known by those who deploy the subject position middle-class white woman. We know and understand the practical, political and personal effects of being "Other" through a consciousness forged from our experiences and oral traditions. The self-presentation in Indigenous women's life writings, and the strategic deployment of different subject positions to resist white cultural domination, is evidence of this consciousness. The position of Indigenous people on the margins of white Australian society means that subjectivity is circumscribed by the cultural practices and material conditions of the white "Other". Indigenous women are the bearers of subjugated knowledges; our different ethics, behaviour and values repudiate the moral and intellectual hegemony of white domination and oppression. Indigenous women's life writings unmask power relations to reveal that the colonised subject has no choice but to be conscious of the subject position middle-class white woman. Indigenous women have to continually negotiate our subject positions in processes of inter-subjectivity in the cultural borderlands.

The female body is not the site of empathy or unity of all women. Indigenous women's relations with white women disrupt the feminist argument that the transcendent Cartesian self is male because it is disembodied and predicated on the separation of the mind and the body. White women are presented as disembodied and disembedded subjects in processes of inter-subjectivity with Indigenous women. Social and cultural distance, unease, cruelty and racial superiority pervade these processes. Lyn Riddett's (1993:89) analysis of white settler women's relationships with Indigenous women in the Northern Territory explains white women's behaviour in relation to the imperatives of survival. White women's conditioning and acceptance of their pioneering role precluded friendship with Indigenous women and some displayed a maternalism that allowed them to maintain a position of superiority (Jolly 1993). However, imperatives of survival and maternalism do not take account of the extent to which white women's sense of superiority is informed by white masculine values of separateness and independence. The appropriation of these values by those wielding the subject position middle-class white woman makes them complicit with the colonial project.

Indigenous women's life writings reveal white women's involvement in gendered racial oppression as unconscious and conscious subjects. The deployment of the subject position middle-class white woman requires an ideology of true womanhood which positions Indigenous women as less feminine, less human and less spiritual than themselves. Indigenous women's resistance to such definitions shows "we have never totally lost ourselves within the other's reality. We have never fallen into the hypnosis of believing that those representations were our essence" (Dodson 1994:9). The domestic white cultural domain provides the context for a process of inter-subjectivity between Indigenous women and white women. In this domain inter-subjectivity is not based on shared knowledges, common experiences and mutual reciprocity. Instead it is based on a form of interpretative indeterminacy arising from different knowledges, different experiences and structural locations that reinforce the subject position middle-class white woman.

The subject position middle-class white woman has been and continues to be invisible yet represented through deployment in feminist theorising and practice. This subject position is structurally located and embodied in various forms of agency and its meanings are historically constituted in discursive and cultural practices. It is the subject position from which most feminists speak, write and theorise about "difference". Differences such as [non-white] race, class, sexuality, abledness and gender are mapped out in this literature, either as structural markers of oppression or as located within the subject. However, the identification, interrogation and elucidation of whiteness as "difference" are missing from the majority of this literature. This works to avoid an engagement with the Indigenous critical gaze on the white racial subject who constructs and represents the "Other".

White feminists in Australia accept, without criticism, anthropological representations of Indigenous women. These representations emerge as constructs of the methodology deployed by white women anthropologists who objectify and essentialise Indigenous women in their texts. They juxtapose Indigenous women to the subject position middle-class white woman within a traditional versus contemporary binary. The subjectivity of Indigenous women is denied by methodological erasure. White women anthropologists subscribe to a positivist dream of science whereby an empirical world can be captured by observation. They do not perceive their writings to be "partisan, or partial, inscriptions in which language becomes the ambiguous factor of 'truth'" (Chambers 1996:51). Knowledge produced through such anthropological techniques has academic stature and credibility, but often conceals colonial processes that have shaped Indigenous cultural domains. Indigenous women live within those domains and we witness and experience whiteness as being visible and omnipresent. White feminists seek to utilise representations of the Indigenous woman, which reinforce their theorising about the cultural construction of gender. Their failure to interrogate such representations means they effect a Cartesian shift to conceal the subject position middle-class white woman deployed in their gaze. The use of anthropological literature by white feminists in their writings about the Indigenous "Other" relegates Indigenous women to the realm of the abstract.

Colonial processes have shaped white feminists' oblivion to their race privilege and their indifference to the history of their relations with Indigenous women. The exercising of white race privilege therefore remains uninterrogated. The power that whiteness confers is normalised within feminist texts and practice. As beneficiaries of colonisation, white feminists have been able to challenge and remake themselves as white women through the state and other institutions. White feminist alliances with the state maintain the centrality of the subject position middle-class white woman in policies and programs designed for all women. This enables racial and cultural differences to be managed without disturbing normative practices or the structural location of white power and privilege.

The history of white feminist relations with Indigenous women reveals that both first- and second-wave feminists defined and normalised themselves within feminist discourse through their centring as the all-knowing subject who constructs the "Other". The mission of first-wave feminists, who embodied respectability and sexual propriety, was to maintain racial purity by civilising Indigenous women. Despite their theorising on "difference" second-wave feminists seek to reconstruct us in the mould of the white woman feminist. What is evident from the relations between white feminists and Indigenous women is that our respective subject positions speak out of different cultures, epistemologies, experiences, histories and material conditions which separate our politics and analyses. The subject position middle-class white woman has functioned in Australian culture as the embodiment of true womanhood. This subject position informs the everyday assumptions and behaviour of white feminists and underpins the prioritising of their goals over those of the most oppressed group of women in Australian society. All women live with the history of their subjectivity but are not necessarily conscious of its impact on their behaviour and attitudes. White women come to feminism with already formed subjectivities linked to different histories, privileges, power and oppression. They are socially situated subjects who are located in power relations where whiteness remains invisible, natural, normal and unmarked.

My research shows the degree to which white feminists' self-presentation belongs to the white centre in Australian society and is enmeshed in its power relations. As evidenced in Chapter 5, white feminist academics, in expressing their views on race, gender and cultural difference, illuminated the contradictory and inconsistent nature of their representations of these differences. They have an engagement with "Other" within the boundaries of academic institutions and practices. The cultural differences of "Others" are subordinated to these white academic values. White feminists do not have to change their pedagogy to include the "Other". Their sociality outside the university is restricted to mixing predominantly with their own race, which diminishes the chances of evaluating their anti-racist practice. The lack of sociality with "Others" reinforces the disparity in experience and meaning between women who are "Other" and white feminists, thereby reinforcing systems of domination and the depth of cultural differences. White feminist academics engage with women who are "Other" predominantly through representations in texts and imaginings. This "Other" offers no resistance and can be made to disappear at will.

The cultural capital that white race privilege confers means that there is no imperative for these white feminists to change their sociality or their pedagogy. Teaching race difference means including in the curriculum representations of the lives and concerns of the "Other" who are predominantly women located overseas with some inclusion of the "Indigenous Other". This neither challenges nor racialises the subject position middle-class white woman. In academic institutions there is no imperative for white feminists to acknowledge, own and change their complicity in racial domination because they believe it to be extrinsic to them. Their anti-racist practice, as an intellectual engagement, is evidence of their compassion, but racism is not a part of their interiority. Their extrinsic and almost extraneous relationship to "race" is why the subject position middle-class white woman is a disembodied, invisible, racialised subject position.

Making the subject position middle-class white woman visible in white feminist academic discourse reveals the power effects of its invisibility. By making visible the subject position middle-class white woman, this book has sought to show the complexity of, and limits to, relations between white feminists and Indigenous women. To change the power relations between these two groups of women is more complex than giving voice, making space or being inclusive within a white feminist politics of difference. The dominance of the subject position middle-class white woman diminishes the inclusiveness of a politics of difference in Australian feminism because it leaves whiteness uninterrogated, centred and invisible. As Davy argues, "white womanhood needs to be theorised as an institution in the service of white control and supremacy in the same way that heterosexuality has been used as an institution in the service of patriarchy" (1997:213). The knowledge produced from such analyses can inform feminist theory and be used in anti-racist practice.

Indigenous women's challenges to white feminism are informed by our sovereignty. We do not want to be white. Our politics are about achieving self-determination as a people. In our critiques of Australian feminism we make visible how white feminists represent the "Indigenous woman". As Huggins notes, white feminists represent the Indigenous woman, "Other", as being

> based on a menial or sexual image: as more sensual but less cerebral, more interesting perhaps but less intellectual, more passive but less critical, more emotional but less analytical, more exotic but less articulate, more withdrawn but less direct, more cultured but less stimulating, more oppressed but less political than they are (1994:77).

Felton and Flanagan (1993:54) argue that "white feminists possess an inability to look outside their own cultural perspective. Yet they constantly speak with some apparent legitimised authority about our experiences". Indigenous women as embodiments of racial difference can never know what it is like to experience the world as a white woman, just as white women can never know what it is like to experience the world as an Indigenous woman.

To know an Indigenous constructed social world you must experience it from within; to *know about* such a world means you are imposing a conceptual framework from outside. These two ways of knowing inform us that there are limits to knowing an "Other" be they black or white and these restrictions impact on inter-subjective relations and the exercising of power.

The subject position middle-class white woman is embedded in material conditions which shape the nature of power relations between white feminists and Indigenous women. As Sykes states, Indigenous exchanges with white women have been imbalanced. White women have been the helpers and Indigenous women the helped (Sykes 1984:64–65). This inter-subjective relationship maintains the structural inequality between white society and Indigenous communities. As I have argued elsewhere:

> White race privilege in Australia is based on the theft of our lands, the murder of our people and the use of our slave labour. Whites' position in our land and the benefits they reap have resulted from the historical fact of White dominance, which was built upon a belief in White racial superiority. If White people today share the beliefs and values of their White ancestors and enjoy the race privileges established by those ancestors, then by "Whitefella" logic they are complicit in that historical dominance (Moreton-Robinson 1998:7).

White feminist imaginings of these power relations serve to erase the actualities of colonialism and reinforce the dominance of the subject position middle-class white woman. The myth of commensurable difference allows white women to position themselves as gendered, classed, sexualised, aged and abled rather than white. However, the myth of commensurable difference does not work the same way for Indigenous women who perceive whiteness to be overwhelmingly and disproportionately predominant. White women occupy the key roles, they constitute the norm and the ordinary and they represent the standard of womanhood in Australia.

White feminists must learn to accept that Indigenous women's involvement in feminism will be partial due to discrepancies in power, incommensurabilities, different histories, experiences, epistemologies and material conditions. This partiality reflects Indigenous women's understandings that white feminists have the dominant position and that conflict, disruption, dissension, incommensurabilities, consensus and commensurabilities will exist in our relations with them. If Indigenous women's interests are to be accorded some priority, white feminists will need to relinquish some power.

This book has shown that whiteness needs to be interrogated as a specific form of privilege. However, the real challenge for white feminists is to theorise the relinquishment of power so that feminist practice can contribute to changing the racial order. Until this challenge is addressed, the subject position middle-class white woman will remain centred as a site of dominance. Indigenous women will continue to resist this dominance by talkin' up, because the invisibility of unspeakable things requires them to be spoken.

Notes

Introduction

1. Indigenous Australians have appropriated English and created a dialect that functions as a fully sufficient language. I have used Australian Indigenous English in the title of the book and in the titles of the chapters as a way of giving recognition to, and maintaining, cultural integrity within the text. The title of the book, "Talkin' Up," means to speak back. The title of the introduction, "Talkin' the Talk", in Australian Indigenous English means to tell people about what you are going to do.

2. In the book I use the term "Indigenous women" to refer to Aboriginal women who identify as such and are accepted by the community as such. I do not include Torres Strait Islander women as Indigenous women, even though they are Indigenous to the Torres Straits, as this would be culturally inappropriate.

3. I use Patricia Hill Collin's definition of subjugated knowledges. Subjugated knowledges are blocks of historical knowledge that are present and disguised, but not naïve, although they may be made to appear so by those who control the knowledge validation in society. Subjugated knowledge is "a particular, local, regional knowledge; a differential knowledge incapable of unanimity who owes its force only to the harshness with which it is opposed to everything surrounding it" (Foucault in Collins 1991:18).

Chapter 1

1. "Tellin' it straight" in Australian Indigenous English means to speak the truth, to address the heart of the matter.

2. "Country" is the term used to denote a person and their people's place/land created by ancestral spirits. For example, my country is Quandamooka (Moreton Bay) of which my people are the custodians.

3. Indigenous women's life writings referred to in this chapter are: *If*

Everyone Cared (Tucker 1983); *Karobran* (Clare 1978); *An Aboriginal Mother Tells of the Old and the New* (Roughsey 1984); *Pride Against Prejudice* (West 1987); *Through My Eyes* (Simon 1987); *My Place* (Morgan 1987); *Ruby Don't Take Your Love to Town* (Langford 1988); *Wandering Girl* (Ward 1988); *Una You Fullas* (Ward 1991); *Me and You* (Walker & Coutts 1989); *Born a Half-Caste* (Kennedy 1990); *When the Pelican Laughed* (Nannup et al. 1992); *No Regrets* (Edmund 1992); *Aunty Rita* (Huggins & Huggins 1994); *Calling of the Spirits* (Morgan 1994); *When You Grow Up* (McDonald & Finnane 1996); *Follow the Rabbit-Proof Fence* (Pilkington 1996). I have not included the autobiography of Roberta Sykes (1997), entitled *Snakes Cradle*, as she does not identify as an Indigenous woman even though her text shares similar experiences to those of Indigenous women. Roberta chooses to write from the standpoint of a black woman, as she has been unable to validate any Indigenous paternity.

4. I use the term "incommensurability" to refer to "the limits of and the partiality involved in all forms of communication and affiliation across lines of cultural division ... Incommensurability then pertains to the residue of the irreducibly particular that cannot, ultimately, be shared" (Ang 1997:58–59).

5. In the cultural borderlands different cultural knowledges operate in spaces that are always ambiguous because of the overlap in different " frameworks, discursive regimes, and repertoires of meaning" (Ang 1997:60).

6. "Nyungar" is the term used by Indigenous people in Western Australia to refer to themselves; "gengar" means white people.

Chapter 2

1. "Look Out White Woman" in Australian Indigenous English means to visualise or see the white woman.

Chapter 3

1. There has not been the same degree of debate in Australia about the problems associated with anthropologists writing culture. However, some anthropologists have been influenced by, or engaged with, the work of Clifford: for example Cowlishaw 1993; Lattas 1993; de Lepervanche 1993.

2. I analyse the Bell–Huggins debate in more detail in Chapter 4.

3. See Kaberry 1935–36; McConnel 1930, 1934, 1935–36; Pink 1991; O'Gormon 1990; Reay 1970; Berndt 1949–50, 1962, 1964, 1978, 1979, 1981, 1983, 1986; Goodale 1971, 1982; White 1978; Hamilton 1970–

71, 1975, 1978, 1980, 1981; Cowlishaw 1978, 1981, 1982; Bell 1981a, 1981b, 1983, 1984/85, 1993; Merlan 1986; Burbank 1985.

4. Reay 1949, 1951/52, 1963; Barwick 1962, 1973, 1978, 1979; Lilley 1989.

5. It should be noted that Cowlishaw's later works, as referenced throughout this book, do engage with the relations between subjectivity and colonisation.

6. Explicit reference to the role of white women in society is made in the works of Kaberry 1939; Berndt 1978, 1979; Hamilton 1981; Barwick 1978.

7. The "traditional" versus "contemporary" binary was also played out in the dispute over secret Indigenous women's business, which arose, in South Australia over Hindmarsh Island. A Royal Commission was established to ascertain whether or not the claims by Indigenous women to the land concerned were legitimate. Male anthropological evidence given to the Royal Commission stated that there was never any women's business associated with the land in question. For further reading, see Hemming, S. 1996, "Inventing Ethnography" in *Journal of Australian Studies*, No. 48, pp. 25–39; Lucas, R. 1996, "The Failure of Anthropology" in *Journal of Australian Studies*, No. 48, pp. 40–51.

Chapter 4

1. The term "little bit woman" means not quite a woman.

2. The British Commonwealth League was a London based women's organisation, which convened International conferences for Dominion women.

3. I am not implying here that the state positioned white women as full citizens; my point is that the state recognised white women as having a legitimate right to make claims.

4 For a comprehensive overview of the feminist agenda on equality before the law, see the Australian Law Reform Commission Reports No 67 and No 69 Parts I and II.

5. I acknowledge that there are other journals that deal with gender in Australia but I have chosen to focus on these three because they are among the oldest and identify as explicitly feminist.

6. For example of such work in *Hecate* is Lyn Riddett 1993, "Watch the White Women Fade: Indigenous and White Women in the Northern Territory 1870–1940", pp. 73–92; Joanne Scott and Raymond Evans 1996, "The Moulding of Menials: The making of the Indigenous Female Domestic Servant in Early Twentieth Century Queensland", Vol. XXII, No. I, pp. 140–57. Also see Lyndall Ryan 1986a, "Indigenous Women and Agency in the Process of Conquest: A Review of Some

Recent Work" in *Australian Feminist Studies*, No. 2 (Autumn), pp. 35–43. Refer to Chapter 3 for why this is problematic.

7. Bell has written a number of papers on Indigenous women, which are cited in the Bibliography. Her most well-known work, *Daughters of the Dreaming* (1993), is a key text in Australian feminism and anthropology.

8. The conference Bell refers to is the 1984 Women and Labour Conference held in Brisbane. One of the African American women Bell refers to is bell hooks and one of the Indigenous women at this conference was Jackie Huggins, who both took issue with Bell about speaking for Indigenous women (pers. comm.).

9. At the conference our discussion was taped; I do not recollect giving my permission for this to occur. Some time after the conference I was told that a copy of the tape had been sent to Diane Bell in the United States for her information. If this was done, it was carried out without my permission, and, as far as I know, without the permission of Jackie Huggins and Jo Wilmot.

Chapter 5

1. "White Women's Way" in Australian Indigenous English refers to the knowledge, concepts and behaviour of white women.

2. See Kaplan 1996 and Grimshaw 1980.

3. I have not used the women's names in this chapter in order to protect their anonymity.

4. The lesbians did not disclose their sexuality to me during the interview and I did expect them to raise it in relation to my question on cultural difference. I believe they did not disclose any information on their sexuality because they viewed cultural difference as belonging to the racialised "Other".

5. I sent the transcripts to each of the women, as I wanted them to have the opportunity to make amendments and correct any errors, because at times some of their comments were muffled and the tape was inaudible. Where I have used their quotes in this chapter I have done so verbatim, as I did not want to alter their text in any way. Therefore some of the quotes are not grammatically correct, which is consistent with most people's speech patterns.

6. The streets in the centre of the majority of Australian capital cities are named predominantly after members of the British royal family: Mary, George, Albert, Adelaide, Alice, Edward, Ann, Elizabeth, Margaret and Mary.

Chapter 6

1. "Tiddas Speakin' Strong" in Australian Indigenous English means Indigenous women speaking powerfully.
2. Source: *Lousy Little Sixpence* 1982. Director Alec Morgan. Producers Alec Morgan and Gordon Bostock. 16 mm, 54 minutes. Sixpence Production, Chippendale, NSW.
3. The Aboriginal Development Commission was established in 1982 to provide enterprise and housing loans to Indigenous people.
4. It should be noted that the same scheme was not introduced for white people until 1997.

References

Abel, E., Christian, B. & Moglen, H. 1997. *Female Subjects in Black and White: Race, Psychoanalysis, Feminism,* University of California Press, Berkeley.

Aboriginal and Torres Strait Islander Commission (ATSIC), 1992. *Aboriginal and Torres Strait Islander Women — Part of the Solution: National Conference Canberra Act 6–10 April 1992 Report.* ATSIC, Canberra.

Aboriginal and Torres Strait Islander Commission (ATSIC), 1993. *"Part of the Solution" Implementation Progress Report August 1993.* ATSIC, Canberra.

Adleman, J. & Enguidanos, G. 1995. *Racism in the Lives of Women: Testimony, Theory, and Guides to Antiracist Practice.* Harrington Park Press, New York.

Affirmative Action (Equal Opportunity for Women) Act 1986 (Commonwealth).

Albrecht, L. & Brewer, R. M. 1990. *Bridges of Power: Women's Multicultural Alliances.* New Society Publishers, Philadelphia, PA.

Allen, T. W. 1994. *The Invention of the White Race.* Verso, London.

Amos, V. & Parmar, P. 1984. Challenging Imperial Feminism. *Feminist Review.* No. 17. pp. 3–20.

Andersen, M. L. & Hill Collins, P. (eds). 1998. *Race, Class and Gender: An Anthology.* 3rd edn. Wadsworth Publishing Company, Belmont.

Andrews, M. 1992. For My People. In *As a Woman: Writing Women's Lives.* Ed. Scutt, J. Artemis Publishing, Melbourne. pp. 83–95.

Ang, I. 1995. I'm a Feminist but — "Other" Women and Postnational Feminism. In *Transitions, New Australian Feminisms.* Eds Caine, B. & Pringle, R. Allen & Unwin, St Leonards. pp. 57–73.

Ang, I. 1996. The Curse of the Smile: Ambivalence and the "Asian" Woman in Australian Multiculturalism. *Feminist Review.* No. 52. Spring. pp. 36–49.

Ang, I. 1997. Comment on Felski's "The Doxa of Difference": The Uses of Incommensurability. *Signs.* Vol. 23. No. 1. Autumn. pp. 57–63.

Anthias, F. & Yuval-Davis, N. 1993. *Racialised Boundaries.* Routledge, London.

Antonios, Z. 1997. *Face the Facts: Some Questions and Answers about Immigration, Refugees and Indigenous Affairs.* Federal Race Discrimination Commissioner, Human Rights and Equal Opp.ortunity Commission, Sydney.

Anzaldua, G. 1987. *Borderlands La Frontera: The New Mestiza.* Aunt Lute Books, San Francisco.

Apple, M. 1997. Consuming the Other: Whiteness, Education, and Cheap French Fries. In *Off White: Readings on Race, Power and Society.* Eds Fine, M. Weis, L. Powell, C. & Mun Wong, L. Routledge, New York. pp. 121–28.

Armstrong, P. & Armstrong, H. 1986. Beyond Sexless Class and Classless Sex: Towards Feminist Marxism. In *The Politics of Diversity.* Eds Hamilton, R. & Barrett, M. Verso, London. pp. 208–37.

Asad, T. 1973. *Anthropology and the Colonial Encounter.* Humanities Press, New York.

Asad, T. 1979. Anthropology and the Analysis of Ideology. *Man* (N.S.), Vol. 14. pp. 607–627.

Asad, T. 1986. The Concept of Cultural Translation in British Social Anthropology. In *Writing Culture: The Poetics and Politics of Enthnography.* Eds Clifford, J. & Marcus, G. University of California Press, Berkeley. pp. 141–64.

Atkinson, J. 1990. Violence in Aboriginal Australia: Colonisation and Its Impact on Gender. *Refractory Girl.* No. 36. pp. 21–26.

Atkinson, J. 1996. A Nation Is Not Conquered. *Aboriginal Law Bulletin.*Vol. 3. No. 80. pp. 4–9.

Attwood, B. & Arnold, J. (eds). 1992. Power, Knowedge and Aborigines. Special edn. *Journal of Australian Studies.* No. 35.

Australian Bureau of Statistics 1994. *Aboriginal and Torres Strait Islander National Survey.* Australian Government Publishing, Canberra.

Australian Law Reform Commission. 1994. Equality Before the Law: Women's Access to the Legal System. Report No. 67 Interim.

Australian Law Reform Commission 1994. Equality Before the Law: Justice for Women. Report No. 69 Part I.

Australian Law Reform Commission, 1994. Equality Before the Law: Women's Equality. Report No. 69 Part II.

Baca Zinn, M. & Thornton, B. Dill. 1996. Theorizing Difference from Multiracial Feminism. *Feminist Studies.* Vol. 22. No. 2. Summer. pp. 321–32.

Bacchi, C. L. 1990. *Same Difference: Feminism and Sexual Difference.* Allen & Unwin, St Leonards.

Barkley, E. Brown 1997. What Has Happened Here?: The Politics of Difference in Women's History and Feminist Politics. In *The Second Wave: A Reader in Feminist Theory.* Ed. Nicholson. L. Routledge, New York and London. pp. 272–87.

Barrett, M. 1980. *Women's Opp.ression Today: Problems in Marxist Feminist Analysis.* Verso, London.

Barrett, M. 1987. The Concept of Difference. *Feminist Review.* No. 26. July. pp. 29–41.

Barrett, M. & Phillips, A. (eds) 1992. *Destablising Theory: Contemporary Feminist Debates.* Polity Press, Cambridge.

Barwick, D. 1962. Economic Absorption Without Assimilation: A Case of Some Melbourne Part Aboriginal Families. *Oceania.* Vol. XXXIII. No. 2. December. pp. 18–23.

Barwick, D. 1973. Coranderrk and Cumeroogunga: Pioneers and Policy. In *Opp.ortunity and Response: Case Studies in Economic Development.* Eds Epstein,T. & Penny, D. C. Hurst & Company, London. pp. 11–68.

Barwick, D. 1978. And the Lubras Are Ladies Now. In *Woman's Role in Aboriginal Society.* Ed. Gale, F. Australian Institute of Aboriginal Studies, Canberra. pp. 51–63.

Barwick, D. 1979. Outsiders: Aboriginal Women. In *In Her Own Right: Women of Australia.* Ed. Rigg, J. Thomas Nelson (Australia), Melbourne. pp. 85–98.

Baxter, J. 1988. Gender and Class Analysis: The Position of Women in the Class Structure. *ANZJS.* Vol. 24. No. 1. March. pp. 106–23.

Behar, R & Gordon, A. 1995. *Women Writing Culture.* University of California Press, Berkeley.

Behrendt, L. 1993. Aboriginal Women and the White Lies of the Feminist Movement: Implications for Aboriginal Women in Rights Discourse. *The Australian Feminist Law Journal.* Vol 1. pp. 27–44.

Bell, D. 1981a. Desert Politics: Choices in the "Marrige Market". In *Women and Colonisation: Anthropological Perspectives.* Eds Etienne, M. & Leacock, E. Cambridge University Press, Cambridge. pp. 239–69.

Bell, D. 1981b. Women's Business Is Hard Work: Central Australian Aboriginal Women's Love Rituals. *Signs.* Vol. 17. No. 21. pp. 314–37.

Bell, D. 1983. Consulting with Women. In *We Are Bosses Ourselves: The Status and Role of Aboriginal Women Today.* Ed. Gale, F. Australian Institute of Aboriginal Studies, Canberra. pp. 24–28.

Bell, D. 1984/85. Aboriginal Women and Land: Learning from the Northern Territory Experience. *Anthropological Forum.* Vol. V. No. 3. pp. 353–63.

Bell, D. 1987. The Politics of Separation. In *Dealing With Inequality.* Ed. Strathern, M. Cambridge University Press, Cambridge. pp. 112–29.

Bell, D. 1990. A Reply from Diane Bell. *Anthropological Forum.* Vol. 6. No. 2. pp. 158–65.

Bell, D. 1991. Letter to the Editors. *Women's Studies International Forum.* Vol. 14. No. 5. pp. 507–13.

Bell, D. 1993. *Daughters of the Dreaming.* 2nd edn. Allen & Unwin, St Leonards, NSW.

Bell, D. & Nelson, T. Napurrula. 1989. Speaking About Rape Is Everyone's Business. In *Women's Studies International Forum.* Vol. 12. No. 4. pp. 403–16

Bellear, L. 1992. Keep Fighting, Keep Speaking Out. In *Breaking Through: Women, Work and Careers.* Ed. Scutt, J. Artemis Publishing, Melbourne. pp. 57–63.

Berndt, C. H. 1949/50. Expressions of Grief Among Aboriginal Women. *Oceania.* Vol. XX. pp. 286–332.

Berndt, C. H. 1962. Mateship or Success: An Assimilation Dilemma. *Oceania.* Vol. XXX III. No. 2. December. pp. 71–89.

Berndt, C. H. 1964. The Role of Women. In *The World of the First Australians.* Eds Berndt, R. M. & Berndt, C. H. Ure Smith, Sydney. pp. 256–58.

Berndt, C. H. 1978. Digging Sticks and Spears, or, The Two-Sex Model. In *Woman's Role in Aboriginal Society.* Ed. Gale, F. Australian Institute of Aboriginal Studies, Canberra. pp. 64–80.

Berndt, C. H. 1979. Aboriginal Women and the Notion of "The Marginal Man". In *Aborigines of the West: Their Past and Their Present.* Eds Berndt, R. M. & Berndt, C. H. University of Western Australia Press, Nedlands. pp. 28–38.

Berndt, C. H. 1981. Interpretations as "Facts" in Aboriginal Australia. In *Woman the Gatherer.* Ed. Dahlberg, F. Yale University Press, New Haven and London. pp. 153–204.

Berndt, C. H. 1982. Aboriginal Women, Resources and Family Life. In *Aboriginal Sites, Rites and Resource Development.* Ed. Berndt, R. M. University of Western Australia Press, Nedlands. pp. 39–52.

Berndt, C. H. 1983. Mythical Women, Past and Present. In *We Are Bosses Ourselves: The Status and Role of Aboriginal Women Today.* Ed. Gale, F. Australian Institute of Aboriginal Studies, Canberra. pp. 13–23.

Berndt, C. H. 1984–85. Women's Place. *Anthropological Forum* Vol. V. No. 3. pp. 347–52.

Berndt, C. H. 1986. Women and The Secret Life. In *Religion in Aboriginal Australia.* Eds Charlesworth, M. et al. University of Queensland Press, St Lucia. pp. 315–36.

Berndt, C. H. 1989. Retrospect and Prospect: Looking Back after 50 years. In *Women's Rites and Sites: Aboriginal Women's Cultural Knowledge.* Ed. Brock, P. Allen & Unwin, St Leonards, NSW. pp. 1–20.

Berndt, R. M. & Berndt, C. H. (eds) 1987. *End of an Era: Aboriginal Labour in the Northern Territory.* Australian Institute of Aboriginal Studies, Canberra.

Blainey, G. 1966. *The Tyranny of Distance.* Sun Books Pty Ltd, Melbourne.

Bottomley, G. 1994. Living Across Difference: Connecting Gender, Ethnicity, Class and Ageing in Australia. In *Australian Women: Contemporary Feminist Thought.* Eds Grieve, N. & Burns, A. Oxford University Press, Melbourne. pp. 59–69.

Bottomley, G., de Lepervanche, M. & Martin, J. (eds) 1991. *Intersexions: Gender/Class/Culture/Ethnicity.* Allen & Unwin, St Leonards, NSW.

Boyle, H. 1983. The Conflicting Role of Aboriginal Women in Today's Society. In *We Are Bosses Ourselves.* Ed. Gale, F. Australian Institute of Aboriginal Studies, Canberra. pp. 44–8.

Brewer, R. 1993. Theorising Race, Class and Gender: The New Scholarship of Black Feminist Intellectuals and Black Women's Labor. In *Theorizing Black Feminisms: The Visionary Pragmatism of Black Women.* Eds James, S. M. & Busia, A. P. A. Routledge, London. pp. 13–30.

Brewster, A. 1996. *Reading Aboriginal Women's Autobiography.* Sydney University Press, Sydney.

Brodkin, K. 1999. *How Jews Became White Folks & What That Says about Race in America.* Rutgers University Press, New Brunswick.

Bruce Pratt, M. 1992. Identity: Skin Blood Heart. In *Knowing Women: Feminism and Knowledge.* Eds Crowley, H. & Himmelweit, S. Polity Press in association with The Open University, Cambridge. pp. 323–33.

Bryan, D., Dadzie, S. & Scafe, S. (eds) 1985. *The Heart of the Race: Black Women's Lives in Britain.* Virago Press, London.

Bryson, L. 1994. Women Paid Work and Social Policy. In *Australian Women: Contemporary Feminist Thought.* Eds Grieve, P. & Burns, A. Oxford University Press, Oxford. pp. 179–93.

Bulbeck, C. 1993. *Social Sciences in Australia: An Introduction.* Harcourt Brace, Sydney.

Bulbeck, C. 1994. Hybrid Feminisms: The Australian Case. *Journal of Women's History.* Fall. Vol. 6. No. 3. pp. 112–25.

Bulbeck, C. 1997. *Living Feminism: The Impact of the Women's Movement on Three Generations of Australian Women.* Cambridge University Press, Melbourne.

Bunch, C. 1991. Not for Lesbians Only. In *A Reader in Feminist Knowledge.* Ed. Gunew. S. Routledge, London & New York. pp. 319–25.

Burbank, V. 1985. The Mirriri as Ritualised Aggression. *Oceania.* Vol. 56. No.1. pp. 47–55.

Burgmann, M. 1984. Black Sisterhood: The Situation of Urban Aboriginal Women and Their Relationship to the White Women's Movement. In *Australian Women and the Political System.* Ed. Simms, M. Longman Chershire, Melbourne. pp. 20–47.

Burgmann, V. 1993. *Power and Protest: Movements for Change in Australian Society.* Allen & Unwin, Sydney.

Burgmann, V. & Lee, J. (eds) 1988. *Staining the Wattle.* McPhee Gribble/Penguin Books, Fitzroy and Ringwood, Victoria.

Busia, A. 1993. 'and this is what we've decided to tell you after everything we've shared'. In *Theorizing Black Feminisms: The Visionary Pragmatism of Black Women.* Eds James, S. M. & Busia, A. P. A. Routledge, London. pp. 283–92.

Butler, J. & Scott, J. W. 1992. *Feminists Theorize the Political.* Routledge, New York.

Caine, B. & Pringle, R. 1995. *Transitions: New Australian Feminisms.* Allen & Unwin, St Leonards, NSW.

Carby, H. 1997. White Woman Listen! Black Feminism and the Boundaries of Sisterhood. In *Black British Feminism: A Reader.* Ed. Mirza, H. S. Routledge, London. pp. 45–54.

Carlson, D. 1997. Stories of Colonial and Postcolonial Education. In *Off White: Readings on Race, Power and Society.* Eds Fine, M. Weis, L. Powell, C. & Mun Wong, L. Routledge, New York. pp. 137–48.

Chambers, I. 1996. Signs of Silence, Lines of Listening. In *The Post Colonial Question: Common Skies, Divided Horizons.* Eds Chambers, I. & Curti, L. Routledge, London. pp. 47–64.

Charlesworth, M., Morphy, H., Bell, D. & Maddock, K. (eds) 1986. *Religion in Aboriginal Australia.* University of Queensland Press, St Lucia.

Chaudhuri, N. & Strobel, M. 1992. *Western Women and Imperialism: Complicity and Resistance.* Indiana University Press, Bloomington.

Christensen, K. 1997. With Whom Do You Believe Your Lot Is Cast? White Feminists and Racism. *Signs.* Vol. 22. No. 3. pp. 617–48.

Clare, M. 1978. *Karobran.* Alternative Publishing Co-operative Ltd, Chippendale, NSW.

Clark, C. & O'Donnell, J. 1999. *Becoming and Unbecoming White: Owning and Disowning a Racial Identity*. Bergin & Garvey, Westport.

Clark, M. 1969. *A Short History of Australia*. Mentor Books, New York.

Clifford, J. & Marcus, G. E. Eds 1986. *Writing Culture: the Poetics and Politics of Ethnography*. University of California Press, Berkeley.

Clough, P. 1994. *Feminist Thought: Desire, Power and Academic Discourse*. Blackwell, Oxford.

Collins, P. Hill. 1991. *Black Feminist Thought: Knowledge, Consciousness, and the Politics of Empowerment*. Routledge, New York.

Collins, P. Hill. 1997. Defining Black Feminist Thought. In *The Second Wave: A Reader in Feminist Theory*. Ed. Nicholson, L. Routledge, New York. pp. 241–63.

Conboy, K., Medina, N. & Stanbury, S. (eds) 1997. *Writing on the Body: Female Embodiment and Feminist Theory*. Columbia University Press, New York.

Coole, M. 1988. *Women in Political Theory: From Ancient Misogyny to Contemporary Feminism*. Wheatsheaf Books, Sussex.

Corbett, H. 1994. An Interview with Helen Corbett. In *Daughters of the Pacific*. Ed. De Ishtar, Z. Spinifex Press, Melbourne. pp. 154–55.

Cosby, C. 1992. Dealing with Difference. In *Feminists Theorize the Political*. Eds Butler, J. & Scott, J. W. Routledge, New York.

Cowlishaw, G. 1978. Infanticide in Aboriginal Australia. *Oceania*. Vol. XLVIII. No. 4. June. pp. 262–83.

Cowlishaw, G. 1981. The Determinants of Fertility among Australian Aborigines. *Mankind*. Vol. 13. No. 1. June. pp. 37–58.

Cowlishaw, G. 1982. Socialisation and Subordination Among Australian Aborigines. *Man* (N.S.). Vol. 17. pp. 492–507.

Cowlishaw, G. 1986a. Aborigines and Anthropologists. *Australian Aboriginal Studies*. No. 1. pp. 2–13.

Cowlishaw. G. 1986b. Colour, Culture and the Anthropologists. *Man* (N.S.). Vol. 22. pp. 221–37.

Cowlishaw, G. 1986c. Race for Exclusion. *Australian and New Zealand Journal of Sociology*. Vol. 22. No. 1. March. pp. 3–24.

Cowlishaw, G. 1988. *Black, White or Brindle: Race in Rural Australia*. University of Cambridge Press, Melbourne.

Cowlishaw, G. 1990. Feminism and Anthropology. *Australian Feminist Studies*. Vol. 11. Autumn. pp. 121–22.

Cowlishaw, G. 1993. Introduction: Representing Racial Issues. *Oceania*. Vol. 63. No. 3. March. pp. 183–94.

Cowlishaw, G. & Morris, B. (eds) 1997. *Race Matters*. Aboriginal Studies Press, Canberra.

Crawford, E. & Walsh, C. 1993. *Over My Tracks: A Remarkable Life.* Penguin, Ringwood, Victoria.

Creed, B. 1994. Queer Theory and Its Discontents: Queer Desires, Queer Cinema. In *Australian Women: Contemporary Feminist Thought.* Eds Grieve, P. & Burns, A. Oxford University Press, Oxford. pp. 151–66.

Crosby, M. 1994. Construction of the Imaginary Indian. In *Feminist Cultural Politics: By, For and About.* Ed. Waring, W. The Women's Press, Ontario, Canada. pp. 85–114.

Crowley, V. 1993. Aboriginality and Feminism: An Interview with Aboriginal Playwright, Eva Johnson. *Social Alternatives*. Vol. 12. No. 1. April. pp. 13–15.

Crowley, V. 1996. The Darkness Before Our Eyes. Paper presented at the 6th International Interdisciplinary Congress on Women, Adelaide, Australia 21–26 April.

Curthoys, A. 1994. Australian Feminism since 1970. In *Australian Women Contemporary Feminist Thought.* Eds Grieve, P. & Burns, A. Oxford University Press, Oxford. pp. 14–28.

Daly, M. 1978. *Gyn/Ecology: The Metaethics of Radical Feminism.* Beacon Press, Boston.

Daniels, J. 1997. *White Lies: Race, Class, Gender and Sexuality in White Supremacist Discourse.* Routledge, New York.

Davidson, D. 1997. *Women on the Warpath: Feminists of the First Wave.* University of Western Australia Press, Nedlands.

Davis, A. 1982. *Women, Race and Class.* The Women's Press, London.

Davy, K. 1997. Outing Whiteness: A Feminist/Lesbian Project. In *Whiteness: A Critical Reader.* Ed. Hill, M. New York University Press, New York. pp. 204–25.

Daylight, P. & Johnstone, M. 1986. *Women's Business: Report of the Aboriginal Women's Task Force.* Australian Government Publishing Service, Canberra.

de Beauvoir, S. 1983. *The Second Sex.* Penguin, Harmondsworth.

de Lepervanche, M. 1975. Australian Immigrants 1788–1940: Desired and Unwanted. In *Political Economy of Australian Capitalism.* Eds Wheelwright, E. L. & Buckley, K. ANZ Books, Sydney. Vol. 1. pp. 72–104.

de Lepervanche, M. 1993. Women, Men and Anthropology. In *First in Their Field: Women and Australian Anthropology.* Ed. Marcus, J. Melbourne University Press, Melbourne. pp. 1–14.

Delgado, R. & Stefancic, J. 1997. *Critical White Studies: Looking Behind the Mirror.* Temple University Press, Philadelphia.

Dodson, P. 1994. The Wentworth Lecture: The End in the Beginning:

Re(de)finding Aboriginality. *Australian Aboriginal Studies*. No. 1. pp. 2–13.

Donald, J. & Rattansi, A. (eds) 1992. *"Race", Culture & Difference*. Sage Publications and The Open University, London.

Donaldson, L. 1992. *Decolonizing Feminisms: Race, Gender & Empire-Building*. Routledge, London.

DuCille, A. 1997. The Occult of True Black Womanhood: Critical Demeanor and Black Feminist Studies. In *Female Subjects in Black and White: Race, Psychoanalysis, Feminism*. Eds Abel, E., Christian, B. & Moglen, H. University of California Press, Berkeley. pp. 21–56.

Dudgeon, P., Oxenham, D. & Grogan, G. 1996. Learning Identities and Difference. In *Feminisms and Pedagogies of Everyday Life*. Ed. Luke, C. State University of New York Press, Albany. pp. 31–55.

Durkheim, E. 1961. *The Elementary Forms of Religious Life*. Collier Books, New York.

Dyer, R. 1988. White. In *Screen*. No. 29. Fall. pp. 44–64.

Dyer, R. 1997. *White*. Routledge, London.

Eatcock, P. 1987. There's a Snake in My Caravan. In *Different Lives:Reflections on the Women's Movement and Visions of Its Future*. Ed. Scutt, J. Penguin, Melbourne. pp. 22–31.

Edmund, M. 1992. *No Regrets*. University of Queensland Press, St Lucia.

Eisenstein, H. 1984. *Contemporary Feminist Thought*. Unwin Paperbacks, London.

Emberley, J. V. 1993. *Thresholds of Difference: Feminist Critique, Native Women's Writings, Postcolonial Theory*. University of Toronto Press, Toronto.

Espin, O. M. 1995. On Knowing You Are the Unknown: Women of Color Constructing Psychology. In *Racism in the Lives of Women: Testimony, Theory, and Guides to Antiracist Practice*. Eds Adleman, J. & Enguidanos, G. Harrington Park Press, New York. pp. 127–36.

Evans, J. 1995. *Feminist Theory Today: An Introduction to Second-Wave Feminism*. Sage, London.

Evans, R., Saunders, K. & Cronin, K. 1975. *Race Relations in Queensland: A History of Exclusion, Exploitation and Extermination*. University of Queensland Press, St Lucia.

Felton, C. & Flanagan, L. 1993. Institutionalised Feminism: A Tidda's Perspective. *Lilith*. No. 8. Summer. pp. 53–59.

Ferguson, R. Gever, M., Minh-ha, T. Trinh & West, C. (eds) 1990. *Out There: Marginalization and Contemporary Cultures*. MIT Press, Cambridge.

Fesl, E. 1984. Eve Fesl. In *Women Who Do and Women Who Do Not Join the*

Women's Movement. Ed. Rowland, R. Routledge and Kegan Paul, London. pp. 109–15.

Firestone, S. 1970. The Women's Rights Movement in the US: A New View. In *Voices from Women's Liberation*. Ed. Tanner, B. The New American Library, New York. pp. 433–43.

Flax, J. 1987. Postmodernism and Gender Relations in Feminist Theory. *Signs*. Vol. 12. No. 4. pp. 621–43.

Flick, B. 1990. Colonization and Decolonization: An Aboriginal Experience. In *Playing the State: Australian Feminist Interventions*. Ed. Watson, S. Verso, London. pp. 61–66.

Foucault, M. 1988. The Ethic of Care for the Self as a Practice of Freedom. In *The Final Foucault*. Eds Bernauer, J. & Rasmussen, D. MIT Press, Boston. pp. 1–20.

Frankenberg, R. 1993. *White Women, Race Matters: The Social Construction of Whiteness*. Routledge, University of Minnesota Press, Minneapolis.

Frankenberg, R. 1994. Whiteness and Americanness: Examining Constructions of Race, Culture, and Nation in White Women's Life Narratives. In *Race*. Eds Gregory, S. & Sanjek, R. Rutgers University Press, New Brunswick. pp. 62–77.

Frankenberg, R. 1997. *Displacing Whiteness: Essays in Social and Cultural Criticism*. Duke University Press, Durham.

Freud, S. 1983. *Totem and Taboo*. Ark Paperbacks, London.

Friedan, B. 1963. *The Feminine Mystique*. Penguin, London.

Friedman, S. S. 1995. Beyond White and Other: Relationality and Narratives of Race in Feminist Discourse. In *Signs*. Vol. 21. No. 1. pp. 1–49.

Frye, M. 1983. On Being White: Toward a Feminist Understanding of Race and Race Supremacy. In *The Politics of Reality: Essays in Feminist Theory*. The Crossing Press, Trumansburg, New York. pp. 110–27.

Frye, M. 1992. White Woman Feminist. In *Willful Virgin: Essays in Feminism 1976–1992*. The Crossing Press, Freedom. pp. 147–69.

Frye, M. 1996. The Necessity of Differences. *Signs*. Vol. 21. No. 4. pp. 991–1010.

Gale, F. 1970. The Impact of Urbanization on Aboriginal Marriage Patterns. In *Australian Aboriginal Anthropology*. Ed. Berndt, R. M. Australian Institute of Aboriginal Studies, University of Western Australia Press, Perth. pp. 305–25.

Gale, F. 1983. *We Are Bosses Ourselves: The Status and Role of Aboriginal Women Today*. Australian Institute of Aboriginal Studies, Canberra.

Ganguly, I. 1995. Exploring the Differences: Feminist Theory in a Multicultural Society. *Hecate.* Vol. XXI. No. I. pp. 37–52.

Gatens, M. 1988. Towards a Feminist Philosophy of the Body. In *Crossing Boundaries.* Eds Caine, B., Gross, E. & de Lepervanche, M. Allen & Unwin, Sydney. pp. 59–70.

Gatens, M. 1991. *Feminism and Philosophy: Perspectives on Difference and Equality.* Polity Press, Cambridge.

Gatens, M. 1992. Power, Bodies and Difference. In *Destablising Theory: Contemporary Feminist Debates.* Eds Barrett, M. & Phillips, A. Polity Press, Cambridge. pp. 120–37.

Gilman, S. L. 1992. Black Bodies, White Bodies: Toward an Iconography of Female Sexuality in Late Nineteenth-Century Art, Medicine and Literature. In *"Race", Culture & Difference.* Eds Donald, J. & Rattansi, A. Sage Publications, London. pp. 171–97.

Giroux, H. 1997. Racial Politics and the Pedagogy of Whiteness. In *Whiteness: A Critical Reader.* Ed. Hill, M. New York University Press, New York. pp. 294–315.

Goldberg, D. T. 1993. *Racist Culture: Philosophy and the Politics of Meaning.* Blackwell, Oxford.

Golden, M. & Richards, S. Shreve (eds) 1995. *Skin Deep: Black Women and White Women Write about Race.* Anchor Books, New York.

Goodale, J. 1971. *Tiwi Wives: A Study of the Women of Melville Island, North Australia.* University of Washington Press, Seattle.

Goodale, J. 1982. Production and Reproduction of Key Resources Among the Tiwi of North Australia. In *Resource Managers: North American and Australian Hunter-Gatherers.* Eds Williams, N. & Hunn, E. Australian Institute of Aboriginal Studies, Canberra. pp. 197–210.

Goodale, J. 1986. Tiwi World Views and Values. In *Religion in Aboriginal Australia.* Eds Charlesworth, M. et al. University of Queensland Press, St Lucia. pp. 373–82.

Gould, J. 1992. The Problem of Being "Indian": One Mixed-Blood's Dilemma. In *De/Colonizing the Subject: The Politics of Gender in Women's Autobiography.* Eds Smith, S. & Watson, J. University of Minnesota Press, Minneapolis. pp. 81–90.

Green, R. 1980. Native American Women. *Signs.* Vol. 6. No. 2. pp. 248–67.

Grieve, N. & Grimshaw, P. 1981. *Australian Women: Feminist Perspectives.* Oxford University Press, Melbourne.

Grieve, N. & Burns, A. (eds) 1994. *Australian Women: Contemporary Feminist Thought.* Oxford University Press, Melbourne.

Grillo, T. & Wildman, S. M. 1995. Sexism, Racism and the Analogy

Problem in Feminist Thought. In *Racism in the Lives of Women: Testimony, Theory, and Guides to Antiracist Practice.* Eds Adleman, J. & Enguidanos, G. Harrington Park Press, New York. pp. 171–80.

Grimshaw, P. 1980. Women and the Family in Australian History. In *Women, Class and History: Feminist Perspectives on Australia 1788–1978.* Ed.Windschuttle, E. Fontana/Collins, Melbourne. pp. 37–52.

Grosz, E. 1989. *Sexual Subversions: Three French Feminists.* Allen & Unwin, Sydney.

Gunew, S. & Yeatman, A. 1993. *Feminism and the Politics of Difference.* Allen & Unwin, St Leonards, NSW.

Gunn-Allen, P. 1992. *The Sacred Hoop: Recovering The Feminine in American Indian Traditions.* Beacon Press, Boston.

Hamilton, R. & Barrett, M. 1986. *The Politics of Diversity.* Verso, London.

Hamilton, A. 1971. The Equivalence of Siblings. *Anthropological Forum.* Vol. III. No. 1. November. pp. 13–20.

Hamilton, A. 1975. Aboriginal Women: The Means of Production. In *The Other Half: Women in Australian Society.* Ed. Mercer, J. Penguin, Ringwood, Victoria. pp. 167–79.

Hamilton, A. 1978. The Role of Women in Aboriginal Marriage Arrangements. In *Woman's Role in Aboriginal Society.* Ed. Gale, F. Australian Institute of Aboriginal Studies, Canberra. pp. 28–35.

Hamilton, A. 1980. Dual Social Systems: Technology, Labour and Women's Secret Rites in the Eastern Western Desert of Australia. *Oceania.* Vol. 51. pp. 4–19.

Hamilton, A. 1981. A Complex Strategical Situation: Gender and Power in Aboriginal Australia. In *Australian Women: Feminist Perspectives.* Eds Grieve, N. & Grimshaw, P. Oxford University Press, London. pp. 69–85.

Hamilton, A. 1982a. Descended from Father, Belonging to Country: Rights in Land in the Australian Western Desert. In *Politics and History in Band Societies.* Eds Leacock, E. & Lee, R. Cambridge University Press, London. pp. 85–108.

Hamilton, A. 1982b. The Unity of Hunting-Gathering Societies: Reflections on Economic Forms and Resource Management. In *Resource Managers: North American and Australian Hunter-Gatherers.* Eds Williams, N. & Hunn, E. Australian Institute of Aboriginal Studies, Canberra. pp. 229–47.

Hannaford, I. 1996. *Race: The History of an Idea in the WeSt* The Johns Hopkins University Press, Baltimore, Maryland.

Harding, S. 1987. *Feminism and Methodology.* Indiana University Press, Bloomington, and Open University Press, Milton Keynes.

Harding, S. 1993. Reinventing Ourselves as Other: More New Agents of History and Knowledge. In *American Feminist Thought at Century's End: A Reader.* Ed. Kauffman, L. S. Blackwell, Cambridge. pp. 140–64.

Hekman, S. 1997. Truth and Method: Feminist Standpoint Theory Revisited. *Signs.* Vol. 22. No. 2. pp. 341–65.

Hemming, S. 1996. Inventing Ethnography. *Journal of Australian Studies.* No. 48. pp. 25–39.

Hiatt, L. R. 1996. *Arguments about Aborigines: Australia and the Evolution of Social Anthropology.* Cambridge University Press, Melbourne.

hooks, b. 1981. *Ain't I a Woman?: Black Women and Feminism.* South End Press, Boston.

hooks, b. 1989. *Talking Back: Thinking Feminist, Thinking Black.* South End Press, Boston.

hooks, b. 1991. Sisterhood: Political Solidarity between Women. In *A Reader in Feminist Knowledge.* Ed. Gunew, S. Routledge, London. pp. 27–41.

hooks, b. 1992. *Black Looks: Race and Representation.* South End Press, Boston.

hooks, b. 1993. *Sisters of the Yam.* South End Press, Boston.

hooks, b. 1996. *Killing Rage: Ending Racism.* Penguin Books, London.

hooks, b. 1997. Selling Hot Pussy: Representations of Black Female Sexuality in the Cultural Marketplace. In *Writing on the Body: Female Embodiment and Feminist Theory.* Eds Conboy, E. Medina, N. & Stanbury, S. Columbia University Press, New York. pp. 113–28.

hooks, b. & McKinnon, T. 1996. Sisterhood: Beyond Public and Private. *Signs.* Vol. 21. No. 41. Summer. pp. 814–29.

Hooton, J. 1990. *Stories of Herself When Young: Autobiographies of Childhood by Australian Women.* Oxford University Press, Melbourne.

Howard, M. C. 1982. Australian Aboriginal Politics and the Perpetuation of Inequality. *Oceania.* Vol. 53. No. 1. pp. 82–101.

Huggins, J. 1987. Black Women and Women's Liberation. *Hecate.* Vol. 13. No. 1. pp. 77–82.

Huggins, J. 1991a. Theories of Race and Gender. *The Olive Pink Society Bulletin.* Vol. 3. No. 1. pp. 6–15.

Huggins, J. 1991b. Black Women and Women's Liberation. In *A Reader in Feminist Knowledge.* Ed. Gunew, S. Routledge. London. pp. 6–12.

Huggins, J. 1992. But You Couldn't Possibly. In *Breaking Through: Women, Work and Careers.* Ed. Scutt, J. Artemis Publishing, Melbourne. pp. 124–30.

Huggins, J. 1994. A Contemporary View of Aboriginal Women's Relationship to the White Women's Movement. In *Australian Women*

Contemporary Feminist Thought. Eds Grieve, N. & Burns, A. Oxford University Press, Melbourne. pp. 70–79.

Huggins, J., Allen, I., Murphy, J., Davies, D., Hammond, R., Repin, Y. & Saunders, S. 1989. *Finding Common Ground: First Indigenous Women's Conference Report*. Government Printers, Adelaide.

Huggins, J., Willmot, J., Tarrago, I., Willetts, K., Bond, L., Holt, L., Bourke, E., Bin-Sallik, M., Fowell, P., Schmider, J., Craigie, V., McBride-Levi, L. 1991. Letter to the Editor. *Women's Studies International Forum*. Vol. 14. No. 5. pp. 506–07.

Huggins, J. & Blake, T. 1992. Protection or Persecution? Gender Relations in the Era of Racial Segregation. In *Gender Relations in Australia: Domination and Negotiation*. Eds Saunders, K. & Evans, R. Harcourt Brace Jovanovich, Sydney. pp. 42–58.

Huggins, J. & Saunders, K. 1993. Defying the Ethnographic Ventriloquists: Race, Gender and the Legacies of Colonialism. *Lilith*. No. 8. Summer. pp. 60–70.

Huggins, R. & Huggins, J. 1994. *Aunty Rita*. Aboriginal Studies Press, Australian Institute of Aboriginal Studies, Canberra.

Human Rights and Equal Opportunity Commission, 1991. *Racist Violence: National Inquiry into Racist Violence*. Australian Government Publishing Service, Canberra.

Humana, C. 1992. *World Human Rights Guide*. 3rd edn. Oxford University Press, Oxford.

Hurtado, A. 1989. Relating to Privilege: Seduction and Rejection in the Subordination of White Women and Women of Color. *Signs*. Vol. 14. No. 4. pp. 833–55.

Hurtado, A. & Stewart, A. J. 1997. Through the Looking Glass: Implications of Studying Whiteness for Feminist Methods. In *Off White: Readings on Race, Power and Society*. Eds Fine, M., Weis, L., Powell, L. C. & Mun Wong, L. Routledge, New York. pp. 297–311.

Jaggar, A. 1994. *Living with Contradictions: Controversies in Feminist Social Ethics*. Westview Press, Boulder.

Jarro, N. 1991. The Socialisation of Aboriginal Children. *The Olive Pink Society Bulletin*. Vol. 3. No. 1. pp. 15–18.

Jeffreys, E. 1991. What is "Difference" in Feminist Theory and Practice? In *Australian Feminist Studies*. No. 14. Summer. pp. 1–13.

Jennings, K. 1993. Sites of Difference: Cinematic Representations of Aboriginality and Gender. *The Moving Image*. No. 1. pp. 6–78.

Johnson, E. 1994. A Question of Difference. In *Taking a Stand: Women in Politics and Society*. Ed. Scutt, J. Artemis Publishing, Melbourne. pp. 250–58.

Jolly, M. 1991. The Politics of Difference: Feminism, Colonialism and

Decolonisation in Vanuatu. In *Intersexions*. Eds Bottomley, G., de Lepervanche, M. & Martin, J. Allen & Unwin, St Leonards, NSW. pp. 52–74.

Jolly, M. 1993. Colonizing Women: The Maternal Body and Empire. In *Feminism and the Politics of Difference*. Eds Gunew, S & Yeatman, A. Allen & Unwin, St Leonards, NSW. pp. 103–27.

Jones, P. & Howard, S. (eds) 1998. *Bringing Australia Together: The Structure and Experience of Racism in Australia*. The Foundation for Aboriginal and Islander Research Action, Brisbane.

Kaberry, P. 1935/36a. Death and Deferred Mourning Ceremonies in Forrest River Tribes, North Western Australia. *Oceania*. Vol. VI. pp. 33–47.

Kaberry, P. 1935/36b. Spirit Children and Spirit Centres of the North Kimberley Division. *Oceania*. Vol. VI. pp. 392–400.

Kaberry, P. 1939. *Aboriginal Woman, Sacred and Profane*. George Routledge and Sons, London.

Kaplan, G. 1996. *The Meagre Harvest: The Australian Women's Movement 1950s–1990s*. Allen & Unwin, St Leonards, NSW.

Keesing, R. 1987. Anthropology As Interpretive Quest *Current Anthropology*. Vol. 28. No. 2. April. pp. 161–69.

Kennedy, M. 1990. *Born a Half Caste*. Aboriginal Studies Press, Canberra.

Kidd, R. 1996. *The Way We Civilise: Aboriginal Affairs — the Untold Story*. University of Queensland Press, St Lucia.

Kirby, V. 1989. Capitalising Difference: Feminism and Anthropology. *Australian Feminist Studies*. Vol. 9. Autumn. pp. 1–21.

Kirby. V. 1991. Comment on Mascia-Lees, Sharpe and Cohen's "The Postmodernist Turn in Anthropology: Cautions from a Feminist Perspective". *Signs*. Vol 16. No. 2 pp. 394–400.

Kirby, V. 1994. Viral Identities: Feminisms and Postmodernisms. In *Australian Women: Contemporary Feminist Thought*. Eds Grieve, N. & Burns, A. Oxford University Press, Melbourne. pp. 120–32.

Klein, R. 1991. Editorial. *Women's Studies International Forum*. Vol. 14. No. 5. pp. 505–6.

Kohn, M. 1996. *The Race Gallery: The Return of Racial Science*. Vintage, London.

Kumar, R. 1994. Identity Politics and the Contemporary Indian Feminist Movement. In *Identity Politics & Women*. Ed. Moghadam, V. Westview Press, Boulder. pp. 274–92.

Lake, M. 1994. Between Old World "Barbarism" and Stone Age "Primitivism": The Double Difference of the White Australian FeminiSt In *Australian Women: Contemporary Feminist Thought*. Eds Grieve, N. & Burns, A. Oxford University Press, Melbourne. pp. 80–91.

Lake, M. 1996. Frontier Feminism and the Marauding White Man. *Journal of Australian Studies*. No. 49. pp. 12–20.

Landry, D. & Maclean, G.1996. *The Spivak Reader*. Routledge, New York.

Langford, R. 1988. *Don't Take Your Love to Town*. Penguin Books, Ringwood, Victoria.

Langton, M. 1988. The Getting of Power. *Australian Feminist Studies*. Vol. 6. Autumn. pp. 1–5.

Langton, M. 1994. Aboriginal Art and Film: The Politics of Representation. *Race & Class*. Vol. 35. April–June. No. 4. pp. 89–106.

Larbalestier, J. 1977. White Women in Colonial Australia. *Refractory Girl*. March. pp. 54–60.

Larbalestier, J. 1980. Feminism as Myth: Aboriginal Women and the Feminist Encounter. *Refractory Girl*. October. pp. 31–39.

Larbalestier, J. 1990. The Politics of Representation: Australian Aboriginal Women and Feminism. *Anthropological Forum*. Vol. 6. No. 2. pp. 143–57.

Larbalestier, J. 1991. Through Their Own Eyes: An Interpretation of Aboriginal Women's Writing. In *Intersexions: Gender/Class/Culture/Ethnicity*. Eds Bottomley, G., de Lepervanche, M. & Martin, J. Allen & Unwin, St Leonards, NSW. pp. 75–91.

Lattas, A. 1993. Essentialism, Memory and Resistance: Aboriginality and the Politics of Authenticity. *Oceania*. Vol. 63. No. 3. March. pp. 240–67.

Lazreg, M. 1988. Feminism and Difference: The Perils of Writing as a Woman on Women in Algeria. *Feminist Studies*. (14). No. 1. Spring. pp. 80–107.

Lee, S., Maracle, L., Marlatt, D. & Warland, B. (eds) 1990. *Telling It: Women and Language across Cultures*. Press Gang Publishers, Vancouver.

Liddy-Corpus, L. 1992. Taking Control Now. In *Breaking Through: Women, Work and Careers*. Ed. Scutt, J. Artemis Publishing, Melbourne. pp. 21–31.

Lilley, R. 1989. Gungarakayn Women Speak: Reproduction and the Transformation of Tradition. *Oceania*. Vol. 60. No. 2. December. pp. 81–98.

Lipmann, L. 1981. *Genderations of Resistence: The Aboriginal Struggle for Justice*. Longman Cheshire, Melbourne.

Lipsitz, G. 1998. *The Possessive Investment in Whiteness: How White People Profit from Identity Politics*. Temple University Press, Philadelphia.

Lloyd, G. 1989. Woman as Other: Sex, Gender and Subjectivity. *Australian Feminist Studies*. Vol. 10. Summer. pp. 13–22.

Lorde, A. 1983a. An Open Letter to Mary Daly. In *This Bridge Called My*

Back: *Writings by Radical Women of Color*. Eds Moraga, C. & Anzaldua, G. Kitchen Table: Women of Color Press, New York. pp. 94–97.

Lorde, A. 1983b. The Master's Tools Will Never Dismantle the Master's House. In *This Bridge Called My Back: Writings by Radical Women of Color*. Eds Moraga, C. & Anzaldua, G. Kitchen Table: Women of Color Press, New York. pp. 98–101.

Lorde, A. 1992. Age, Race, Class and Sex: Women Redefining Difference. In *Knowing Women: Feminism and Knowledge*. Eds Crowley, H. & Himmelweit, S. Polity Press, Blackwell and The Open University, Cambridge. pp. 47–54.

Lousy Little Sixpence. 1982. Director, Alec Morgan, Producers. Alec Morgan and Gerry Bostock. 16mm, 54 minutes. Sixpence Production, Chippendale, NSW.

Lucas, R. 1996. The Failure of Anthropology. *Journal of Australian Studies*. No. 48. pp. 40–51.

Lucashenko, M. 1994. No other Truth? Aboriginal Women and Australian Feminism. *Social Alternatives*. Vol. 12. No. 4. January. pp. 21–24.

Luke, C. 1996. *Feminisms and Pedagogies of Everyday Life*. State University of New York Press, Albany.

Ma Rhea, Z. 1998. *Production, Reproduction and Dissemination of the Idea of "White" Superiority: A Study of an Academically-Generated Idea in the Universities of the Empire And Commonwealth*. Unpublished paper.

Mackay, N. 1993. Acknowledging Differences: Can Women Find Unity Through Diversity? In *Theorizing Black Feminisms: The Visionary Pragmatism of Black Women*. Eds James, S. M.& Busia, A. P. A. Routledge, London. pp. 267–82.

Magarey, S. Ryan, L. & Sheridan, S. 1994. Women's Studies in Australia. In *Australian Women: Contemporary Feminist Thought*. Eds Grieve, N. & Burns, A. Oxford University Press, Melbourne. pp. 285–96.

Marcus, J. 1993. *First in Their Field: Women and Australian Anthropology*. Melbourne University Press, Carlton, Victoria.

Markus, A. 1994. *Australian Race Relations 1788–1993*. Allen & Unwin, St Leonards, NSW.

Martin, B. 1992. Sexual Practice and Changing Lesbian Identities. In *Destablising Theory: Contemporary Feminist Debates.*. Eds Barrett, M. & Phillips, A. Polity Press, Cambridge. pp. 93–119.

Martin, J. 1980. Non English-Speaking Migrant Women in Australia. In *Australian Women: New Feminist Perspectives*. Eds Grieve, N. & Burns, A. Oxford University Press, Melbourne. pp. 233–47.

Matthews, J. J. 1984. *Good and Mad Women: The Historical Construction of*

Femininity in Twentieth Century Australia. Allen & Unwin, St Leonards, NSW.

McConnel, U. H. 1930. The Wik-Munkan Tribe of Cape York Peninsula: Part 1. *Oceania.* Vol. 1. pp. 97–104.

McConnel, U. H. 1934. The Social Organisation of the Wik-Munkan Tribe. *Oceania.* Vol. IV. pp. 1–3.

McConnel, U. H. 1935/36. Myths of the Wik-Munkan and Wik-Natara Tribes. *Oceania.* Vol. VI. pp. 66–93.

McDonald, C. & Finnane, J. 1996. *When You Grow Up.* Magabala Books, Broome, Western Australia.

McGrath, A. 1984. Black Velvet: Aboriginal Women and Their Relations With White Men in the Northern Territory 1910–1940. In *So Much Hard Work: Women and Prostitution in Australian History.* Ed. Daniels, K. Fontana/Collins, Sydney. pp. 233–93.

McGrath, A. 1993. Beneath the Skin: Australian Citizenship, Rights and Aboriginal Women. *Journal of Australian Studies.* No. 37. pp. 99–114.

McIntosh, P. 1992. White Privilege and Male Privilege: A Personal Account of Coming to See Correspondences Through Work in Women's Studies (1988). In *Race, Class and Gender: An Anthology.* Eds Andersen, M. & Collins, P. Hill. 3rd edn. Wadsworth Publishing, Belmont. pp. 94–105.

McNay, L. 1992. *Foucault and Feminism.* Polity Press, Cambridge.

Meekosha, H. & Pettman, J. 1991. Beyond Category Politics. *Hecate.* Vol. 17. No. 2. pp. 75–92.

Merlan, F. 1986. Australian Aboriginal Conception Beliefs Revisited. *Man* (N.S.) 21. pp. 474–93.

Merlan, F. 1988. Gender in Aboriginal Social Life: A Review. In *Social Anthropology and Australian Aboriginal Studies.* Eds Berndt, R. M. & Tonkinson, R. Aboriginal Studies Press, Canberra. pp. 17–76.

Milech, B. 1996. Counter-Memories, Counter-Identifications: Aboriginal Women's Life Writings. *Australian Feminist Law Journal.* Vol. 7. September. pp. 3–20.

Minh-ha, T. Trinh 1989. *Woman Native Other.* Indiana University Press, Bloomington and Indianapolis.

Mitchell, J. & Oakley. A. 1986. *What Is Feminism?* Basil Blackwell, Oxford.

Moghadam, V. (ed) 1994. *Identity Politics & Women.* Westview, Boulder.

Mohanty, C. 1988. Under Western Eyes: Feminist Scholarship and Colonial Discourses. *Feminist Review.* No. 30. Autumn. pp. 61–88.

Mohanty, C. 1990. On Race and Voice: Challenges for Liberal Education in the 1990s. *Cultural Critique.* Winter. pp. 179–208.

Mohanty, C. Russo, A. & Torres, L. (eds) 1991. *Third World Women and the Politics of Feminism*. Indiana University Press, Bloomington and Indianapolis.

Molloy, M. 1995. Imagining (the) Difference: Gender, Ethnicity and Metaphors of Nation. *Feminist Review*. No. 51. Autumn. pp. 94–112.

Momsen, J. H. & Kinnaird,V. (eds) 1993. *Different Places, Different Voices: Gender and Development in Africa, Asia and Latin America*. Routledge, London.

Moore, H. 1988. *Feminism and Anthropology*. Polity Press, Cambridge.

Moraga, C. & Anzaldua, G. 1983. *This Bridge Called My Back: Writings by Radical Women of Color*. Kitchen Table: Women of Color Press, New York.

Moreton-Robinson, A. 1998. Witnessing Whiteness in the Wake of Wik. *Social Alternatives*. Vol. 17. No. 2. pp. 11–14.

Moreton-Robinson, A. 1999. Unmasking Whiteness: A Goori Jondal's Look at Some Duggai Business. *Queensland Review*. Vol. 6. No. 1. May. pp. 1–7.

Morgan, E. 1994. *The Calling of the Spirits*. Aboriginal Studies Press, Canberra.

Morgan, S. 1987. *My Place*. Freemantle Arts Centre Press, South Freemantle, Western Australia.

Morris, B. 1983. From Underemployment to Unemployment: The Changing Role of Aborigines in a Rural Economy. *Mankind*. Vol. 13. No. 6. pp. 499–516.

Morris, B. 1985. Cultural Domination and Domestic Dependence: The Dhan-Gadi of New South Wales and the Protection of the State. *Canberra Anthropology*. Vol. 8. Nos. 1 & 2. pp. 87–115.

Morris, B. 1989. *Domesticating Resistance: The Dhan-Gadi and the Australian State*. Berg, Oxford.

Morris, M. 1988. *The Pirate's Fiancee*. Verso, London.

Morrison, T. 1993a. *Playing in the Dark: Whiteness and the Literary Imagination*. Picador, London.

Morrison, T. 1993b. *Race-ing Justice, En-Gendering Power*. Chatto & Windus, London.

Moss, I. 1991. *Racist Violence: Report of National Inquiry into Racist Violence in Australia*. Human Rights and Equal Opportunity Commission, Australian Government Publishing Service, Canberra.

Murdolo, A. 1996. Warmth and Unity with All Women? Historicising Racism in the Australian Women's Movement. *Feminist Review*. No. 52. Spring. pp. 69–86.

Nakayama, T. K. & Martin, J. N. 1999. *Whiteness: The Communication of Social Identity*. Sage Publications, Thousand Oaks, London.

Nandy, A. 1994. Culture, Voice and Development: A Primer for the Unsuspecting. *Thesis Eleven.* No. 39. pp. 1–18.

Nannup, A., Marsh, L. & Kinnane, S. 1992. *When the Pelican Laughed.* Freemantle Arts Centre Press, South Freemantle, Western Australia.

Napangardi, G., Nakamarra Long, J. & Vaarzon-Morel, P. 1995. *Warlpiri Women's Voices: Our Lives Our History.* IAD Press, Alice Springs.

Narogin, M. 1990. *Writing from the Fringe: A Study of Modern Aboriginal Literature.* Hyland House, Melbourne.

Neill, H. 1989. One of the Mission Blacks: Girlhood and Education on a Queensland Aboriginal Reserve. In *Battlers and Bluestockings: Women's Place in Australian Education.* Eds Taylor, S. & Henry, M. Australian College of Education, Canberra. pp. 65–75.

Nelson, T. Napurrula. 1991. Letter to the Editor. *Women's Studies International Forum.* Vol. 14. No. 5. pp. 507.

Nicholson, L. 1998. *The Second Wave: A Reader in Feminist Theory.* Routledge, New York.

Nile, R. & Ryan, L. (eds) 1996. Secret Women's Business: The Hindmarsh Island Affair. Special edn. *Journal of Australian Studies.* No. 48. May. University of Queensland Press, St Lucia.

Northern Territory (Land Rights Act) 1975.

Oakley, A. & Mitchell, J. 1997. *Who's Afraid of Feminism: Seeing through the Backlash.* Hamish Hamilton, London.

O'Donoghue, L. 1992. Setting the Scene. In *Aboriginal and Torres Strait Islander Women — Part of the Solution: National Conference Report.* Aboriginal and Torres Strait Islander Commission, Canberra. pp. 17–20.

O'Gorman, A. 1990. Ursula McConnel: A Woman of Vision. *Olive Pink Society Bulletin.* Vol. 2. No. 2. December. pp. 4–9.

O'Shane, P. 1976. Is There Any Relevance in the Women's Movement for Aboriginal Women? *Refractory Girl.* September. pp. 31–34.

Omond, A. 1983. Federation of Aboriginal Women. Aboriginal Women's Action Group Report. Unpublished manuscript.

Oram, D. 1995. *The Enlightenment.* Cambridge University Press, Cambridge.

Paisley, F. 1993a. "Don't Tell England!": Women of Empire Campaign to Change Aboriginal Policy in Australia Between Wars. *Lilith.* No. 8. Summer. pp. 139–52.

Paisley, F. 1993b. Vron Ware, Beyond the Pale: White Women, Racism and History. *Lilith.* No. 8. Summer. pp. 164–67.

Paisley, F. 1997. No Back Streets in the Bush: 1920s and 1930s Pro-

Aboriginal White Women's Activism and the Trans-Australia Railway. *Australian Feminist Studies.* Vol. 12. No. 25. pp. 119–35.

Pateman, C. 1988. *The Sexual Contract.* Stanford University Press, Stanford.

Pattel-Gray, A. 1995. Not Yet Tiddas: An Aboriginal Womanist Critique of Australian Church Feminism. In *Freedom and Entrapment: Women Thinking Theology.* Eds Confoy, M., Lee, D. A. & Nowotny, J. Dove-Harpers Collins, Sydney. pp. 165–92.

Payne, S. 1990. Aboriginal Women and the Criminal Justice System. *Aboriginal Law Bulletin.* Vol. 2. No. 46. October. pp. 9–11.

Perera, S. 1985. How Long Does It Take To Get It Right? Migrant Women And The Women's Movement. *Refractory Girl.* May. pp. 13–15.

Perreault, J. & Vance, S. (eds) 1993. *Writing the Circle- Native Women of Western Canada: An Anthology.* University of Oklahoma Press, Norman and London.

Pettman, J. 1988. Whose Country Is It Anyway? Cultural Politics and the Construction of Being Australian. *Australian Journal of Intercultural Studies.* Vol. 1. No. 9. pp. 1–24.

Pettman, J. 1991. Racism, Sexism and Sociology. In *Intersexions: Gender/Class/Culture/Ethnicity.* Eds Bottomley, G., de Lepervanche, M. & Martin, J. Allen & Unwin, St Leonards, NSW. pp. 187–202.

Pettman, J. 1992. *Living in the Margins: Racism, Sexism, and Feminism in Australia.* Allen & Unwin, St Leonards, NSW.

Phelan, S. 1991. Specificity: Beyond Equality and Difference. In *Differences.* Vol. 3. No.1. pp. 128–43.

Pilkington, D. 1996. *Follow the Rabbit-Proof Fence.* University of Queensland Press, St Lucia.

Pink, O. 1935–36. The Landowners in the Northern Division of the Aranda Tribe, Central Australia. *Oceania.* Vol. VI. No. 2. pp. 275–322.

Pink, O. 1991. Australian Aborigines: What Is Their Future? Dictation or Freedom in Civilisation. *Olive Pink Society Bulletin.* Vol. 3. No. 1. March. pp. 4–5.

Pollock, G. 1988. *Vision and Difference.* Routledge, London.

Prakash, G. 1995. *After Colonialism: Imperial Histories and Postcolonial Displacements.* Princeton University Press, Princeton, New Jersey.

Pritchard, S. 1998. *Indigenous Peoples, the United Nations and Human Rights.* Zed Books, The Federation Press, Leichhardt.

Radcliffe-Brown. A. R. 1930. Editorial. *Oceania.* Vol 1. No.1. April. pp. 1–4.

Reagon, B. J. 1983. Coalition Politics: Turning the Century. In *Home Girls:*

A Black Feminist Anthology. Ed. Smith, B. Kitchen Table: Women of Color Press, New York. pp. 356–68.

Reay, M. & Sitlington, G. 1948. Class and Status in a Mixed-Blood Community. *Oceania.* Vol. XVIII. pp. 179–207.

Reay, M. 1949. Native Thought in Rural New South Wales. *Oceania.* Vol XX. No. 2. December. pp. 89–118.

Reay, M. 1951–52. A Survey of the Marital Conditions of 264 Aboriginal and Mixed-Blood Women. *Oceania.* Vol XXII. pp. 116–29.

Reay, M. 1962. Subsections At Borroloola. *Oceania.* Vol XXXIII. No. 2. pp. 90–115.

Reay, M. 1963. The Social Position of Women. In *Australian Aboriginal Studies.* Eds Stanner, W. E. H. & Sheils, H. Oxford University Press, Oxford. pp. 319–45.

Reay, M. 1970. Decision as Narrative. In *Australian Aboriginal Anthropology.* Ed. Berndt. R. M. University of Western Australia Press, Nedlands. pp. 164–73.

Reddy, M. 1994. *Crossing the Colour Line: Race, Parenting and Culture.* Rutgers University Press, New Brunswick, New Jersey.

Renouf, E. 1991. *Remote Area Aboriginal and Torres Strait Islander Women's Meeting July, 1991 Report.* Women's Policy Unit, Office of Cabinet, North Quay, Brisbane.

Reynolds, H. 1981. *The Other Side of the Frontier.* James Cook University Press, Townsville.

Reynolds, H. 1987. *The Law of the Land.* Penguin, Ringwood.

Reynolds, H. 1989. *Dispossession, Black Australians and White Invaders.* Allen & Unwin, St Leonards, NSW.

Reynolds, H. 1990. *With the White People: The Crucial Role of Aborigines in the Development of Australia.* Penguin, Ringwood.

Rich, A. 1977. *Of Woman Born: Motherhood As Experience and Institution.* Virago, London.

Rich, A. (ed.) 1979. Disloyal to Civilization: Feminism, Racism, Gynephobia (1978). In *On Lies, Secrets and Silence: Selected Prose 1966–1978.* W. W. Norton & Company, New York. pp. 275–310.

Riddett, L. 1993. Watch the White Woman Fade: Aboriginal and White Women in the Northern Territory 1870–1940. *Hecate.* Vol. IV. No. 2. pp. 73–92.

Roediger, D. R. 1998. *Black on White: Black Writers on What It Means To Be White.* Schocken Books, New York.

Rosaldo, M. 1980. The Use and Abuse of Anthropology: Reflections on Feminism and Cross-Cultural Understandi.ig. *Signs.* Vol. 5. No. 3. pp. 389–417.

Rosaldo, M. 1984. Towards an Anthropology of Self and Feeling. In

Culture Theory: Essays on Mind, Self and Emotion. Eds Shweder, R & LeVine, R. A. Cambridge University Press, Cambridge. pp. 137–57.

Rothfield, P. 1994. A Narrative on the Limits of Theory. In *Australian Women: Contemporary Feminist Thought.* Eds Grieve, N. & Burns, A. Oxford University Press, Melbourne. pp. 108–20.

Roughsey, E. 1984. *An Aboriginal Mother Tells of the Old and the New.* McPhee Gribble/Penguin Books, Fitzroy, Victoria.

Rowland, R. 1987. *Made to Order: The Myth of Reproductive and Genetic Progress.* Pergamon Press, London.

Rowley, C. D. 1972a. *The Remote Aborigines.* Penguin Books, Ringwood.

Rowley, C. D. 1972b. *Outcasts in White Australia.* Penguin Books, Ringwood.

Rowley, C. D. 1986. *Recovery: The Politics of Aboriginal Reform.* Penguin, Melbourne.

Runciman, C. 1994. *Elevating Choice: A Study of Aboriginal Women's Labour Market Participation in South-East Queensland.* Australian Government Publishing Service, Canberra.

Russo, A. 1991. We Cannot Live without Our Lives: White Women, Antiracism and Feminism. In *Third World Women and the Politics of Feminism.* Eds Mohanty, C., Russo, A. & Torres, L. Indiana University Press, Bloomington and Indianapolis. pp. 297–313.

Ryan, L. 1986a. Aboriginal Women and Agency in the Process of Conquest: A Review of Some Recent Work. *Australian Feminist Studies.* No. 2. Autumn. pp. 35–44.

Ryan, L. 1986b. Reading Aboriginal Histories. *Meanjin.* Vol. 45. No.1. pp. 49–57.

Sacks, K. Brodkin 1994. How Did Jews Become White Folks? In *Race.* Eds Gregory, S. & Sanjek, R. Rutgers University Press, New Brunswick. pp. 78–102.

Said, E. W. 1993. *Culture and Imperialism.* Chatto & Windus, London.

Said, E. W. 1994. *Representations of the Intellectual.* Vintage, London.

Saunders, K. 1991. All the Women Were White? Some Thoughts on Analysing Race, Class and Gender in Australian History. In *Hecate.* Vol 17. No. 1. pp. 157–60.

Saunders, K. & Bolton, G. 1992. Girdled for War: Women's Mobilisations in World War Two. In *Gender Relations in Australia, Domination and Negotiation.* Eds Saunders, K & Evans, R. Harcourt Brace Jovanovich, Sydney. pp. 376–95.

Saunders, K. & Evans, E. 1992. *Gender Relations in Australia: Domination and Negotiation.* Harcourt Brace Jovanovich, Sydney.

Scott, J. & Evans, R. 1996. The Moulding of Menials: The Making of the

Aboriginal Female Domestic Servant in Early Twentieth Century Queensland. *Hecate.* Vol XXII. No. 1. pp. 140–57.

Sheridan, S. 1988a. Introduction. In *Grafts: Feminist Cultural Criticism.* Versco, New York. pp. 1–9.

Sheridan, S. 1988b. Wives and Mothers Like Ourselves, Poor Remnants of a Dying Race: Aborigines in Colonial Women's Writing. In *Aboriginal Culture Today.* Ed. Rutherford, A. Dangaroo Press, Sydney. pp. 76–91.

Simms, M. 1981. The Australian Feminist Experience. In *Australian Women Feminist Perspectives.* Eds Grieve, N. & Grimshaw, P. Oxford University Press, Melbourne. pp. 227–39.

Simon, E. 1987. *Through My Eyes.* Collins Dove, Blackburn, Victoria.

Smallwood, G. 1992. Demanding More Than a Great Vocabulary. In *Breaking Through: Women, Work and Careers.* Ed. Scutt, J. Artemis Publishing, Melbourne. pp. 71–80.

Smith, B. 1983. *Home Girls: A Black Feminist Anthology.* Kitchen Table: Women of Color Press, New York.

Smith, D. 1991. Writing Women's Experience into Social Science. *Feminism & Psychology.* Vol.1. No.1. pp. 155–69.

Smith, D. 1999. *Writing the Social: Critique, Theory and Investigations,* University of Toronto Press, Toronto.

Spearritt, K. 1992. New Dawns, First Wave Feminism 1880–1914. In *Gender Relations in Australia, Domination and Negotiation.* Eds Saunders, K & Evans, R. Harcourt Brace Jovanovich, Sydney. pp. 325–49.

Spelman, E. 1990. *Inessential Woman: Problems of Exclusion in Feminist Thought..* The Women's Press, London.

Spivak, G. 1988a. Can the Subaltern Speak? In *Marxism and the Interpretation of Culture.* Eds Nelson, C. & Grossberg, L. University of Illinois Press, Illinois. pp. 271–313.

Spivak, G. 1988b. *In Other Worlds: Essays in Culural Politics.* Routledge, New York.

Spivak, G. 1992. The Politics of Translation. In *Destablising Theory: Contemporary Feminist Debates.* Eds Barrett. M. & Phillips. A. Polity Press, Cambridge. pp. 177–200.

Stanner, W. E. H. 1979. *White Man Got No Dreaming.* Australian National University Press, Canberra.

Stephenson, P. 1994. Difference or Indifference?: Aboriginal Women and Australian Feminism. Honours Thesis. Faculty of Humanities, Griffith University.

Stokes, G. 1997. *The Politics of Identity in Australia.* Cambridge University Press, Melbourne.

Stivens, M. 1994. The Gendering of Knowledge: The Case of Anthropology and Feminism. In *Australian Women: Contemporary Feminist Thought*. Eds Grieve, N. & Burns, A. Oxford University Press, Melbourne. pp. 133–41.

Sullivan, B. 1995. Rethinking Prostitution. In *Transitions: New Australian Feminisms*. Eds Caine, B. & Pringle, R. Allen & Unwin. St Leonards, NSW. pp. 184–97.

Sunder Rajan, R. 1993. *Real and Imagined Women: Gender, Culture and Postcolonialism*. Routledge, London.

Summers, A. 1975. *Damned Whores & God's Police: the Colonization of Women in Australia*. Penguin, Ringwood.

Sykes, R. 1975. Black Women in Australia — A History. In *The Other Half: Women in Australian Society*. Ed. Mercer, J. Penguin Books, Ringwood. pp. 313–21.

Sykes, R. 1984. Bobbi Sykes. In *Women Who Do and Women Who Do Not Join the Women's Movement*. Ed. Rowland, R. Routledge and Kegan Paul, London. pp. 63–69.

Sykes, R. 1989. *Black Majority*. Hudson Publishing, Hawthorn.

Sykes, R. 1997. *Snakes Cradle*. Allen & Unwin, St Leonards, NSW.

Sylvester, C. 1995. African and Western Feminisms: World-Traveling the Tendencies and Possibilities. *Signs*. Vol. 20. No. 4. pp. 941–69.

Taylor, J. M. Gilligan, C. & Sullivan, A. M. 1995. *Between Voice and Silence: Women and Girls, Race and Relationship*. Harvard University Press, Cambridge.

Thomas, N. 1994. *Colonialism's Culture: Anthropology, Travel and Government*. Polity Press, Cambridge.

Thompson, D. 1994. Feminism and Racism: What Is at Stake? Unpublished paper presented at the Australian Women's Studies Conference. Deakin University, Melbourne. December.

Threadgold, T. & Cranny-Francis, A. 1990. *Feminine, Masculine & Representation*. Allen & Unwin, St Leonards, NSW.

Tong, R. 1992. *Feminist Thought: A Contemporary Introduction*. Routledge, London.

Tonkinson, M. 1988. Sisterhood or Aboriginal Servitude? Black Women and White Women on the Australian Frontier. *Aboriginal History*. Vol. 12. No. 1–2. pp. 27–39.

Trask, H. K. 1996. Feminism and Indigenous Hawaiian Nationalism. *Signs*. Vol. 21. No. 41. Summer. pp. 906–16.

Tucker, M. 1983. *If Everyone Cared*. Grosvenor, Melbourne.

Vasta, E. & Castles, S. 1996. *The Teeth Are Smiling: The Persistence of Racism in Multicultural Australia*. Allen & Unwin, St Leonards, NSW.

Wade-Marshall, D. & Loveday. P. 1985. *Employment and Unemployment*.

Monograph, Australian National University, North Australia Research Unit, Darwin.

Walker, D. & Coutts, T. 1989. *Me and You*. Aboriginal Studies Press, Canberra.

Walker, F. 1997. A Very Different Mission: Myora Aboriginal Mission on Stradbroke Island, 1892–1940. In *Stradbroke Island: Facilitating Change*. Ed. Ganter, R. Queensland Studies Centre, Griffith UniPrint, Brisbane. pp. 9–19.

Wanganeen, R. 1990. The Aboriginal Struggle in the Face of Terrorism. In *Playing the State: Australian Feminist Interventions*. Ed.Watson, S. Verso, London. pp. 67–70.

Ward, G. 1988. *Wandering Girl*. Magabala Books, Broome, Western Australia.

Ward, G. 1991. *Unna You Fullas*. Magabala Books, Broome, Western Australia.

Ware, V. 1992. *Beyond the Pale: White Women, Racism and History*. Verso, London and New York.

Waring, W. 1994. *By, For and About: Feminist Cultural Politics*. Women's Press, Ontario.

Waters, M. 1998. Optional Ethnicities: For Whites Only? In *Race, Class and Gender: an Anthology*. 3rd edn. Eds Andersen, M. L. & Collins, P. Hill. Wadsworth Publishing Company, Belmont. pp. 403–12.

Watson, I. 1992. Surviving as a People. In *Breaking Through: Women, Work and Careers*. Ed. Scutt, J. Artemis Publishing, Melbourne. pp. 177–86.

Watson, L. 1987. Sister, Black is the Colour of my Soul. In *Different Lives: Reflections on the Women's Movement and Visions of Its Future*. Ed. Scutt, J. Penguin, Melbourne. pp. 45–52.

Weedon, C. 1987. *Feminist Practice & Poststructuralist Theory*. Blackwell, Cambridge and Oxford.

West, C. & Fenstermaker, S. 1995. Doing Difference. *Gender and Society*. Vol. 9. No. 1. February. pp. 8–37.

West, I. 1987. *Pride Against Prejudice*. Aboriginal Studies Press, Canberra.

Western, J. 1983. *Social Inequality in Australian Society*. MacMillan, South Melbourne, Victoria.

Whelehan, I. 1995. *Modern Feminist Thought: From Second Wave to "Post-Feminism"*. New York University Press, New York.

White, I. 1978. Aboriginal Women's Status: A Paradox Resolved. In *Woman's Role in Aboriginal Society*. Ed. Gale, F. Australian Institute of Aboriginal Studies, Canberra. pp. 36–45.

White, I. 1990. The Lives of Aboriginal Girls and Women According to

Daisy Bates. *Olive Pink Society Bulletin.* Vol 2. No. 2. December. pp. 26–28.

Willets, K. 1991. Health, Education and Child-Rearing Practices among Aboriginal and Islander Australians. *The Olive Pink Society Bulletin.* Vol. 3. No. 1. pp. 18–24.

Williams, E. 1987. Aboriginal First, Woman Second. In *Different Lives: Reflections on the Women's Movement and Visions of Its Future.* Ed. Scutt, J. Penguin, Melbourne. pp. 67–73.

Williams, P. J. 1991. *The Alchemy of Race and Rights: Diary of a Law Professor.* Harvard University Press, Cambridge.

Wilson, R. 1997. *Bringing Them Home: National Inquiry into the Separation of Aboriginal and Torres Strait Islander Children from Their Families Report.* Sterling Press, Sydney.

Winant, H. 1994. *Racial Conditions.* University of Minnesota Press, Minneapolis.

Wingfield, J. 1994. An Interview with Joan Wingfield. In *Daughters of the Pacific.* Ed. De Ishtar, Z. Spinifex Press, Melbourne. pp. 152–54.

Wollstonecraft, M. 1971. The Prevailing Opinion of a Sexual Character. In *Voices from Women's Liberation.* Ed. Tanner, L. B. The New American Library, New York. pp. 35–37.

Yeatman, A. 1991. Postmodernism and the Politics of Representation. *Olive Pink Society Bulletin.* Vol. 3 (2). pp. 14–19.

Yeatman, A. 1993. Voice and Representation in the Politics of Difference. In *Feminism and the Politics of Difference.* Eds Gunew, S. & Yeatman, A. Allen & Unwin, St Leonards, NSW. pp. 228–45.

Yeatman, A. (ed.) 1994. The Place of Women's Studies in the Contemporary University. In *Postmodern Revisionings of the Political.* Routledge, New York. pp. 42–56.

Yeatman, A. 1995. Interlocking Oppressions. In *Transitions: New Australian Feminisms.* Eds Caine, B. & Pringle, R. Allen & Unwin, St Leonards, NSW pp. 42–56.

Young, I. 1990. *Justice and the Politics of Difference.* Princeton University Press, Princeton, New Jersey.

Young, R. 1995. *Hybridity in Theory, Culture and Race.* Routledge, New York.

Zetlein, S. & Brook, H. 1995. The 5th Women and Labour Conference. *Australian Feminist Studies.* No. 22. Summer. pp. 155–60.

Index